PSYCHOLOGY AND PSYCHOTHERAPY
Current Trends and Issues

Edited by
DAVID PILGRIM
Derby Psychotherapy Unit

ROUTLEDGE DIRECT EDITIONS

ROUTLEDGE & KEGAN PAUL
London, Boston, Melbourne and Henley

First published in 1983
by Routledge & Kegan Paul plc
39 Store Street, London WC1E 7DD, England
9 Park Street, Boston, Mass. 02108, USA
464 St Kilda Road, Melbourne,
Victoria 3004, Australia and
Broadway House, Newtown Road,
Henley-on-Thames, Oxon RG9 1EN, England

Printed and bound in Great Britain by
Redwood Burn Ltd, Trowbridge, Wilts

Library of Congress Cataloging in Publication Data

Main entry under title:
Psychology and psychotherapy
    (Routledge direct editions)
    Includes bibliographies and references.
    1. Psychology - practice. 2. Clinical psychology.
3. Psychotherapy. I. Pilgrim, David, 1950-   .
(DNLM: 1. Psychotherapy. 2. Psychology. WM 420 P97415)
BF75.P76   1983   616.89   83-11137
ISBN 0-7100-9551-1

CONTENTS

EDITOR'S ACKNOWLEDGMENTS

Thanks are owing to Marilyn Maloney and Kay Coulson for their time and typing skills. Keith Nichols extends his gratitude to Polly Woodhams, Nurse in Charge at Exeter Renal Unit, for her patient tutoring and to Lorna Donnelly for her invaluable help in preparing his script. Dorothy Rowe acknowledges the permission of Methuen & Co. Ltd to quote material from John M. Heaton's contribution to 'Philosophical Problems in Psychology', ed. Neil Bolton, 1979. I am grateful that all the contributors met their deadline despite clinical and academic pressures. I am particularly indebted to Don Bannister for showing me the ropes peculiar to publishing and to Miller Mair, who could not, unfortunately, contribute to this edition but whose energy pushed the PPA boat out on its journey.

NOTES ON CONTRIBUTORS

DON BANNISTER, BA, PhD, is on the external staff of the Medical Research Council, at High Royds Hospital, Ilkley.

BILL BARNES, BA, BPhil, Dip Psychother, is a Principal Clinical Psychologist working for Liverpool Health Authority and is a teacher at the University of Liverpool.

ERIC BROMLEY, BA, Dip Psychol, is a Top Grade Clinical Psychologist working for Liverpool Health Authority and a teacher at the University of Liverpool.

DAN GOWLER, MA, is University Lecturer in Management Studies (Organisational Behaviour) at the Oxford School of Management Studies.

PETER HILDEBRAND, LesL, PhD, is a Training Analyst for the British Psychoanalytic Society, Chief Psychologist at the Tavistock Clinic, and Professor Associate of Psychology at Brunel University.

SUE LLEWELYN, BA, MSc, is Lecturer in Psychology at the University of Nottingham.

KEITH NICHOLS, BSc, MSc, is Lecturer in Psychology at the University of Exeter and a Senior Clinical Psychologist in the Exeter Health District.

PAUL O'REILLY, BSc, MSc, is a clinical psychologist and family therapist in the Department of Clinical Psychology at the Exe Vale Hospital, Exeter, and the Department of Psychology, University of Exeter.

KATE OSBORNE, BA, MSc, is a Psychologist and Psychotherapist and was a founder member of Bristol Women's Therapy Centre.

GLENYS PARRY, BA, Dip Psychol, is a Research Psychologist at the MRC/SSRC Applied Psychology Unit, Sheffield University.

DAVID PILGRIM, BSc, MPsychol, Dip Psychother, is Principal Clinical Psychologist at the Psychotherapy Unit in Derby.

ix

DOROTHY ROWE, BA, PhD, Dip Clin Psych, is a Top Grade Clinical Psych-ologist working for the Lincolnshire Health Authority.

PHILLIDA SALMON, MA, PhD, is a Senior Lecturer in Child Development at the Institute of Education at the University of London.

DAVID SMAIL, BA, PhD, is a Top Grade Psychologist working for Nottingham Health Authority and is an Honorary Professor of Clinical Psychology at Nottingham University.

ANDREW TREACHER, BA, PhD, is Lecturer in Mental Health at Bristol University.

EDITOR'S INTRODUCTION
David Pilgrim

The clinical psychologist practising psychotherapy is like a work horse burdened with an inappropriate academic legacy and chafed by an ill-fitting medical collar. Not surprisingly many find the profession inhospitable and leave for what are perceived to be more rewarding pursuits (White 1972 and Barden 1979). Kear-Colwell (1972) pointed to conflict with other professions, especially medicine, and poor morale in relation to role status, as aspects of the high wastage rate from clinical posts.

The medical constraints operating are twofold. First, the professional domination of health-care structures by medicine militates against the democratic inter-dependence of autonomous professions. Instead, a power pyramid is evident, which stifles democracy in the workplace and the free flow of professional practices and ideas, concerning health-care goals and models. Second, a hospital- and cure-oriented technical medicine swallows up resources and limits the imaginative implementation of community-oriented projects, which could prevent distress and make more humane psycho-social provision for people with psychological problems, be they acute or chronic, primary or secondary in nature.

Unfortunately psychology itself has an impersonal tradition which leaves clinical psychologists at the outset of their careers hamstrung by the false hope and security of scientific competence to add to their frequent personal insecurity, which is an intelligible function of relative youth. Technique-oriented workshop manuals peddled by behavioural psychology and psychometric devices are a great comfort to neophyte psychologists but are of dubious value to the inevitably complex personal and contextual variation of psychological distress in the real world. The personal needs of clients are just that: personal. Psychological theories of course exist, the depth psychologies and the phenomenological and existential traditions, which offer ways of working personally, but all too often in graduate and even post-graduate training these are ridiculed and marginalised in the name of science. For those of us on the other side of the fence this is scientism. The maverick

1

psychiatrist, Laing, captures this sorry state of affairs with the following words:

> The science of personal relations is not assisted by the fact that only a few psychologists are concerned to discover valid personal ways in which persons, and relations between persons can be studied by persons. Many psychologists feel that if psychology is not a branch of natural science it is not a science at all - - - - . It is impossible to derive the basic logic of a science of persons from the logic of non-personal sciences. No branch of natural science requires to make the peculiar type of inferences that are required in a science of persons. (1980, pp.27-8)

It is unclear at an individual level whether Laing's own zig-zag career has actually provided a basis for such a science of persons (see Sedgwick, 1982). However, the central criticism he is making has a solid feel to it. In 1973, a group of academic and clinical psychologists formed the Psychology and Psychotherapy Association, both confirming and seeking to rectify the type of charge being made by Laing. Those writing in this volume, though expressing their individual views, provide a sample of a range of opinion which indicates the development of the PPA as an anti-reductionist project in its first decade of life. Typically, psychologists immersing themselves in psychotherapeutic ventures have creatively reacted against reductionist assumptions bound up with the ratology and sterile empiricism, which have traditionally dominated academic life. A positive consequence of this has been that personal psychology has fed back into university departments, in terms of numbers of personnel and the ideas and values they carry with them. In this way the cultural characteristics of psychology have become modified as an intellectual as well as an applied pursuit. Whether the modification has been profound enough is a moot point.

The provision of personal ways of theorising and practising in psychology would require a massive increase in the numbers of psychotherapists as one aspect. A second and broader aspect though is not to do with formal psychotherapy so much, as the provision of basic psychological practices in health care, fitting for all the personal ramifications of illness behaviour and the sick role. This would involve the invasion of a personal psychology into an impersonal territory of tubes, drugs and electrodes, as well as the political pursuit of humane alternatives to our hospital oriented legacy. Presently psychological provision lacks depth in terms of the availability of psychotherapy services, free at the time of need, to the public, and lacks breadth because technical responding to physiological functioning is all too often pursued at the expense of personal responding to the psychological needs of people facing biological inefficiency and deterioration. Returning to psychotherapy, those psychologists who pursue psychotherapeutic projects face a number of difficulties, which are an additive effect of their speciality and their parent profession. Psychologists can unobtrusively experiment with their role, provided that they pose no serious threat to the values and practice of medical hegemony. This often leads to psychologists

oscillating between quiet isolation and controversial conflict in
relation to health structures and their medical managers. If
isolation is tolerated and conflict survived and the will and
wherewithal linger to pursue helpful conversations with clients,
then the challenge of psychotherapy still has its problematic
aspects. First, there is professionalism itself. Is private or
State funded friendship being offered or is psychotherapy something
over and above this? The present analysis and debate concerning
technical and non-technical, 'real' and 'transference' and 'being
with' and 'doing to' aspects of therapy address themselves to this
question. Second, it is difficult for psychotherapists to avoid a
pattern of chronic self-justification in the face of tough minded
cynicism from behavioural psychologists. Third, it is often
anxiety provoking to live with the uncertainty and impotence that
evolve at times from sharing the more tragic aspects of other
people's lives. There is little wonder that professionals have
buffered themselves against this anguish by placing advice, pills,
tests or statutory procedures between themselves and their clients.
Even transference has its defensive function for therapists (Szasz
1963), although this view is not shared by all psychoanalytical
dissidents (Lacan 1979). Finally it is saddening to have to
recognise realistically the limitations of psychological
interventions, in the face of developmental damage from the past
and social deprivations in the present. Such an exposure to the
vicissitudes of family relations and the impact of prevailing
contemporary stressors provides the basis of a political learning
experience; this experience, as with others, may be used creatively
or it may be squandered.

REFERENCES

BARDEN, V. (1979), Basic data for manpower planning in Clinical
Psychology, 'Bull. Brit. Psychol. Soc.', 32, 12-16.
KEAR-COLWELL, J.J. (1972), A study of Clinical Psychology job
movements during the period 1.10.67 to 30.9.70, 'Bull. Brit.
Psychol. Soc.', 25, 25-7.
LACAN, J. (1979), 'The Four Fundamental Concepts of Psychoanalysis',
Harmondsworth, Penguin.
LAING, R.D. (1980), 'Self and Others', Harmondsworth, Penguin.
SEDGWICK, P. (1982), 'Psychopolitics', London, Pluto Press.
SZASZ, T.S. (1963), The concept of transference, 'Int. J.
Psychoanal.', 44, 432-43.
WHITE, J.G. (1972), What's wrong with Clinical Psychology?, 'Bull.
Brit. Psychol. Soc.', 25, 101-6.

Part one
THEORY AND PRACTICE

Chapter 1

PSYCHOTHERAPY AND PSYCHOLOGY
David Smail

Telling somebody about your troubles in order to find some relief
from them is neither an unfamiliar nor a new experience for most
people: it happens every day, in families, between friends, in bars
and barbers' shops, vicarages and doctors' surgeries, and has been
happening, in one form or another, for a very long time.

As far as psychotherapy involves this kind of activity, then, it
would not seem to need much in the way of justification. But, of
course, there is much more to psychotherapy than this. Psychotherapists are, or are supposed to be, especially expert in the
nature of human psychological ills, have degrees and qualifications,
professional organizations, and expect to be paid for whatever
comfort they dispense. And so it seems reasonable to expect them to
have something more to offer than just a sympathetic ear or a piece
of friendly advice. When professional claims are made, expectations
established among clients, and money changes hands (even if only
indirectly, as in the British National Health Service), it becomes
important to establish a solid justification for psychotherapy as a
discipline.

Because, perhaps, of the uncritical faith which we tend to invest
in our established institutions, it is hard for the layman to doubt
that such justification must exist. Psychotherpists are, after all,
like other professional experts, specially educated, trained, and
accredited; they are, in some cases at least, supported by academic
and medical authority; their services may be sought through the
official channels of the National Health Service. Such a person
could scarcely be thought to exist in such a setting were he or she
offering nothing more than what could be obtained from a spouse,
mother, best friend or barmaid.

It is not my intention to suggest that no psychotherapist has more
to offer than this, but I do wish to argue that the kind of
justification for our activities commonly stated, or at least
implied, cannot be substantiated in any convincing way. In
particular, those of us whose involvement in the psychological
therapies stems from a background in psychology, often like to think,

I suspect, that our therapeutic practice is guided by the psychological discoveries which have been made in academic laboratories - that we are, in other words, applied psychologists who can, in defence of our professional activities, appeal to established scientific laws and principles. For reasons which will, I hope, become apparent, I do not believe that this is a tenable position, and if we try much longer to hold onto it we shall find ourselves, from a theoretical point of view, less rather than more credible than the sympathetic layman. This is not to say that I see credibility, pure and simple, as an end in itself; it is more my hope that by achieving an adequate theoretical understanding of the process of psychotherapy we may in the long run make it easier for effective psychological help to be available to people without recourse to any particular groups of experts.

Ever since the beginnings of psychoanalysis, psychotherapists have been desperately anxious to establish the validity of their credentials - both in order to earn the respect of psychological and medical colleagues and, no doubt, to justify their professional (fee-taking) status. To be rather more charitable, they have also been concerned to establish the degree to which their undertaking works. During the past century, of course, the way to justify an activity of this kind has been scientifically - it is the scientific community which has to be satisfied that therapeutic treatments are reputable and claims supported by satisfactory evidence. However, as an object of scientific study, psychotherapy has not stood great in repute. From the moment that Freud put pen to paper, experimental psychologists, as well as many medical specialists, have looked with mistrust at the activities and theories of those calling themselves psychotherapists, largely because of the difficulties encountered in framing these activities and theories in a sufficiently disciplined and well defined form to allow them to be scientifically tested and validated. As far as it goes, the 'scientific evidence' supports such a mistrustful attitude. Libraries full of published research aimed at establishing the effectiveness of or clarifying the processes involved in a wide range of psychotherapies still give no really clear indication of what the important ingredients are or what is the nature of their operation. Despite this being the case, however, and despite the almost universal importance attached to scientific justification of his or her activities, no psychotherapist of any of the myriad schools of psychotherapy which exist has as far as I know given up practising on the grounds of lack of adequate evidence. There may be a number of reasons for this. It may be, for instance, that psychotherapists are by and large a collection of charlatans who are making too much money to allow their scientific scruples to interfere with their interests. They may be misguided, stupid, or mistaken. They may be pinning their faith on potential rather than actual scientific support for their position. Often, however, they may be being guided by a kind of evidence which, while not 'scientific' in the orthodox sense, seems to have a kind of validity which they are reluctant to discount.

I do not myself believe that this state of affairs has arisen because psychology is a young science which cannot yet reasonably be expected to deliver the goods. Rather, I suspect, it is because the

conception of psychological science most widely adopted both in and
outside academic institutions is one which, because of the assumptions
it makes and the aspirations it embraces, is doomed to failure when
applied to psychotherapy. One must of course acknowledge that such
assumptions and aspirations have not remained unchallenged in recent
years, even from within the institutions where they tend to hold sway;
nevertheless, they survive as those conventionally accepted among the
vast majority of those who conduct research into psychotherapy as well
as by therapists who are conscious of a need to pay lip service to the
demands of 'science'.

The assumptions and aspirations which I mean may perhaps best be
illustrated by reference to the definition of psychotherapy (taken
from Meltzoff and Kornreich, 1970) which has found most favour with the
British Psychological Society recently. This sees psychotherapy as an:
informed and planful application of techniques derived from
established psychological principles by persons qualified through
training and experience to understand these principles and to
apply these techniques with the intention of assisting individuals
to modify those personal characteristics as feelings, values,
attitudes and behaviors ... as are judged to be maladaptive or
maladjusted.

Despite its surface plausibility, this definition seems to me to
beg just about every factual and moral question which can be asked
about psychotherapy. For example, it assumes (a) that there <u>are</u>
techniques which can be applied to individuals; (b) that the
application can be planful; (c) that there are established psychological principles on which they can be based; (d) that qualificiation
and experience will reveal what the techniques and principles are,
and (e) that judgements about what is maladaptive and maladjusted can
be made relatively unproblematically.

My objection to these assumptions is not that they are not in
principle attractive or reasonable or what I should like to be the
case. It is that in my experience they simply do not seem to be
valid, and I could believe in their validity only if I suspended
belief in my own experience of psychotherapy. For example, I have
never found that I can say or suggest things to one patient on the
grounds that either my own of other people's patients have in the
past been helped by the identical utterances or procedure: in other
words, I have not found that I can rely on techniques, as such.
Instead, I have to take account of how the patient understands, what
he makes of what I say and suggest: I have to negotiate with him or
her the meaning of what we are talking about. Over and over again
I have to abandon preconceived notions because of the influence the
patient has on me. As for 'planfulness', I almost never find that
I can predict the way a therapeutic interview is going to go, but can
only formulate ideas about what has taken place after the event.
Again, I know of no 'established psychological principles' in the
formal academic sense: the psychological literature seems rather to
attest to the fact that any attempt to establish a psychological
principle has been met with a more vigorous attempt to establish a
range of opposing 'principles', with the result that in no sphere of

research have stable paradigms emerged.

The implicit claim in the above definition of psychotherapy that training and experience qualify one to understand and apply techniques blithely ignores the fact that psychotherapists are split into a wide range of different schools, with fundamentally different and often mutually exclusive theoretical ideas. It would be truer to say that qualification reflects more often an allegiance to a prejudice than privileged access to established knowledge. Finally, the making of judgements about what is maladaptive or maladjusted has, as surely nobody remotely connected with the field of mental disorder could be unaware, been the centre of a violent and unresolved controversy for at least the past twenty years.

The assumptions embodied in this definition of psychotherapy, then, reflect wish rather than reality; they are the creation of a scientific mythology which in fact takes almost no account of our actual experience of psychotherapy.

Academic psychology seems to breed in its adherents an unhealthy obsession concerning how far they are or are not 'scientific'. Indeed, what seems to have happened is that what it is to be scientific has in psychology become a question of dogma, which is itself centred upon an appraisal of the methods which natural scientists appear fairly consistently to have used to pursue their enquiries. What inspires this dogmatic approach to scientific thinking seems to be a tacit faith that, by following a prescribed methodological path, scientific authority can be rendered absolute and impersonal; can, in guiding human activity and human intervention, exclude the frailty of human judgement by appealing to such principles as objectivity, lawfulness, quantifiability, generality, stability, determinism (prediction and control), and so on. It is possible that principles such as these are helpful in understanding and manipulating the inanimate and mechanical aspects of our world, and perhaps also the behaviour of organisms 'lower' than man, though even in these spheres of scientific achievement and relatively stable scientific paradigms orthodox methodological dogma has been questioned by a number of eminent natural scientists (the reader is likely by now to be familiar with most of these arguments – if not, I can do no better than recommend Polanyi, 1958). But whatever is the case with the natural sciences it seems to me now beyond question that the view of scientific method conventionally accepted in psychology has not helped us in our attempts to understand psychotherapy. Confronted with this, we have, presumably, at least two choices: we may conclude, as some certainly seem prepared to do, that scientific psychology must concern itself only with those phenomena which will leave its methodological purity uncontaminated, relegating psychotherapy to the realm of the 'healing arts', or, alternatively, we may begin to wonder whether our traditional scientific concepts need revising in order to cope with phenomena to which they should, if we are to remain psychologists rather than physiologists or biochemists, be applicable.

In considering the question of the applicability of a scientific psychology to the field of psychotherapy, it is of course important to distinguish the practice of psychotherapy from the theoretical understanding of it. Szasz (1979) has argued, in my view convincingly, that psychotherapy cannot in itself be seen as a scientific undertaking, but rather as a moral enterprise. That, however, is not to say that the processes of psychotherapy are not mediated by psychological phenomena which can be studied scientifically. That such study does not seem to be facilitated by the impersonal set of dogmas we have taken to represent science does not release us from an obligation to get properly to grips with the intellectual (as distinct from the moral) problems presented in the experience of psychotherapy. What alternatives could there be to a scientific understanding, apart from believing in magic, or being ready to accept that something is the case just because somebody says so?

Science, freed from a dogmatic interpretation, has its own special appeal not because it guarantees an impersonal route to objective truth, but because it embodies a particular set of values. Most centrally, what is, or in my view ought to be valued is an under- standing, elaboration and, where possible, explanation of our experience of the world which is, precisely, not based on dogma or arbitrary authority. Ideally, science is thus a means whereby we convince or persuade ourselves and others of the adequacy of our understanding by appealing to experience which we and they cannot in good faith deny. The fact that science may have developed methods which have proved useful in this undertaking, particularly perhaps in spheres unrelated to psychology, does not mean that such methods are sacrosanct - if at any point they prove inadequate for our purposes, they can be jettisoned without a qualm. What conventional psycho- logical science has failed consistently to do is to take our experience seriously, and yet that is exactly what should have been its task.

It is not even on the whole considered necessary to a scientific psychological understanding to have any experience of the phenomena under consideration. For example, some academic psychologists seem to feel quite at liberty to give 'scientific' opinions about or to conduct research in psychotherapy without having any first hand knowledge of it. This presumably stems from a misguided belief that 'objectivity', in the sense of approaching a problem uncontaminated by any familiarity with it, somehow guarantees a more accurate appraisal of its nature. And yet, surely, the very first thing a scientist should do is make himself thoroughly acquainted with the phenomena whose nature he wishes to understand. I find it completely mystifying to see how anyone can know, except in a completely empty and abstract sense, anything with which he or she has not been in intimate physical relation. One can only know the taste of oranges by having had one in one's mouth, and nobody could learn to play the piano by reading a treatise about it. The structure of orthodox, dogmatic psychology is such that it permits people to pronounce with apparent authority upon whole ranges of psychological phenomena about which they know nothing simply because the methodology it espouses is applicable to any set of data, no matter how meaningless, and as long as methodology is seen as the criterion of scientific excellence, we shall continue to be subjected to an apparently endless stream of meaningless research. One cannot know anything about psychotherapy unless one has been in some way bodily involved in it. Those who have been so involved often do know a lot about psychotherapy, but they are on the whole unable to elaborate their knowledge because the structure of official scientific psychology is uninterested in their experience and unwilling to alter its methods and assumptions in order to take account of it. Almost inevitably, to say something truthful about psychotherapy is to violate the dogmas of conventional academic psychology; to be an accurate student of psychotherapy is to be a psychological heretic.

There are many instances of this kind of difficulty in the literature on research into psychotherapy, where often only those 'findings' are taken seriously which conform to current standards of methodological purity. Sloane et al. (1975), for example, in their well known study of psychotherapy versus behaviour therapy, obtain objective measures of personal characteristics of therapists as well as seeking directly the views of patients on the same characteristics of their therapists. Because there is some conflict between the two sets of evidence, the authors are persuaded to pay more attention to the objective measures, though the logical grounds for doing so are far from clear, solely because this is more in accordance with methodological dogma. Again, Jerome Frank (1973), having soberly and dispassionately taken stock of many of the important phenomena of psychotherapy (thereby, one would have thought, advancing the cause of science), then despairingly witholds the possibility of scientific study from psychotherapy on the gounds that the processes involved cannot be reduced to physiological or biochemical events. What seems to be happening in these and other cases is that our assumptions are blinding us to the significance of what is in front of our noses.

If our theoretical structures turn out to be such that our experience cannot be fitted into them without doing it violence, then our theoretical structures will have to be revised. Galileo (see Drake, 1980) complained that the professors of philosophy of his day 'would have us altogether abandon reason and the evidence of our senses in favour of some biblical passage...'. If one substitutes 'methodological dogma' for 'biblical passage', and professors of psychology for professors of philosophy, we find ourselves faced by similar dogmatic constraints. If we took a leaf from Galileo's book, and characterized science simply as the conjunction of practical experience and reason, we might find ourselves free to think about, for example, the phenomena of psychotherapy with results far more fruitful than those we have come to expect from orthodox research. Laying our scientistic prejudices on one side, the first thing we should do is to take our experience of psychotherapy absolutely seriously, and only then use our powers of reasoning to construct a theoretical framework which can do it justice. If in the process we find ourselves in need of conventional philosophical concepts, that is no immediate cause for alarm and despondency.

Any statement which purports to be scientific in the end stands or falls on the evidence presented in subjective experience, not on its conformity to established dogma. Where our subjective experience overlaps, we are presented with the possibility of debating, persuading, and negotiating with each other the significance of the phenomena experienced. Objectivity thus becomes, not a magic methodology for guaranteeing truth in an impersonal world of ideas, but rather what emerges from a consensus of subjectivities.

If one approaches the psychotherapy literature with the intention of learning from those who have gained experience in psychotherapy, it is my impression that there are sufficient areas of commonality, enough recurring foci of interest, to suggest at least embryonic forms and questions with which a science of psychotherapy might concern itself.

For example, Freud, when not lost in the intricacies of theory-building or carried away by his own mystique, develops undeniable insights into the way neurotic symptoms and defences can disguise painful and distressing dilemmas. Jung, long before Rogers, is clarity itself when discussing the nature of the therapist-patient relationship. Sullivan expounds brilliantly the importance and influence of interpersonal relations in the formation of personality and psychopathology, foreshadowing in many respects the later contributions of Laing as well as of Kelly. Horney develops very helpfully a framework in which to view the kinds of neurotic problems and strategies familiar to all of us. More recently, Peter Lomas (1973, 1981) goes further than anyone in laying bare the nature of what is therapeutic in the therapist's stance towards his patients and its inescapably personal nature, and both Lazarus (1971) and Wachtel (1977) confront with great honesty the commonalities between psychotherapy and behaviour therapy.

More widely, the literature on psychotherapy research is laden with quite consistent hints about what the likely effective ingredients and central problems of therapy are, though frequently these are relegated to the realm of the 'non-specific', not because they are in the least peripheral, vague or irrelevant, but simply because they do not conform to the kind of technical specification dictated by our dogmas. One central conclusion which seems to me inescapable is that fundamentally psychotherapy cannot satisfactorily be cast in terms of anything other than a personal relationship, so that any attempt to standardize or technicize therapy is certain to detract from its proper understanding (see Smail, 1978, for an extended elaboration of this view).

It is unfortunate that a central concern of many writers on psycho-therapy has been to defend the theoretical claims of their school against the rival claims of other schools. This has naturally led to an emphasis on the differences rather than the similarities between the ways in which therapists construe their experience. If, however, one approaches the literature with a more charitable attitude, sifting from it those observations and statements which accord with one's own experience of psychotherapy, it may be possible to arrive at a set of statements which could form the basis for a rudimentary consensus around which, eventually, it might be possible to construct a science of psychotherapy which would invite allegiance because of

the sense it made of our experience. An extremely preliminary attempt
of my own to generate such a set of statements, to map out, very
roughly, some of the psychotherapeutic phenomena which seem to me to
occur fairly generally in therapists' experience, has resulted in the
following list:
   Most patients, on first consulting a therapist, do not really
   know what is troubling them, and their 'symptoms' cannot,
   therefore be treated at face value.
   The '.truth' of the situation has to be negotiated between
   therapist and patient, and this takes time.
   Patients have to trust their therapist, and whether or not they
   can will depend in part on how honest (genuine) the therapist
   is able to be.
   Therapists cannot avoid influencing patients. To understand
   patients, also, they cannot avoid drawing on personal experience.
   Empathy is of course important, but arises between people, and
   is not a quality (or'skill') possessed by individuals in some
   finite amount.
   Patients are not the passive victims of psychological (or any
   other kind of) determinism, but are agents in a social world.
   Techniques, as such, are unlikely to be effective, but need to
   be placed in a context of meaning.
   Mutual affection between patient and therapist is one of the
   most powerful therapeutic factors encouraging change.
   In order to change patients need courage, which may be only to
   be found in the context of a confirming relationship.
   Self-deception is a universal human phenomenon, and is a
   particularly strong and ubiquitous feature of 'neurotic'
   strategies. Thus what people tell themselves about their conduct
   will often conflict with the apparent meaning to others of
   their conduct. One is not in a specially privileged position
   to interpret the meaning of one's own conduct. (This view is,
   of course, closely related to concepts of conscious and
   unconscious.)
   Therapists cannot always act from reflection and deliberation,
   and much of their contribution to therapy will be spontaneous,
   understandable only after the event.
   There is no standard way of being therapeutic, and hence the
   ideal of the technical handbook, however complex and detailed, is
   doomed to failure.
   In the vast majority of cases, 'patients' are not 'ill', and
   'therapy' is not a 'treatment' or a 'cure'.
   Patients' problems hinge on emotional pain and psychological
   distress having origins in their experience and relationships
   and recognisable to us all.

   I have in fact exposed this set of statements to the critical
comments of a number of groups of therapists over the last year or so,
so far without causing, apparently, great dissent. However, even if a
collection of statements such as this could command a measure of assent,
one is of course still a very long way from a scientifically viable
structure in which to place the phenomena of therapeutic experience.
What is still needed is a theoretical psychology which is capable of
accommodating and elaborating, not to say refining and extending such

observations as these. Personally, I think the nature of our observations suggests the form that such a psychology must take, and indeed it may well turn out that psychotherapeutic experience has a part to play in revolutionizing psychology, rather than, as is more the case at present, psychotherapeutic practice straining itself to conform to the mechanistic ideals of an 'applied psychology' in the conventional sense.

There are indeed signs that a theoretical structure capable of accommodating the phenomena of psychotherapy is beginning to develop on the fringes of official psychology. Behaviourism, although still the predominant theoretical force in clinical psychology, is no longer as popular in many university departments of psychology as it once was, and indeed academics seem to be becoming increasingly aware of the inapplicability of their traditional preoccupations to the living psychological problems of the outside world. Over the past few years Anglo-American psychologists seem also to have become more conscious of a European philosophical tradition which has avoided the positivist and empiricist excesses of our own intellectual establishment, and while phenomenological, existential and structuralist writers from France and Germany tend to have an expressive opacity which fails to lift their views above the contempt of most British academic philosophers and psychologists, a number of their more central concerns (e.g., to do with freedom, meaning, subjectivity, the phenomenology of the body) have recommended themselves to a significant minority of people working in the clinical fields of psychology and psychiatry. These views, combined with an increasing awareness that natural scientists no longer find (if ever they really did) a simple philosophy of objectivity adequate for the understanding of their particular theoretical puzzles, leads to a conception of man not as a passive responder to stimuli, but as, in an important sense, the creator as well as the interpreter of his world, the institutions within it, and the relations between people.

In many ways, things are getting more complicated than might have seemed likely a few decades ago: our theoretical dilemmas can no longer be encompassed within simple oppositions between idealism and realism, mind and body, free will and determinism. For example, psycho-therapeutic experience suggests that a person may be both responsible for his actions, and yet unable to account for them (see Smail, 1978 for an account of this apparent paradox); able to initiate action and yet incapable of decision in the sense in which that concept is normally used. Attention has been drawn (Harré and Secord, 1972) to the way we negotiate our reality through the accounts we give of it, and yet, to complicate matters, the problematic relations between language and conduct are only just beginning to surface in the consciousness of experimental psychologists (see, for example, Nisbett and Wilson, 1977; Gur and Sackheim, 1979). The inevitability of man's experience of the world determining his scientific and philosophical (as well as personal) constructions of it also ushers on to the psychological scene a revived preoccupation with moral issues, so that psychology becomes undetachable from morality (see in this respect Poole, 1972; Shotter, 1980).

We have scarcely begun to think, in the English-speaking psychological world, in terms of these categories, but as we gain the ability
to do so, I suspect that we shall find ourselves developing a psychology
which looks very little like today's orthodox version. The most
fundamental difference we are likely to see, in my view, is a psychology
which up-ends our established dogma, and takes man as primarily subject
rather than primarily object. Instead of a mechanical organism
behaving in reaction to a specifiable environment, man becomes a focus
of activity himself, in relation to others, in what Roger Poole calls
'ethical space'. It may well be that from a God's-eye-view human
beings could be studied objectively, their behaviour subject to
prediction and control, much as we might study rats. But unless
psychologists manage to close themselves off entirely from commerce with
the rest of the world and keep their scientific observations completely
secret, there is no logical hope of our achieving a viable psychology
of this kind.

The practical consequences of looking at men and women as subjects
rather than objects might not be uninteresting. One of the main
effects of this might be to turn our attention from what we are to what
we do, from our 'objective selves' to our conduct. In suggesting this
I am certainly not advocating a modified form of behaviourism: in
splitting behaviour from its intention, or meaning, behaviourism
lost, in the cause of mechanism, whatever it might have gained from
recognizing the difficulties implicit in verbal accounts of psychological processes. The use of the word 'conduct' here is meant to
correct behaviourism's mistake by placing activity firmly within the
context of its ethical intention, while acknowledging that intentions
are not things which people have in their heads.

Traditional psychology has above all else concerned itself with the
objective characteristics of people, i.e. with traits, descriptions,
diagnoses, self concepts, self/ideal self discrepancies, presentations
of self, and so on. All of which suggests that the individual person
can be emptied out into a finite number of accurate descriptive labels
by which he or she can be fixed, as it were, as an object in psycho-
social space. This kind of enterprise takes place in a wider culture
in which almost everyone is obsessed with self-as-object. This
pervasive concern is most evident in the extent to which people are
preoccupied (a) with what people think of them and (b) with what they
look like - the body becomes the ultimate object in which we are
trapped, inescapably vulnerable to the lust, disgust, derision or
adulation of others. We live in, and have helped to create, a society
in which a person's entire life can be reduced to an agonized
consciousness of being too fat, too thin, too short, too tall; a
society in which what people actually do matters not at all in
relation to the appearance of success or status they manage to give.
In this setting, it can be no surprise that 'therapeutic' psychologies
become more and more concerned with the management of appearance and
the development of 'skills' by means of which others may be deceived
into believing that we are invulnerable. Many so-called neurotic
patients seem to me to be people who have not been able to conceal
from themselves an inarticulate awareness that they have been
mystified and crippled by the bludgeon of objectivity, and have not

been able to obliterate totally the defencelessness which lies, I believe, at the centre of our being.

A culture, and indeed a psychology, which took proper account of subjectivity, however, might release people from this kind of objectified status, and allow them to concentrate on what they are trying to do rather than on how successfully thay are managing their presentation of self. Bodies might become instruments rather than objects, valuable for what they create rather than valued for what they look like. Beauty would become a relational characteristic (in the eye of the beholder) rather than a fixed possession obtainable from a bottle of skin cream or the consumption of low-calorie bread.

The future course of our relations with each other, from the personal to the global, must in fact depend on what we do to and with each other, not on the success with which we manage to convince each other of our lies. It is only at the cost of despair and, very probably, eventual destruction, that we learn to adapt to a world which takes manipulation and deceit as the fabric of relation, in which the actual consequences of our conduct are obscured by an ever more strident insistence on the rational necessity of our objective constructs, a world in which we are led by moral imbeciles whose actions are presented to us by the image makers as the inevitable response to rational, objective (economic) necessity. Psychologists and psychotherapists must, I believe, decide upon what their stance toward such a world should be, if only because, through their own activities and in their own small way, they either help or hinder its construction.

A psychology adequate to deal with the phenomena of psychotherapy must, certainly, be reflexive, and must acknowledge people as agents in a social world, whose conduct cannot be considered out of the context of its ethical intention. As psychologists and psychotherapists we contribute to an ethically evolving social world in which we cannot validly dissociate ourselves from a process of constant negotiation (concerning what is true, real and good) with its other inhabitants. Nor can we validly maintain the pose of technical experts privileged to stand back and guide others to some kind of objectivity determined or morally self-evident goal.

The recent history of clinical psychology in Britain (and pre-sumably even more so in the USA) suggests that psychological therapists are no less vulnerable than any other groups to the temptations of professionalization - indeed, we show every sign of rushing to be seduced by them without even a sideways glance at the kind of moral pitfalls (so ably described by Illich, 1977) we are likely to dig for ourselves and our clients in so doing. And yet if we are to take seriously the reflexiveness of psychology, we shall I think need to consider very carefully what it means to be a professional psychologist or psychotherapist. As far as 'being a psychologist' may be identified by others as an implicit claim to expertise about human nature, it is an embarrassment. It is always painful for psychologists to be asked at social gatherings what they do for a living. The most apt response I ever got to the somewhat

shamefaced confession that 'Well, I'm a psychologist, actually', was
from a man who, with a patient but rather tired smile, replied 'Ah.
Aren't we all'. And, of course, we all are - highly skilled and
experienced psychologists who have spent a lifetime developing ways
of living in a world which contains other people, observing the
regularities of their conduct, and conducting ourselves in accordance
with our observations. We can with extraordinary accuracy read the
significance of a glance or a minute vocal inflection, react
sensitively to the mood of those around us, make lightening judgements
about the appropriateness of what to do in this or that situation.
In the face of this kind of expertise, when the professional
psychologist, because of his commitment to the dogmas of quantifiability,
generality, objectivity, etc., attempts, for instance, to reduce human
personality to the interaction of two or three so-called personality
traits, he risks making himself a laughing stock.

   Not only, then are psychologists people, but, much more important,
people are psychologists. This being so, it seems to me unreasonable
for psychologists to regard psychology as their own special property.
Psychology cannot, in other words, be considered a special discipline
understandable only to a particular group of professional experts,
but consists rather in a conceptual network embedded, at least
implicitly, in the general culture, and is in principle accessible to,
and is certainly operated by, the members of that culture. I would
thus argue that a psychology is successful, or accurate, to the
extent to which it unearths or makes explicit the psychological
practices and processes of ordinary people.

   Now it may well fall to a particular group of people to interest
itself in the psychological processes of people in general, but once
the nature of such processes has been to some extent revealed, the
'discoveries' involved should not be appropriated by a professional
group for it to exploit in its own interest, but should be reflected
back into the culture, which may well in turn be modified by them. To
be effective, psychological theories have to be practised by the very
people to whom they apply. In support of this argument, I would
suggest that Freud's discoveries, if one chooses to regard them as
such, have gained their significance much more from the way in which
they have been assimilated and made manifest in the general culture
than from the use to which they have been put by the professional
groups of analysts which have tried to make them their own property.

   One practical consequence of this for psychotherapy, I suggest,
is that more important than the technical 'cure' of individual
patients (in which the professional therapist acts as an intellectual
usurer, lending his concepts, as it were, at interest) may be the
enrichment or modification of the psychology implicit in our
conceptual culture as a whole. This may be difficult to achieve in
any deliberate kind of way, but, if our insights have any significance,
it is likely in the long run to be achieved accidentally.

   It is possible that a number of observations derived (not
necessarily exclusively) from therapeutic practice might prove of
more practical value if they were offered up, so to speak, for public

consumption, rather than kept simply as the theoretical property of professional therapists. One may perhaps illustrate this through the use of one or two examples of observations already made above. For instance, popular psychology, if one may call it such, has even more difficulty than professional psychology in recognizing explicitly that there is much more to the explanation of conduct than merely the individual's verbal report of what he or she is intending. In fact, of course, even the most psychologically naive layman is all the time judging other people's intentions from their actions rather than their words, and yet when it comes to making the grounds of such judgements explicit, is likely to find himself at a loss; people feel unhappy if they have not got verbal evidence of another's intentions to back their hypotheses about why he or she did something. I have often been struck, for example, by the lengths to which even experienced residential child care workers will go in their attempts to extract from a recalcitrant child, who clearly cannot say why it did what it did, a motivational account of its actions; it would often seem more appropriate on such occasions to offer to the child a suitable explanation for its conduct. Considerations such as these in turn raise questions about the ways in which, popularly, we conceptualize responsibility, blame and fault, etc. From experience of psychotherapy, it seems to me quite clear that people can do something intentionally without being able to say, either to themselves or to others, what they are doing, and are thus responsible for their actions, though perhaps not blameworthy if the actions turn out to be socially unfortunate. Whatever one might feel about the philosophical or linguistic complexity of such issues, it is clear that our everyday conceptual language is not subtle enough to handle the psychological complications which underlie much human conduct. Decisions, again, seem not on the whole to be things which people make in their heads before they act, and many patients, in my experience, are hampered by their culturally determined inability to recognize this as being so; they feel that before they can do something, they have to await the occurrence of a decision.

Now what is important about such insights as these (assuming for the moment that they are insights) is not that psychologists or psychotherapists should attempt to patent them as their own property to be used for their own material gain, but that they should be exposed to a critical scrutiny so that, if valid, they may become part of common conceptual property. What, to take a Utopian view, may follow from this is the psychotherapy may contribute to a popular psychology which could in the end render almost obsolete the need for any specific professional group of psychotherapists. As psychotherapists, certainly, we shall never expunge emotional pain, distress and friction from the world, and indeed the reasons for these are probably political and moral much more than psychological. What we may help to do is develop a more effective understanding of their psychological consequences and complications than seems current at present. The practitioners of such a psychology, however, will not be professional psychologists and psychotherapists, but people themselves.

REFERENCES

DRAKE, S. (1980), 'Galileo', Oxford, Oxford University Press.
FRANK, J.D. (1973), 'Persuasion and Healing', Baltimore and London, Johns Hopkins University Press.
GUR, R.C. and SACKEIM, H.A. (1979), Self-Deception: a concept in search of a phenomenon, 'Journal of Personality and Social Psychology', vol. 37, pp. 147-69.
HARRÉ, R. and SECORD, P.F. (1972), 'The Explanation of Social Behaviour', Oxford, Blackwell.
ILLICH, I. (1977), 'Disabling Professions', London, Boyars.
LAZARUS, A. (1971), 'Behaviour Therapy and Beyond', New York, McGraw Hill.
LOMAS, P. (1973), 'True and False Experience' London, Allen Lane.
LOMAS, P. (1981), 'The Case for a Personal Psychotherapy', Oxford, Oxford University Press.
MELTZOFF, J. AND KORNREICH, M. (1970), 'Research in Psychotherapy', New York, Atherton Press.
NISBETT, R.E. AND WILSON, T.C. (1977), Telling more than we know: verbal reports on mental processes, 'Psychological Review', vol. 84, pp. 231-59.
POLANYI, M. (1958), 'Personal Knowledge', London, Routledge & Kegan Paul.
POOLE, R. (1972), 'Toward Deep Subjectivity', London, Allen Lane.
SHOTTER, J. (1980), Men the magicians: the duality of social being and the structure of moral worlds, in A.J. Chapman and D.M. Jones (eds), 'Models of Man', Leicester, The British Psychological Society, pp. 13-34.
SLOANE, R.B., STAPLES, F.R., CRISTOLL, A.H., YORKSTON, N.J. and WHIPPLE, K. (1975), 'Psychotherapy Versus Behavior Therapy', Cambridge, Mass., and London, Johns Hopkins University Press.
SMAIL, D.J. (1978), 'Psychotherapy: A Personal Approach', London, Dent.
SZASZ, T. (1979), 'The Myth of Psychotherapy', Oxford, Oxford University Press.
WACHTEL, P.L. (1977), 'Psychoanalysis and Behavior Therapy. Toward an Integration', New York, Basic Books.

Chapter 2

DOUBTS AND CERTAINTIES
IN PRACTISING PSYCHOTHERAPY
Bill Barnes

For Certainties Either are past remedies; or timely knowing, The
remedy then borne. (Shakespeare)
There are two types of experience of reality, one being derived from
the duality of subject and object in which everyday life is governed
by the principle of creating meaning in the face of non-being whilst
in the other, the experience of enlightenment, subject and object,
being and non-being are the same. This chapter is concerned with
the first type of experience, that of ordinary people, of psychologists
and psychotherapists, of the author; for us the Absolute is only
theoretical. Psychotherapists function dualistically and believe,
with Freud, that people can be helped to overcome unnecessary misery
so that they can face the normal suffering of everyday life. That is
as far as psychotherapy goes, and it is a long way. At its best it is
one way (not the way) in which people can come to a maturity which
enables then to stand in the inevitable suffering of an existence
perceived dualistically but it does not attempt to solve the suffering
itself. Psychotherapy ends precisely where the great contemplative
traditions begin, where the Absolute is actual, dualism is transcended
and suffering becomes transparent. I completely accept that reality
can be perceived in this second way but think that, for most of us,
our truths are only ever partial and our philosophies no more or less
than attempts to find meaning in ordinary life. That systems and
philosophies of psychology are the attempts of human beings to make
sense of their lives is obvious enough, and yet how often do our
theories confuse meaning with truth and seem to be statements about
the nature of reality? Dogmatic assertions about reality are offered
with certainty as philosophies appear to spontaneously sprout out of
one another somewhere on the darkened shelves of libraries, with
little reference to the actual people who philosophised. The great
Spanish philosopher Miguel de Unamuno (1921) insisted that it is not
a person's theory that makes him an optimist or a pessimist but his
optimism or pessimism that makes his theory. The theory is, he said,
the work of 'the man of flesh and bone' needing to find his conception
of the world, it is a personal act not a direct print-out of reality;
we can only know uncertainty and relative truth. However our 'Quest
for Certainty' continues as Dewey (1929) suggests, in a book of that
title, out of our need for security which compels us to seek the

certain, regular and repeated aspects of life. This necessitates an
appeal to reason as a means of control because relying on simple
experience of life reveals only the unruly and the chaotic; so
knowledge itself is power, as Bacon said, for it promises security.
The use of reason obstructs objects of knowledge which can be treated
instrumentally but which remain abstract. They are very useful, but
one must be careful not to reverse the process and assert the nature
of reality on the basis of man made instruments 'so as to infer that
scientific ways of thinking of objects give the inner reality of
things' (Dewey, p. 135).

There are so many theories, man made instruments and partial truths
contesting to have the last work to say about life. One way of
introducing order into this rivalrous confusion was offered by Harry
Guntrip (1971) when he set forth a hierarchical model of the structure
of knowledge
    that is like a building with a ground floor which is physics and
    chemistry, and then rises tier by tier upwards, with physiology,
    biology, ethology, sociology, and finally psychology, first
    behaviouristic, and finally truly personal psychology (p. 309).
His point is that the process of thought can only be moved forward
and upwards, not backwards and downwards. It is not that better
thinking is done the higher up you go but that at each level on the
way up new phenomena arise which call for new concepts not used on the
floor below. However much sense this model might make it seems that,
in most of our Universities, we are educated into using the same
concepts on all floors. This is largely the legacy of Descartes's
insistence, centuries ago, that we should not bother with anything
about which we cannot have a certainty equal to the demonstrations of
mathematics. His 'Rules for the Direction of the Mind' (1955) are
still followed implicitly by most inhabitants of our hypothetical
building; whatever you are investigating, be it cabbages or kings,
reason can be your only guide and objective mathematical certainty
your only criterion. Moreover, the conceptual shift, which was there
for Descartes himself, from seeing the knowledge borne of his Rules
as an interpretation of phenomena to seeing it as a revelation of
reality itself is still operating whenever those phenomena which elude
objective measurement are dismissed as not being real. Reality, it
seems, is only knowable by the masters of mathematics and objectivity,
the physical scientists on the ground floor. They are emulated
throughout the building by social 'scientists', philosophers undertaking the logical study of language, students of literature (the
New Criticism) and, of course, by their greatest fans of all,
psychologists.

That psychologists remain in the thrall of the physical scientists
can only be evidence of some maladaptive habit which has not been
extinguished by experience, for example by being warned by none other
than Oppenheimer (1956) precisely against using early twentieth-
century physics as our model. In a similar vein we have been told
that our belief in mathematics is not shared by eminent mathematicians
like Kline (1980), who has argued that the concept of a universally
accepted and infallible body of reasoning called mathematics is an
illusion and that there are now so many conflicting mathematics that

doubt and uncertainty have replaced the certainty and complacency of the past. Worse still, our cherished objectivity has been called into question by philosophers of science. Polanyi (1958) has shown that even in the physical sciences one has to take into account the personal acts of the scientist. Objectivity is a personal act and scientific achievement must always imply the creative agency of the scientist. To include objectivity in the personal is, I think, more than just a nice intellectual point because to forget that objectivity is a personal act can lead, once more, to its identification with an immutable reality out there in a universe of causes rather than as an intelligible act in a universe of meaning. If the personal disappears in this shift from methodology to metaphysics then the consequences in psychology are both absurd and sinister. The absurd part is the disappearance of the scientist, in this case of the psychologist, as an agent in the manner described by Polanyi. The sinister part is the disappearance of the patient or experimental subject as an agent. A disembodied and value-free objectivity-reality 'out there' can easily exculpate the social status quo because there is no way of seeing the responses of the patient or subject as being valid or intelligible in such a world.

Physical scientists, going about their work, have also shown us that the goal of impersonal objectivity has practical limitations to go with the philosophical ones. At the most homely level it has been seen that different people harbour different assumptions as to exactly how to measure the level of the humble meniscus in a burette (Abercrombie, 1960), the thing is rounded so do you take the highest bit or the lowest bit for your measurement? Psychologists harbour assumptions too. On a more lofty place of science it has been demonstrated that you cannot pinpoint an electron in space and time because observing it alters its behaviour. Psychologists observe things too and yet it is quite remarkable that the impossibility of eliminating the observer from the observed should be declared by physicists and ignored by psychologists rather than the other way round. Perhaps this has something to do with a third consideration not shared with physical scientists and that is that not only do psychologists have assumptions, and not only does their observation affect the things they are having assumptions about, but the things they are having assumptions about can actually affect the psycho-logists unless they are very careful, that is to say very objective. As the building rises tier by tier upwards and the subject matter becomes less and less inanimate-predictable the harder it is to maintain a semblance of impersonal objectivity until, in applied psychology, it becomes almost impossible not to be moved by comparison, annoyance, or some other response toward the person sitting there with you. It is here that we misuse our objectivity and reason if we slavishly harness them to the methodologies of physical science, not only out of an eagerness to please the new establishment but also in an effort to rub out the human dimension because it makes us feel uncomfortable. I am not criticizing objectivity itself, especially when it is seen as a function of a participant-observer, but I think it is legitimate to protest against the claim that absolute objectivity is the only route to knowledge, particularly to knowledge about people. That is scientism, not

science. It would be most odd to be 'against science', it is one of
our great achievements. It can tell us all sorts of things about the
world which are fascinating and life-enhancing but, equally, there is
no reason in science itself why it should not be used to destroy and
oppress. It cannot give us the meanings and values of human relationships and one can hardly blame it for that, its job lies elsewhere.
Psychologists, however, do meet these new phenomena of meaning and
value and what they do with them is not a matter of intellectual
deliberation but an act of faith - 'Credo ut intelligam'. If psychologists see man in a mechanistic universe of causes then there will
be no place for these new phenomena because the psychologists' faith
obviates their very existence, and yet despite avuncular tickings-off
from their heroes on the ground floor this is precisely what psychologists continue to do; they persist in using a range of convenience,
which is quite appropriate in physical science, to try to understand
what simply cannot be understood in this way, that is to say, to try
to understand thinking subjects. Having set (a) the thinking subject
('res cognitans') against (b) the material universe ('res extensa')
the problem of how (a) can know (b) becomes intractible and it is
indeed tempting to try to approach it objectively by committing
oneself to determinism in a universe of causes, and it is by this act
of faith that many psychologists choose their level of investigation.
Others, however, see (a) as an abstraction of existence and for them
the problem takes a different form, it becomes one of how the
thinking subject gives meaning to the world, their commitment is to
intelligibility in a universe of meanings, to the possibilities of
unique agents rather than the properties of interchangeable objects.
This is not to deny determinism but to work in that margin of 'new
phenomena' within which people can be aware of and confront what is
determining them; within the radical subjectivity of Kierkegaard that
recognizes subjectivity as truth and affirms truth in a more personal
way than is possible when using epistemological conceptions.
Kierkegaard sought to abstract faith from reason and insisted that
they were different; just as a lover does not justify his love
rationally so does faith say, simply, 'I believe' (and then perhaps
finds reasons later on). Although the truth to which Kierkegaard
referred was not ordinary truth but Christian truth his 'Concluding
Unscientific Postscript' (1941) is of relevance to the worldly
concerns of psychology and psychotherapy. His truth is about the
individual human existence rather than general laws, it concerns
active, never-finished, relations to the external world rather than
static, completed statements about that world. Relational truth is
not concerned with objective certainty but with how the person
relates to objective uncertainty, it is about divergent problems which
cannot be solved by convergent thought. Kierkegaard was not a
subjective idealist, for him to exist means to reckon with the not-me,
much of which would 'be there' if there were no humans on earth and
yet as there are, at present anyway, he showed that everything we say
must be said from a human standpoint. Everything said from a human
standpoint is relative, partial; even in physical sense, when it
confronts the infinitely large and the infinitely small, the
relativity of realities is recognized. Indeed, according to
Dr Fritjof Capra in a BCC radio talk (1982), modern physics can be
seen to be suggesting a reality beyond that which is perceived

dualistically, the very reality of the great contemplative traditions
which is also beyond psychotherapy. It is as though on every level of
the hypothetical building of knowledge dualistic models are being
applied which reveal, in a balance between the knower and the known,
by acts of 'men of flesh and bone', different realities and partial
truths; different worlds are created, none more true than the other
and all are personal acts derived from the duality of subject and
object in the face of non-being.

> that grey subject
> of dread that Søren Kierkegaard
> depicted crossing its thousands
> of fathoms. the beast that rages
> through history; that presides smiling
> at the councils of the positivists.
>   (R.S. Thomas, 1978, p. 44)

Perhaps it is true that the limits of a personal psychology and
the limits of physics both point in the same direction to another
experience of reality outside the building of knowledge. Inside it,
however, we cannot speak of absolutes, the artistic world is just as
real as the scientific world and there need be no conflict between
them so long as we recognize the personal stance of the artist or
the scientist and take it seriously. Similarly, the psychotherapist
view of man is not more real than, say, a chemical view, it is just
more fitting when dealing with the new phenomena of value and meaning,
it means taking the personal more seriously than would be necessary
in natural science. It is not just the patient's personal view which
must be taken seriously but also that of the psychotherapist. In
other sciences, the personal element has to do with what you choose
to look at, what you choose to look for in it, how you choose to look
for it and what you make of what you are eventually see. It concerns
how you work with your impersonal apparatus. In psychotherapy,
however, the psychotherapist is the apparatus which is observing the
patient and it is his or her thinking and feeling which is objectively
and subjectively interpreting what is going on. The psychotherapist
is a participant-observer however much we may wish to deny one half
or other of this equation in order to avoid taking it seriously. The
'scientific' psychologist would not wish to be involved in such an
investigation because, being objective, there is no woolly
participant (however this is an illusion and can lead to oppression
by objectivity); the 'spontaneous' psychologist would not want to know
either because, being so genuine, there is no po-faced observer (this
is a manic dream of self-transcendence and can lead to oppression by
subjectivity). Most psychotherapists do not harbour the enviable
certainty of these two extremes and for them psychotherapy is
intriguing and enjoyable work in which, to borrow Shakespeare's words,
'Modest Doubt is cal'd The Beacon of the wise'.

PSYCHOTHERAPY AND REALITY

Personal interpretive psychotherapies have learned from, but are not
the same as, psychoanalysis. Psychoanalysis is a long, intensive and
detailed way of working which has revealed phenomena which need be

taken into account in modified forms in other settings. Unconscious
acts are the most important of these phenomena, especially those of
phantasy - the schemas to which people assimilate their realities.
Psychoanalysts have further shown that, in psychotherapy, the phantasies
which are disturbing the patient's capacity for relating to the psychotherapist may well be the same as those that are preventing the
establishment of relationships in everyday life. Given this acknowledgment of unconscious activity, the psychotherapy referred to here
can be defined as a conversation within the setting of a personal
relationship in which someone in distress can work towards personal
change through understanding. This is not usually how the patient sees
it, however, and he or she typically has a theory about some causes
existing outside the sphere of his or her responsibility; something
in the body (nerves) or environment (spiders) or in the forgotten past
(something nasty in the wood shed and 'do you do hypnosis?'), something happening which you are to stop happening whilst the patient
remains passive throughout - cure by treatment, 'While-U-Wait'.
Although the psychotherapist's goal is change by understanding
meanings and accepting personal responsibility, rather than cure by
treatment, it would be quite wrong to insist that the patient agrees
with this from the start as he or she is seeking cure by treatment
precisely because to see it in any other way would be intolerable;
the patient has come for the very reason that he or she dare not
accept responsibility. The patient's theory demands respect and is to
be treated with tact as the psychotherapist slowly and patiently comes
to suggest meanings where none were thought to exist. The theory which
the psychotherapist uses in order to do this consists of notations
which are meaningful but not empirically true (Heaton, 1979). Psychotherapy is about the patient's theory and cannot be understood in terms
of the psychotherapist's theory as being one which has some direct
relation to reality, to the Reality to which the patient's theory also
eventually accommodates itself. It is, instead, a process of
negotiation, it is two people treating with one another (which is one
definition of negotiation) rather than the treating of one person by
the other. They are sitting together and attempting to arrive at a
mutual understanding of the reasons why the patient selects and directs
a particular painful existence. It is indeed reclamation work as Freud
said, but reclamation of disclaimed action. Action is meaningful
activity, that which we do for a reason, and this includes bringing
about that from which we suffer. A symptom is not something you have
but something you do, defences do not act on the person they are
actions of the person. Things that happen to us (like reflexes) have
causes, but things we do have reasons and meanings, maybe multiple
reasons and meanings. Although Freud moved from meaning to mechanism
and gave us a positivistically conceived metapsychology around which
we have typically spun our confusion between meaning and truth in
identifying the homuncular fallacies of ids and egos with reality, the
person as agent can still be understood in terms of depth psychology
without falling back on ideas about the play of substantive, almost
personified forces. Roy Schafer (1976) has provided a framework
within which the formulations of psychodynamics and its forces can be
translated into an action language of reasons which does the same kind
of job as psychodynamics whilst making actions more comprehensible to
the patient - as impersonal forces are, by definition, forever beyond

the patient's reach. Interpretations, instead of being explanations about propulsive entities happening to us in reality and making us do things become, instead, ways of throwing light on the extent to which we are the authors, consciously and unconsciously, of our own lives and on how much we are disclaiming our own creation of our own worlds. Incidentally, it must be noted in passing the process is not only about claiming the falsely disclaimed but also about disclaiming the falsely claimed, as certain events do 'happen' which are not our responsibility. I am thinking of a young man who, since childhood, has felt responsible for his little brother having been born handicapped. Whatever other meanings are involved in this relationship, the actual syndrome afflicting his brother was determined in a universe of causes and it was falsely claimed on a personal level as this patient's responsibility. In general, however, psychotherapy does not deal with things that happen because of causes but relates to a universe of actions and the reasons people give for them, that is, with their theories. The psychotherapist does not have a theory which will furnish the patient with secure and certain answers; as Lacan said, the psychotherapist is not the 'subject who is presumed to know' (Turkle, 1979). The process is, instead, a practice in which the patient finds his or her own answers. The psychotherapist's communications are indirect, cultivating the slow mulling over of experience and the patient's discovery of his or her own truth, rather than what Kierkegaard calls direct communications which are didactic instructions to do with the psychotherapists's theory. It is here that Schafer's action language is particularly important. If we speak of the patient as though he or she is possessed by some malevolent entity which is denying him or her the salvation promised by the eternal verities of our theory. Now although Schafer's translations are often quite a mouthful, his translation of The Resistance is simple and direct. He treats the concept in its verb form, to resist, and speaks of the person doing the resisting as being engaged in two opposing actions at once. The person is not simply being negative and not collaborating but is doing something else as well, something with positive, affirmative reasons such as maintaining self-esteem. Schafer (op. cit.) believes that questions about resistance are really questions about these affirmations - what are they for? Rather than being a matter of resisting the psychotherapist and the psychotherapist's theory, these questions are about the patient and the patient's theory, about how the patient is opposing any change in the phenomenal world he of she has constructed.

Patients bring along their theories and, being people not objects, they can create new meanings, new worlds. Patient and psychotherapist work together toward the mutual understanding of a new version of reality. Ever since Freud had to abandon his seduction hypothesis it has been seen that the truth arrived at in this process cannot be understood solely in terms of historical facts about the past, but must include the person's relational truth about the events whether or not they actually 'happened' (which is a different matter entirely). We cannot reconstruct the historical past that explains the present but we can construct a personal past which is truth in terms of something emerging in the present that makes sense, an existential reality to live by; what else, indeed, could psychotherapy offer other than this, apart from some delusional system of certainty? Our commonsense reality originated in the seventeenth century with the rise of science, that is, there was a different one before that and there will clearly now be a different one after it. In psychology there is no real agreement about what the 'average expectable environment' to which people adapt actually is, and consensually validated reality provides no secure framework within which to work either. So perhaps in psychotherapy any old reality will do? No, the test of the reality is its fruitfulness, and that test is ultimately the patient's. Meanwhile, along the way, the process does not become solipsistic because the emergent must make sense to both theorists (consciously and unconsciously) which is why it is important to take the psychotherapist seriously as a participant-observer, as someone who has a vision of reality, as a person who is involved every step of the way. First, however, it is the psychotherapist's theory that must be considered. His or her best knowledge about the importance of past experiences in general (arrivals, departures and so on) will help the psychotherapist to privately construct a possible past for this patient, but this is no more than a starting point for negotiations about the individual's personal past; the same goes for the possible present. Obviously, psychotherapists have theories, they have consistent frameworks of criticism. What is important is the way these criticisms are articulated. It matters, quite literally, how they are put into words. If the impersonal passive is used, both patient and psychotherapist can disappear; the psychotherapist disappears by disclaiming any responsibility for the opinion conveyed by the interpretation and the patient disappears by being denied any agency in the matter it concerns. The interpretation hovers in the air above the heads of the two people in the room, having little to do with either of them. It is not attributable to the psychotherapist but to some higher authority like Freud or Freud-Reality and has much the same alienating effect as a letter from the tax man that begins 'it is regretted' (by whom?). The patient is eliminated when the statement carries on in the passive voice to refer to a mental process vaguely but inexorably going about its business while he or she sits helplessly by. Therefore I believe it is important to use the words 'I' ('I reckon') and 'You' ('You are doing such-and-such') rather than resorting to impersonal references to, for example, there being 'something persecutory in the air'. The use of personal words means, moreover, that the psychotherapist can phrase things in such a way as to convey a wish to understand even if what is said is wrong. This is impossible with impersonal statements delivered ex cathedra as they are not open to correction, and being open to correction is central to a view of psychotherapy that sees the work as a series of negotiations leading toward a mutual understanding. The alternative, that of viewing it as the patient's gradual acceptance of the psychotherapist's priestly omniscience, may be a simple extension of the way the patient's parents dealt with earlier communications by acts of attribution based on their own phantasies, to which the patient complied just as he or she is complying now by learning the psychotherapist's theory in order to be understood (thereby amply proving to the psychotherapist that the theory is, yet again, confirmed!). Of course, all psychotherapists want their theories to be right, but so do patients and I think it is important that patients experience being right in psychotherapy. Indeed, the most important attitude for us to bear in mind as psychotherapists, according to Meares and Hobson in their study of 'The

persecutory therapist' (1977), is that we should be ready and willing
all the time to look for evidence that we are wrong and that we should
be capable of adjusting our approach accordingly; this is not to abandon
theory and technique but to approach them in the spirit of Keats's
'negative capability', 'that is, when a man is capable of being in
uncertainties, mysteries, doubts, without any irritable reaching after
fact and reason' (Meares and Hobson, p. 353). I think the key word
there is 'irritable', it is the irritable reaching after formulations
that produces the closure of premature and alienating conclusions.
Clinging to what we already know produces more of the same, 'past
remedies', yet much of the psychotherapy concerns what we and the
patient do not know, that which can only be apprehended intuitively by
a leap into the unknown. In trying hard to understand we may mis-
understand rather than simply, for the moment, not understand. As in
myths, creation comes out of uncertainty. Of course, we have to use
our critical abilities eventually to form an interpretation to which we
are committed, but the point is that this can only arise creatively
after patience in the face of ambiguity and frustration otherwise our
response may well be an attempt to deal with our anxiety about the
unknown, and therefore possibly dangerous, situation; it will be theory
only. The patient does not want an impersonal theory and I would now
like to suggest that there can in a sense be no impersonal theory for
us psychotherapists either.

The psychotherapist is a man, or woman, 'of flesh and bone'. Heaton
(op. cit.) comments that when Freud 'discovered' the Oedipus complex he
was not acting like someone who had made a discovery at all, but more
like someone who was trying to make sense of his experiences; and
Guntrip (op. cit.) points out how different Adler and Freud were as
people, and how this difference reflected their backgrounds, influenced
their theories and more-or-less guaranteed that they would never be
able to work together. All of which is to say that our theories imply
views of life, health and sickness and that our theories are based on
these views and not the other way round. If we acknowledge the
relativity of reality we can then speak in terms of visions of reality,
of acts of imagination that mean looking at reality in certain ways and
not others. As visions of reality influence what we see and label as
'facts', clashes between theories based on different visions cannot be
resolved by appealing simply to these facts alone. When one's theory
is being attacked in terms of the evidence against it one feels
personally got at; there are several reasons for this but one is that
one's theory is the rhetoric of one's vision so it seems that one's
whole way of looking at the world is being belittled (and this is how
patients feel when we make our reality the measure of theirs). So
perhaps it is important to stand back from theory and look at the vision
of reality inherent in psychotherapy, and the different visions behind
the different types of psychotherapy (as opposed to rehabilitative and
training approaches, which are outside the scope of this investigation).
In the discussion that follows the terms used are derived from Schafer's
(op. Cit) transposition of some of Northrop Frye's difficult ideas to
the study of psychoanalysis. However, Schafer deals exclusively with
psychoanalysis whereas I intend to use his basic thesis as a framework
for looking at other approaches; first at the behavioural level, then
at the humanist or 'third force' therapies and finally at what Guntrip

(op. cit.) called 'truly personal psychology', a psychology which he believed was not the sole property of any one orthodoxy. In so doing I will deal consecutively with the four features which, Schafer says, go to make up the complex vision of reality inherent in psychoanalysis; the comic, the romantic, the tragic and the ironic - four mythic forms through which reality can be viewed.

   The comic vision seeks evidence for optimism and maintains itself by emphasising the secure, familiar, perdictable and controllable aspects of life - the quest for certainty of which Dewey spoke. Problems are situation-bound and can be dealt with by manipulative action, we laugh (at collapse of stout party) when they are overcome, they were not really dangerous after all! The vision embraces the concept of 'cure', definite goals and sure techniques for attaining them. Of course, all therapies involve optimism and taking steps to make things better; and on the comic level, the level of psychotherapy outcome research, all therapies seem as good as each other in this respect. But much more is involved in personal psychotherapy than this comic vision and this is why it can never by reconciled with behavioural approaches because behavioural therapy views man entirely from the comic point of view. This is not to say that the behavioural method is a joke, it is just that it follows the typical structure of dramatic comedy in which no blow is so final that it cannot be made up for, no dilemma so great that it cannot be relieved and so on. There is always an answer and the article 'Behaviour analysis, terminable and interminable' has yet to be written. Patients are encouraged to do things that will make them feel better, according to the psychologist's comic vision that is. This is nicely illustrated in a story that I once heard on the radio by the humourist Stephen Leacock. It concerned a miserable man complaining to his doctor of all sorts of melancholy and pessimism. The doctor, pragmatic and optimistic in the best spirit of the comic vision, suggested that the man needed taking out of himself and that the surest way of doing this would be to go to the theatre and see the great clown, Grimaldi; this would definitely lift all the gloom and make him a happier chap, said the doctor - to which the patient glumly replied, 'Yes, but I am the great Grimaldi!'

   In the romantic vision life is a quest undertaken by a hero in search of some idealized principle, some golden age. The quest ends, after perilous individualistic struggles (and dragons to be slain) with exaltation and joy. In contrast to the comic where steps are taken toward cure, here risks are taken toward liberation. The sense of adventure into the unknown is shared by the humanist and personal psychotherapies and is not to be found in the behavioural ones with their fixed target goals decided in the first session of therapy. However, the difference between the humanist perspective and what I am calling personal psychotherapy begins here as the individualistic quest of third force psychology seems lop-sidedly rooted in the romantic vision. In talking about human potential and growth there is inevitably some idealization involved. For example, people are promised a return to some nostalgic golden age in which the experiences of childhood (or even foetus-hood!) can be relived by a person regardless of the fact that he or she now has an adult body and body-image and a self-image to which all manner of experience has since been assimilated. Others speak of authenticity or spontaneity, but however the message is put it always seems to involve some triumph and a return to an idealized relationship with the world (our parents). I know that many humanist psychotherapists see behind this vision to the tragic sense of life, but a great deal of third force writing, particularly the psychobabble, emphasises the romantic vision to the exclusion of everything else. Modern Man in Search of a Crutch limps along from workshop to seminar to marathon always hoping that next time he will 'get it together', that he will gloriously fuse with reality and leave the suffering behind. The romantic vision is important in personal psychotherapy too and yet, as Balint said, although the wish for an idealized relationship is an honourable one it is one that we must help our patients to bury with honour (Wolff, 1982).

The tragic vision is reflected in an awareness of the uncertainties, paradoxes, ambiguities and trials of living. Earlier it was mentioned that psychotherapy deals with the possibilities of human beings; the tragic vision concerns the opposite to possibility, the limited factor in existence which the existentialists call facticity - the doors that close around our openness. Thus, personal psychotherapy does not run away with itself in wishful thinking because each decision made on the romantic quest determines, to some extent, the choices that remain for the future, there is loss in gain, guilt in justified action and defeat in victory as well as victory in defeat. Facticity is the inner aware-ness that one's own view of reality is relative and that there will always be something missing, it is a recognition of finitude and determinism. The tragic vision is central to the ideas presented in this chapter; the partial nature of experience perceived dualistically; the retreating horizon in the quest for certainty; the goal of psycho-therapy being Freud's normal suffering rather than the transcendence of dualism mistakenly claimed by certain existentialist psychotherapists; 'the man of flesh and bone' seeking intelligibility in a finite world; the insidious influence of unconscious phantasies; the realization of one's active role in bringing about passive suffering; the reality negotiated in psychotherapy, whilst not any old reality, being still no more than a version of the patient's life and mind; no idealized relation with the world (and no fully analysed person!); and lastly, to anticipate the final section, the tragic vision is the source of empathy (the participant) and the safeguard against omnipotence (the observer) in the psychotherapist. The tragic vision is nothing to do with being hopeless and miserable, indeed it is the most searching and involved perspective on human life that there is. In accepting facticity it sees that only in adversity can people grow and change. Psychotherapy works within the margin of the person's relation to facticity rather than by ignoring it in the search for a happy ending. The romantic quest is tempered by what Miguel de Unamuno calls 'The Tragic Sense of Life' (op. cit.) through which the hero finds not despair but a new affirmation.

The ironic view concerns the same appreciation of ambiguity and uncertainty as the tragic view but treats it in a different way. Whilst the tragic vision is passionate and involved the ironic is detached, it keeps things in perspective and in so doing it challenges grandiosity and safeguards good judgment. The assurance of the comic, the exultation of the romantic and the momentousness of the tragic are all vulnerable to irony which seeks contradictions and ambiguities, the antithesis to every thesis. Irony takes the relativity of reality very seriously and undermines any claim to certainty. Certainty means that the facts can be relied upon as being so and so and not called to question. Doubt, as a verb used transitively, means just the opposite, it calls in question. In personal psychotherapy doubt is radical in the face of the arbitrariness of absolutes. This is not to mystify psychotherapy, there is nothing in the least mysterious about its technique, its view of persons, however, does acknowledge their mystery. The ambiguity sought by the ironic vision is especially disconcerting for people (patients and psychotherapists) who have been prematurely forced into orderly and unambiguous functioning in childhood, who were not able to enjoy trying out nonsense and risks secure in the conviction that their parents would be able to manage the outcome. The ironic vision in psychotherapy involves learning to overcome this and accepting the indeterminate and the enigmatic - hence the importance of the 'negative capability' on the part of the psychotherapist.

I believe that all truly personal psychotherapy, whether it is that of Guntrip (op. cit.) or Smail (1978), involves these four visions and that there four visions limit the extent to which one can be an eclectic psychotherapist. The sense of optimism, progress (comic) and adventure (romantic) are appreciated and relied upon but, as therapy progresses, their natures change in the light of the ambiguous and inexorable. The tragic and ironic visions are the depth of depth psychology, a psychology that has a 'reality principle' that recognises the depth of existence and unremittingly questioning all absolutes, the psycho- therapist whose theory proceeds from this composite vision can no longer be seen as an expert who knows the answers to all the questions asked by great writers and ordinary people alike who are worrying their heads about what it all means. This omniscient and impersonal object- ivity is an illusion, and if there is a place for objectivity in psycho- therapy then it is objectivity of a different kind - that of a participant observer.

THE PARTICIPANT-OBSERVER

Becoming a psychotherapist is a complex project which we undertake for reasons of our own. Although some adventitious influences are involved, it is largely no accident that we end up doing what we are doing. When I left school I had no idea about what to do with myself in career terms so I just drifted around for a while. Then I chanced upon a book called 'What Jung Really Said' (Bennet, 1966). I am sure I did not understand a word of it but, at the time, I found it fascinating so I decided to go to University to study psychology. Needless to say, I never heard of Jung once in the five years that followed. Freud's name came up only occasionally, usually as an illustration of how daft you can get, and people like Rogers and Kelly were consigned to the marginalia of courses about personality and its assessment. There are two points to this anecdote. The first is that I was drawn to psychology in the hope that I would learn to understand myself (and maybe other people as a bonus), and the second is that psychology, at present, is not about understanding people. Its universe of

determinism provides no basis for the practice of psychotherapy. Had
my professional route been through psychiatry or social work I would
still be doing much the same kind of work as I am now (although life
would be easier were I a psychiatrist). Moreover, it seems, according
to Henry, Sims and Spray (1971), that people who do psychotherapy have
more in common with each other than they do with non-psychotherapist
members of their own profession. This finding rather raises questions
about the economy of maintaining professional routes like psychology
and psychiatry to what amounts to the separate enterprise altogether
of psychotherapy that has no theoretical or ideological bases in these
parent professions at all. So in order to make sense of becoming a
psychotherapist we have to consider the reasons we give for doing it
rather than the route we took to get to it. The most common reasons
we give are to do with being interested in people and wanting to help
them. Of course we actually have to be interested in people or we
would soon get fed up with psychotherapy, and I am not questioning
the authenticity of human kindness either, but if we take ourselves
seriously as participant-observers we come to appreciate paradoxes
and ambiguities involving the disclaimed elements of these motives.
Behind these apparent strengths lie our weakness: our need for
intimacy and safe tenderness; the satisfactions of voyeurism and
control; illusions of omnipotence (and the impotence behind them); the
wish to make amends for some imagined damage done. However, through
our experience of doing psychotherapy, of getting supervision with a
supervisor who is not omnipotent or persecutory, of arrivals and
departures in our own lives and, if we can get it, of psychotherapy
for ourselves, we come to see that our weakness is our strength.
These less laudible reasons are problems only in so far as they are
kept out of awareness and psychotherapy is done to meet the psychotherapist's needs rather than those of the patient. However in
coming to know these reasons, especially in so far as anxiety
diminishes and guilt becomes tolerable, the psychotherapist is actually
enhanced; he or she will be more able to relinquish intimacy when the
time comes, the patient's separateness and autonomy will be better
respected, the psychotherapist's omnipotence is not treasured at all
costs, his or her temporary feelings of failure can be understood
within the context of the relationship and perhaps used to the
patient's advantage and, finally, unequivocal failure can be lived
with. So it seems that each of the previously mentioned 'neurotic'
reasons has a therapeutic seed within it, which suggests that psychotherapeutic ability is developed rather than acquired. It grows from
one's own far from perfect personality in which, to quote Churchill,
the greatest handicap of all is to have no handicap.

However, psychotherapeutic ability is often seen as something
separate from ourselves, something promising certainty that can be
obtained 'off the peg' from an Institute in order to clothe our
inadequacies. This idealized image of the omnipotent psychotherapist
is, of course, an illusions and one that makes it hard for the
beginning psychotherapist to learn to be weak. It is, however, an
illusion that is actually fostered by the various Schools and
Institutes of psychotherapy themselves. This is partly because
psychotherapists know little and can do even less, whereas their rivals
have clearly demonstrable techniques concerning treatments (surgical,

electrical, behavioural or chemical) that at least sound more scientific and persuasive to other people - including employing authorities! The Institutes, therefore, have to protect the profession, as all scientific societies do, but in the case of psychotherapy this can subvert what is most subversive about it, that is, its radical doubt; truths become established and techniques codified that are actually antithetical to the spirit of psychotherapy itself which, being a form of truth-seeking, can never be identified with any such certitudes (Turkle, op. cit.). These certitudes, however, offer the security of the comic and romantic visions, in the first case as a defence against the inevitable uncertainties of our work and in the second case by promising an idealized emotional relationship with our parents in the guise of the founding Father or Mother of the theory. That is, they protect us against the tragic and the ironic. Moreover, the discomfort of being a psychotherapist in a competitive and results-oriented service industry further tempts one into dogmatism because in the process of imagining one's own theory to be better than the rest there somehow arises the illusion that it is better than it actually is itself. The psychotherapist is then faced with the discrepancy between the rhetoric of the School and his or her own day-to-day experience of psychotherapy, warts and all. The result is that either one becomes dejected and gives up or, more likely, one clings even more to the theory and blames infidel psychiatrists, 'unsuitable' patients or something else for one's perplexities; the theory, however, remains above reproach because of the emotional investment one has in it for the sake of security. In this way psychotherapy repeats the schismatic history of religious sectarianism; the narcissistic illusion of certainty is unsusceptible to criticism and views other than those of one's own School are treated as heresies. Doctrinaire rigidity becomes a dead hand stifling creativity in any direction. None of which is to depreciate theory in itself but to say that theory can be used in a faintly paranoid way in our quest for certainty. A further parallel with religion illustrates this distinction. A few months ago a copy of Watchtower mysteriously turned up in the staff toilet of one of the places where I work. There being nothing else to hand I read the contents closely. It was a special issue called 'Why are there so many Religions?' in which the writer went on to ask 'Have you ever wondered about this? Most thinking people have' and 'Is there any way of telling which one is right?' There are no prizes for guessing the answer to the last question, and there is no arguing with it - as anyone who has tried to exchange views with a Witness all know. When you close the front door you will not have made the slightest dent in his certainty that Truth is revealed in his own particular book. How different this is to the Buddhist idea of 'ehi-passika' which means do not believe a word of it just because it is in a book, look and see in your own experience, work out your own way in terms of what proves fruitful in action, no passive adherence to any dogma for the sake of security. This spirit is essential if psychotherapeutic theory is to be open-ended and ever developing. Life is short and one obviously has to confine oneself to a particular style of theory, one that makes sense intellectually (some seem beneath my dignity and some go right over my head), one that proves fruitful in practice, one that suits one's personality and fits one's vision of reality. Theories are valuable instruments, but when they are reified they can soon get deified and when this happens, as Tennyson said, 'There lives more faith in honest doubt, Believe me, than in half the creeds.'

Techniques, like theory, can either be used or abused. Unfortunately, it is by definition concerned with the mechanical part of an artistic performance (Chambers Dictionary) and this implies an orderly sequence of how to go about psychotherapy that can be acquired and then mechanically applied to all comers without reference to their uniqueness. As part of the quest for certainty technique, in this sense, becomes an essentially comic engagement with only the regular and repeated common denominators of human existence. When this happens, the technique is the therapy and this, I think, is implicitly the case not only in package behavioural treatments like Anxiety Management Training but also in package non-behavioural treatments like Gestalt therapy. In personal psychotherapy, however, the patient's uniqueness is something to be discovered, not something to be put in brackets so that the technique can work. This means that the technique must be flexible enough to follow the unpredictability and ambiguity recognized in its vision of reality. Naturally, in developing a technique everyone goes through the movement from loose-to-tight-to-loose construing familiar to personal construct theorists, and beginning psychotherapists generally adhere more closely to the 'proper' technique of their own particular School than do their more experienced elders (Strupp, 1955). So initially technique is a source of security, hence the idea of acquiring it. However, as it gradually develops as a function of experience it becomes modified to suit the person, and the other way round; it comes to be valued differently and used more flexibly. Technique is of value and to say that it is not can often be seen as a cover for inexperience. We all have a lot to learn from each other and it is only seeing what we have to learn as being a mechanical technique and how we learn it as being a process of acquisition that is being questioned. David Malan's 'Universal Technique' (1979), for example, provides a generous, clear and accessible account of what he has learned from others and from his own experience which demystifies technique whilst demonstrating that it can never be mechanical. It looks orderly and sequential but is far from being a Workshop Manual as its governing principle is rapport, so that understanding comes before technique and not vice versa. Given this, however, Malan has shown in plain terms the horse-sense and tact of a certain stepwise approach toward unlocking the 'à clef' elements of the patient's story as it unfolds within the relationship, but he warns (p. 93)

> that all this is only a rough guide, which may help the therapist to find his way through the maze of the patient's material, but will certainly be a treacherous guide if followed slavishly.

This reminds me of my once finding my way to a particular place in France using only a ridiculously small and garish Map of Europe given free with some petrol. I always knew what was roughly the right direction but never really knew what to expect round the next corner. Consequently I was lost much of the time and forced back upon my own resources, such as they were, but I carried on because I thought it was worth it. Similarly, in psychotherapy one is often lost and thrown back upon oneself. Technique is a useful guide but only if one thinks that the journey is worth it, that is if one thinks people are worth

it. As Fromm-Reichman (1950) wrote
   It is my firm belief that the first prerequisite for successful
   psychotherapy is the respect that the psychiatrist must extend
   to the mental patient. Such respect can be valid only if the
   psychiatrist realizes that his patient's difficulties in living
   are not too different from his own. (p. xi)
The 'consumer' research of Strupp et al. (1964) suggests that the
patient's conviction that he or she has the psychotherapist's respect
is the cornerstone of helpful therapy and that technical skill only
serves to capitalize on this. However, if respect is construed in
Fromm-Reichman's terms then this quality of relationship cannot be
offered by an impersonally objective and largely bullet-proof observer
but only by someone who knows that we are all in the same boat and is,
therefore, objective in a different way, that is, in a way that
recognizes the creatureliness of the observer. So far, the participant-
observer has been discussed in relation to assumptions about reality,
ways of conceptualizing theory and so on, but if the principle is
really to be taken seriously it must be finally be seen to relate to
what actually happens in practice.

   An objectivity that implies that, of the two people in the room, one
is 'sick' and that the other is observing from some Olympian plane of
'health' is a myth. The truth is that we are all more similar than
otherwise. When patient and psychotherapist come together the content
of the session is about just one of them, but the process involves
both, each responding consciously or unconsciously to everything that
happens whilst they are interacting (Racker, 1968). That they do not
both drown in subjectivity has nothing to do with the psychotherapist
averting the issue by turning his or her objectivity towards the whole
field of what is going on in the room, and this includes what is going
on in the psychotherapist. This is the difference between the two
people, one of them is maintaining a private division between participation in subjective experience and critical observation of that
experience in order to help the other person to do something similar,
to possess experience rather than, as it seems to the patient, to be
possessed by it. In this way, objectivity is an achievement of the
patient and not a self-imposed methodological precondition of the
psychotherapist, as would be the case for other scientists. The
psychotherapist is affected by a participant but, instead of acting-
out his or her personal responses, the psychotherapst observes them
and, if possible, uses them in the service of the patient's struggle
towards personal acts of objectivity in the reclamation work they are
undertaking together. Thus, as a participant-observer, the psychotherapist has to glide in and out of both modes of action, shifting
and blending inlook and outlook. The actions of the observer are
rational and consist of reasoning, synthesizing, scrutinizing what is
going on in the light of knowledge about past patients, remembering
previous attempts to help; they involve theory, experience, technique
and the idiosyncratic cast of the psychotherapist's critical and
intellectual life in general. The rational is essential, but the
psychotherapist has to be able to let go of this mode of functioning
in order to gain access to the very information necessary for understanding the patient. It is the psychotherapist's personal experience
of the movement of the relationship that furnishes the 'observer' with

the raw data that has then to be critically scrutinized. It is preferable not to call this raw data irrational, thereby implying that rationality is precluded, but to see it as flowing from the non-rational actions of the psychotherapist as 'participant', that is, from those imaginative activities involved in what is called empathy.

Unfortunately, empathy has come to be seen as some sort of substance that can exist, as though in tubes, at different levels in different people with the implication that you can get topped up with it if your level is low by taking a course. Thus appropriated by the comic vision, Carl Rogers's important concept is now often treated as a catalyst - as a substance involved in a process but not affected by it - a 'constant' offered at a uniformly high level to all patients from the beginning to the end of all therapies. The idea that one can have a large quantity of empathy and therefore be accurate is one's dealings with patients obscures the essential quality of empathic action, which is only ever approximate and marked by an openness to being, and being seen to be, wrong - inaccurate. Moreover, empathy is not really a comic constant, but a way of responding that gradually develops in each individual case as therapy deepens and you come to know the person through the slow unfolding of crises and adversities in his or her life; indeed, Schafer (op. cit.) believes that empathy is eventually associated with a way of responding depressively to the patient as a tragic hero. A final problem with the idea of empathy as a commodity is that it suggests something to be consciously striven after and this can lead to one's attention to the other person becoming one's attention to one's attention to the other person making the psychotherapist a combination of puppeteer and marionette who is more likely to end up in knots than respond with empathy. What empathy seems to be, instead, is a way of imagining the other person's experience that is arrived at pre-consciously and unconsciously with only its final reaction registering in consciousness, that is, we find to our surprise that we are acting in the way the other person is at the end of a series of actions that took place outside awareness. This is not a esoteric practice, people do it all the time, so it is nothing to be strained after; we simply find ourselves privately acting empathically in viewing ourselves differently and only make sense of it after we have done it. The process involves a temporary 'dip' into identification from which the psychotherapist then emerges as a separate person (sometimes we resist this because we fear that we will not be able to find our way back into separateness). I once worked with a mother and daughter who were in such close empathic communication with each other that the poor girl literally did not have a mind of her own; similarly, in psychotherapy, the raw data of empathy on its own does not liberate the patient, memories from childhood or even from earlier on in the day that pop up in the psycho-therapist's mind are not mutative for the patient, without thought they can lead to confusion or even to fusion. The psychotherapist has to stand back and submit them to the intellectual scrutiny of the observer. However, there has to be the empathic action of the participant as well or there will be nothing to be thought about and this requires the free play of projection and introjection and a relative freedom from defensive manoeuvres in response to the panics and sadnesses sensed in this way; we cannot understand anything in another person unless we have first understood it in ourselves. As empathy involves identifying

with the patient on the basis of corresponding actions of my own, if I
have not understood these actions in my own life then I can hardly
expect my patient to do any better. Sometimes, however, the demand on
the psychotherapist's understanding is even greater than this and he or
she has actually to personally resolve a sense of disquiet before the
process can move again for the patient. In this case the psychotherapist may not be identifying with the patient but with what the
patient is making of the psychotherapist in phantasy, with the worried,
hated, feared, threatened or rejected aspects of the patient's
unconscious imagination. When this happens, the psychotherapist's
empathic understanding goes down the drain because he or she is not
just being treated as someone else, which is common enough, but feels
treated as someone else and is surprised by an upsurge of unaccountable
emotion that is, therefore, a 'symptom' to be taken just as seriously
as any other 'symptoms' in the field of the session. The essential
ingredient of psychotherapy has been temporarily lost, the lively
interest in, and affection for, the patient involved in the attitude of
respect and its resulting acts of empathic understanding are all
eclipsed for the psychotherapist finds that he or she has been driven
into a different kind of relationship altogether; that is, into a
phantasy relationship in which the psychotherapist's identification is
not concordant with the conscious and unconscious actions of the
patient as agent, as in empathy, but complementary to them (see Racker,
op. cit.). In such instances the psychotherapist is a participant in
a very real sense and is experiencing the relationship from the point
of view of a protagonist in the private drama of the patient's
imagination. Thus the psychotherapist's understanding fails when the
patient is struggling with a personal conflicted relationship that
involves the psychotherapist in a way that the latter does not understand in himself, or herself (having been , as Jung said, possessed by
the demon of sickness). The patient will be unable to tolerate the
anxiety and guilt attendant upon the conflicted relationship until the
psychotherapist can. They are in it together and, to some extent to
the patient's relief, it is up to the psychotherapist, using the
negative capability, to tolerate what is intolerable for the patient;
this is not all that heroic because these transient feelings of, say,
being under threat are only a diluted form of just how dreadful the
patient feels all the time. When this form of identification registers
in consciousness it provides the observer with very important information for understanding the patient and, although it is disturbing for
the psychotherapist, it is therefore not a matter of the therapy 'going
wrong' - indeed the complementary feelings of the psychotherapist
feelings of the psychotherapist often mean that the patient now feels
safe enough for the conflicted relationship to be enacted. The only
problem is that as the psychotherapist is representing, for example,
the angry parent of the patient's imagination the psychotherapist's
response will reflect the attitude of that very object of distortion.
So, in being treated as, and feeling treated as, an angry parent the
danger is that one may respond accordingly particularly because there
is the additional irritation of being frustrated in one's therapeutic
strivings. However, if one does react with a harsh comment the
viscious circle of the imaginary relationship takes another inexorable
turn in maintaining the projections and introjections that were at the
root of the problem in the first place, and this is how the poor get

poorer in psychotherapy. Unfortunately, the completion of the viscious circle is paradoxically what the patient is after in the sense that it confirms the patient's theory and saves him or her from the risks that any change in it might have involved. Rather than this the patient needs to be offered something new and this necessitates the psychotherapist's finding a way back to the attitude of friendly interest towards the agent provocateur, that patient as agent. That is, one must experience for oneself the feelings of guilt, anxiety and so on and tolerate them as a participant before the 'observer' can recognize what is distorting the positive relationship and work out the part the patient is playing in it. The 'correctness' of the resulting formulation matters far less than the degree to which it is neither defensive towards the impact of the patient nor towards the impact of one's own feelings. If this is not accomplished and vengefulness at being thwarted gets the better of one in the form of a sarcastic remark I think it would be quite appropriate to apologise, as one would in most other conversations. Assuming, however, that this is not the case and one has tolerated the feelings of the participant, whether concordant, complementary or an alternation between the two, and submitted them to the critical evaluation of the observer there is one final consideration before opening one's mouth, and that is the question of tact. This is a mixture of the actions of the participant-observer as a whole person for, ideally, the participant will know from the inside through empathic understanding and the observer from the outside through experience whether or not putting the formulation into words will be too disturbing to be intelligible and useful to the patient at the present moment. When all has gone well in the manner described and the psychotherapist finally suggests a new meaning there is clearly a great deal more being conveyed in the interpretation than just its intellectual content (see Rycroft, 1956) as it is the creation of the psychotherapist as a person. It contains something that is missing in impersonal interventions - the implicit message that the patient has the psychotherapist's respect and this, I think, is what the patient really wants to hear. This respect is disclosed by all the actions of the participant-observer that have been discussed in the preceding pages in terms of empathy, patience, tact and so on. A background in academic psychology or psychiatry is clearly irrelevant to these actions and people who do psychotherapy have not acquired them from anywhere; everyone can be empathic et cetera and all the psychotherapist has over the man in the street is a setting in which these actions can be effectively performed and a way, developed from experience, of observing and making relative sense of what is going on that facilitates these ordinary human actions where the understandable temptations for others might be to act as a lover, guru, victim, judge, aggressor, comforter or expert instead.

In psychotherapy patients do not receive just an impersonal interpretation and no such thing is transmitted by the psychotherapist either. As with choosing theory and technique, choosing an interpretation is a personal act; no two psychotherapists, even if they belong to the same School, would say exactly the same thing at any given moment. Neither interpretation would bear the imprimatur of the School and each psychotherapist would arrive at a different truth, one of which might be more fruitful than the other but not more empirically

true. They would say different things because they are different people
with different experiences rather than identical impersonally objective
observers who have triumphed in their quest for certainty. The
development of a psychotherapist is never completed and unless one is
a slave to a rigid doctrine there is always something new to discover
in each session. Unlike in other sciences, this means that the
apparatus is mutable as one cannot remain static whilst dealing with
such dynamically changing material as a person's life. Not only does
one come to intellectually understand more from patients and colleagues
but one also changes personally in the emotional give and take of the
work itself, from the concordant identifications that enrich one's
general scope for empathy in the future to the specific small changes
involved in coming to understand one's complementary feelings in
relation to a particular person before that person is free to move
again and, in turn, change on a larger scale. Thus, personal psychotherapy is of necessity quite a different enterprise to those
undertaken elsewhere in the hypothetical building of knowledge. Its
vision embraces new concepts in a universe of meanings in which the
quest for certainty is tempered by radical doubt. Its truth is not
absolute but negotiated on the basis of relative realities in the
ordinary dualistic experience of people of flesh and bone - a species
that includes psychologists and psychotherapists, however much we may
wish to arrogate to ourselves a more advanced stage of evolution in
order to gain distance on our subject matter by a self-deceit
unnecessary in other sciences. In psychotherapy truth is relational
and Kierkegaard's concept applies equally to the truths of patient and
psychotherapist. The significance of this is that, rather than
distancing oneself to attain absolute objectivity, one can find
personal objectivity only by clarifying one's reactions as a participant
in the field of the relationship, one's own experience in session. Of
course, this personal experience will be fallible and subject to
distortions but, as Racker says (op. cit.), it is the best we have of
its kind. Our imagination is never irrelevant to what is going on in
any given moment and the dangers of ignoring it are far greater than
those attendant upon giving it freedom. It is only what we make of it
that is important and this is where the 'observer' acts rationally in
trying to make sense of our feelings, phantasies and memories instead
of letting them be followed blindly or acted out. Nothing about the
observer, from becoming a psychotherapist to coming to an interpretation,
is impersonal but it is rational in terms of the best we can do to make
timely and good-enough sense of the therapeutic process for it to move
again intelligibly for the patient. This critical scrutiny of our own
non-rational actions is a function of experience and will reflect our
own School of thought about theory and technique, but it only comes
into play when unconscious activity has finally registered something to
be thought about in consciousness. Coming to a formulation involves
head and heart in an interplay between rational and non-rational action
that has a closer affinity to creative activity in art than it has to
the problem-solving methodologies of psychology. Picasso, for example,
had learned from the Schools and could paint 'proper' pictures as well
as anyone could. He had absorbed the traditions of Western Art but
created something new by relying on unconscious inspiration for his
work. However, like the psychotherapist formulating an interpretation,
he then had to subject this very personal unconscious inspiration to

the disciplines of critical organizing activity in order to communicate
his new meaning to other people - for as he said after looking at some
paintings by Jackson Pollock, you should not let the unconscious have
all its own way. The same holds for personal psychotherapy, we cannot
expect defences to melt in the warmth of our unconscious inspiration,
they have to be made malleable by words that communicate understanding
in an intelligible way. Our understanding is shaped into words on the
basis of a consistent but open-ended framework of criticism. For
systematic purposes I think a private framework of action language is
the most fitting, but what is actually said will depend upon the
patient's theory too and will therefore reflect a developing common
language in the light of the psychotherapist's experience and evolving
technique. Thus, the intuitive actions of the non-rational participant
and the critical actions of the rational observer are necessary in
psychotherapy, either function in isolation being an insufficient
basis from which to negotiate a mutual understanding with another
person. Practitioners of personal psychotherapy, whatever their
School, are participant-observers who, unlike their 'spontaneous' or
'scientific' colleagues caricatured above, recognize degrees of
subjectivity and objectivity in personal action without resorting
either to the romantic idealization of anti-intellectualism or to the
comic pedagogy of expertise. The tragic vision deepens participation
into respect for the other person's autonomy in a shared finite world
and the ironic vision sharpens observation to a point that deflates
certainty; what remains is the humility of the participant-observer.
Psychologists are taught to be impersonal observers and this Cartesian
teaching acts like a magnet in attracting some people and repulsing
others so that in neither case is there independence from its field.
From the two resulting positions of 'nothing but' Reason and 'anything
but' Reason the notion of a participant-observer might seem to be both
weak-minded and faint-hearted, a sort of passive compromise unworthy
of consideration in the theoretical great debate about the truth of
psychotherapy. However, I think that the participant-observer is far
from passive in practice and that the concept embraces the actions of
the whole person in a way that the two extremes do not. In 'Continuous
Excursions' by Marshall Colman(1982) the following passage by
E. M. Forster was used to portray the false dichotomy between the
personal and the political; I too would like to borrow Forster's words
as they apply most fittingly to the actual practice of psychotherapy
and also illustrate the thesis that one does not have to be exclusively
a participant or an observer in order to do it. The psychotherapist
who clings to rational observation and the psychotherapist who lets
the unconscious have all its own way, like the

> businessman who assumes that this life is everything and the
> mystic who asserts that it is nothing, fail, on this side and
> on that, to hit the truth. 'Yes, I see, dear; it's about half-
> way between', Aunt Juley had hazarded in earlier years. No;
> truth, being alive, was not halfway between anything. It was
> only to be found by continuous excursions into either realm,
> and though proportion is the final secret, to espouse it at the
> outset is to ensure sterility. (p. 72)

Personal psychotherapy involves the faith of the participant and
the works of the observer through continuous excursions into either

realm, However, in compliance to personal and political demands for
manifest expertise we place undue emphasis publicly on theory, research
and technique with the private experience of the psychotherapist being
seen at best as a very peripheral subject of inquiry. Of course the
rational actions of the observer are important, too important to be
rejected out of hand in a counter-dependent backlash against anything
to do with head-work, they are worthy of study and development throughout life. Nevertheless, if we fail to recognise the limitations of the
intellectual side of psychotherapy we can come to see the rational and
predictable aspects of the work as being its essence and the perfect
psychotherapist as being an expert who, knowing all the theory and
having acquired all the skills, is 'the subject who is presumed to
know'. It is quite reasonable, although usually misguided, to presume
that a mechanic knows how to fix your car but to think of the psychotherapist in exactly the same way is to belie the very vision of
personal psychotherapy. Theory and technique are learned and, as we
go along, they gradually melt into experience but there is no question
of aiming for perfection. The best we can hope for is to be good-
enough psychotherapists which, in view of the relativity of realities,
partial truths and radical doubt, means that we cannot deal in certainties. People are inconceivably complex and it is a source of great
intellectual gratification to sense a pattern in someone's life as it
emerges in our work and to put this understanding to the test of
negotiation. There is always something new to discover and preconceived past remedies only serve to rob us of this satisfaction; even
the security thus gained in attending only to the certain, the regular
and the repeated is, in the end, hollow. As Meredith wrote, 'Ah, what
a dusty answer gets the soul, When hot for certainties in this our
life'. However, in the humility of knowing that we are all in the
same boat of ordinary experience perhaps we can make the best of those
partial conceptions we have developed in our practice that have proved
most fruitful as an open-ended basis for negotiation whilst remaining
true to our vision of reality. This vision embraces psychotherapists
too and puts our rational actions into the perspective of our being
people first and psychotherapists second. Helping people to overcome
unnecessary misery means making continuous excursions into either
realm and not just a one-way journey in the quest for certainty.
Expert knowledge promises personal and political security but if we
cannot tolerate the ambiguous, the non-rational and the weakness of
not knowing we can hardly expect any better of our patients. To mimic
the beatitudes it can be said both of psychotherapists and of their
patients that blessed are the confused for they will find their way,
cursed are the certain for that's the way they'll stay.

REFERENCES

ABERCROMBIE, M.L.J. (1960), 'The Anatomy of Judgement', London,
Penguin.
BENNET, E.A. (1966), 'What Jung Really Said', London, Macdonald.
CAPRA, F. (1982), Einstein and the Buddha - Part One, 'The Listener',
11 March, pp. 12-13.
COLMAN, M. (1982), 'Continuous Excursions: Politics and Personal Life',
London, Pluto Press.

DESCARTES, R. (1955), 'Rules for the Direction of the Mind', in
E.S. Haldane and G.R.T. Ross (trans.), 'The Philosophical Works of
Descartes', vol. 2, New York, Dover.
DEWEY, J. (1929), 'The Quest for Certainty', New York, Plenum.
FROMM-REICHMAN, F. (1950), 'The Principles of Intensive Psychotherapy',
University of Chicago Press.
GUNTRIP, H. (1971), The Ego Psychology of Freud and Adler Re-examined
in the 1970's, 'British Journal of Medical Psychology', vol. 46,
pp. 305-18.
HEATON, J.M. (1979), Theory in Psychotherapy, in N. Bolton,
'Philosophical Problems in Psychology', London, Methuen.
HENRY, W.E., SIMS, J.H. and SPRAY, S.L. (1971), 'The Fifth Profession',
San Francisco, Jossey-Bass.
KIERKEGAARD, S. (1941), 'Concluding Unscientific Postscript', trans.
D.F. Swenson, Princeton University Press for the American Scandinavian
Foundation.
KLINE, P. (1980), 'Mathematics, the Loss of Certainty', Oxford
University Press.
MALAN, D.H. (1979), 'Individual Psychotherapy and the Science of
Psychodynamics', London, Butterworths.
MEARES, R.A. and HOBSON, R.F. (1977), The Persecutory Therapist,
'British Journal of Medical Psychology', vol. 50, pp. 349-59.
OPPENHEIMER, R. (1956), Analogy in Science, 'American Psychologist',
vol. 11, pp. 127-35.
POLANYI, M. (1958), 'Personal Knowledge', London, Routledge & Kegan
Paul.
RACKER, H. (1968), 'Transference and Countertransference', London,
The Hogarth Press and The Institute of Psychoanalysis.
RYCROFT, C. (1956), The Nature and Function of the Analyst's
Communication to the Patient, 'International Journal of Psychoanalysis',
vol. 37, pp. 469-72.
SCHAFER, R. (1976), 'A New Language for Psychoanalysis', Yale
University Press.
SMAIL, D.J. (1978), 'Psychotherapy: A Personal Approach', London, Dent.
STRUPP, H.H. (1955), Psychotherapeutic Technique, Professional
Affiliation and Experience Level, 'Journal of Consulting Psychology',
vol. 19, pp. 97-102.
STRUPP, H.H., WALLACH, M.S. and WOGAN, M. (1964), Psychotherapy
Experience in Retrospect: Questionnaire Survey of Former Patients and
their Therapists, 'Psychological Monographs', Vol. 78 (11. Whole
No. 588).
THOMAS, R.S. (1978), Synopsis, in 'Frequencies', London, Macmillan.
TURKLE, S. (1979), 'Psychoanalytic Politics, Freud's French Revolution',
London, Burnett Books in association with Andre Deutsch.
UNAMUNO, M. de (1921), 'The Tragic Sense of Life', London, Macmillan.
WOLFF, H.H. (1982), Teaching Dynamic Psychotherapy: An Overview,
paper given at Oxford Conference on Teaching Dynamic Psychotherapy.

Chapter 3

THE MEANING AND INTENTION OF HELPING
Dorothy Rowe

Over the ten years that I have been in charge of a department of
clinical psychology, I have interviewed many applicants for the
probationer posts. In each interview, the question has to be asked,
'Why do you want to become a clinical psychologist?' I always feel
sorry for the candidate as she or he fumbles for an answer, since no
answer sounds satisfactory. Of course, some candidates are simply after
a job, any job, but most candidates seem to be impelled by some drive or
need which appears to be as strong as that which impelled many young men
or women in past centuries to give their lives to the Church. Unlike
the religious applicant, our candidates cannot claim to have a vocation,
much less to have been called by the Great Psychologist in the Sky, but
while the word 'vocation' is forbidden in this godless science, the
sense of vocation is certainly there - the sense of being on a journey
to some great and wondrous goal, and the sense of discovering and using
one's talents to the glory of the dicipline and the betterment of mankind. Even in those psychologists who are driven by a need for personal
advancement, prestige and power, there is the belief that to be a
therapist is to be someone special. A therapist is someone who really
knows what life is about. He has sorted out all of life's problems and
he knows how to live happily and successfully.

This is the myth. The reality is different. Perhaps there are lots
of happy and successful therapists around, but I have not met them.
Even the great Sheldon Kopp, (1) whose books chart his painful progress
in self-knowledge, still describes himself as shy, unable to engage
easily in social conversation. Some of my therapist friends have
periods of profound sadness, while others engage in somewhat frantic
activity which seems to indicate a desperate desire to experience all
the pleasures of this world. Such greed, they sooner or later find,
does damage to their relationships with their nearest and dearest. I
view all this with the eyes of a survivor whose last five years have
been the happiest of a very fraught life. I have worked out some
solutions, but these are very personal ones, not generalizable to rules
about how we should all live our lives. This is why I always feel
sorry for our candidates for posts in clinical psychology. They are
hoping to be let into The Secret. And, of course, the secret is that
there is no secret.

What we do have, though, instead of a Secret, is Great Confusion. Part of this confusion is well known - the confusion over techniques, behaviourist or psychoanalytic, cognitive or personal construct, Gestalt, Transactional Analysis, Rational Emotive, social skills, problem-solving, Primal Scream and so on. Some therapists try to reduce their confusion by cleaving to one technique with the narrow passionate faith of a religious convert. Others dabble in a variety of techniques, call themselves 'eclectic', and often fail to see that they change the technique not as a step forward in the therapeutic process but in the way that some doctors change the patients' drugs - in the desperate hope that something new will work. However, the 'eclectic' therapists can often see quite clearly that the variety of therapeutic techniques arise from a variety of theories about why people behave as they do and that theories are simply ways of organizing experience and do not in themselves contain the truth about reality. Egoes and ids, reinforcers and stimuli, constructs, tightening and loosening, Child and Adult, Psyche and Shadow, and so on are simply ideas, concepts, what John Heaton (2) calls 'notations and myths' which 'do not stand in any direct relation to observable reality'. The myths of every psychological theory 'are meaningful but are not empirically true'. (3)

The passionate believer in one psychological theory is always in danger of regarding the concepts of the theory as having an independent reality, as if people do walk around as the containers of an id and superego, or a Child, Adult and Parent, or an array of interlocking constructs, or a set of responses or habits, or a schizophrenic process or a variety of moods. Such internal objects are considered to have some optimal arrangement; neurosis occurs when there is a divergence from this optimal arrangement; and therapy is the process of creating or returning to this optimal arrangement. This is a neat way of thinking, but it does not match reality. I work in therapy using some of the concepts of Personal Construct Theory. My client and I discuss and compare our constructs, and some of my clients go on to live their lives in modest happiness. I can observe enormous changes in my client's construct system, but such changes are apparent only after the client begins to behave differently. Why the client can now act differently is not known, either to the client or to me. All we can both say is that the client now finds himself free to make choices different from his previous choices.

This is another reason for the Great Confusion of Therapists. If we believe that our theory of why people behave as they do is a true representation of reality then we expect that our theory will reveal causal connections and therefore show how change can be effected. Thus an historian can choose between conspiracy theories or cock-up theories of history, look for the conspirators or the idiots, and, if he wishes to alter history, seek more powerful conspirators or cleverer world leaders.(4)   The Azande of Southern Sudan believe that everything can be understood in terms of the causal properties of magic and so they resolve problems like adultery, sickness, jealousy, crop failure by looking for the magical process and reversing it.(5)   Now it is a wonderful thing to be in possession of a theory which works. When my car makes a new sound and I think 'That's a wheel-bearing gone,' I feel quite pleased when the mechanic confirms my diagnosis, even though I

have to pay for an expensive repair. But what I need to remember is
that my theory about wheel-bearings is of a different kind from my
theory as to why my client suffers mental anguish. I could not tell you
what a wheel-bearing looks like. Since I only know the sound it makes
when it is not functioning properly, my word 'wheel-bearing' refers
simply to an idea that I have. Likewise, I know the sounds people make
when they are not functioning well. I have lots of words to use in
explaining why they make these sounds - 'a punitive super-ego', 'low
self-esteem', 'rigid constructs', 'inability to accept their shadow'
and so on. On the surface both theories look the same, but in reality
they are not. The mechanic can show me the damaged wheel-bearing; the
client cannot show me his punitive super-ego and his battered ego. The
client simply acts, and I stick my labels on his actions. Another
important difference between these two kinds of theories is that in the
wheel-bearing theory the mechanic can show me the step-by-step causal
connections between the broken wheel-bearing and the sound I heard, and
from this show me the causal connections necessary to remove the sound.
In all the psychotherapeutic theories no such step-by-step causal
connections can be seen. The therapist committed to a particular
theory can make splendid leaps to preserve the theory, but the gaps are
always there. Any causal theory of human behaviour must be incomplete
since it cannot account for the choice which is part of every action.
People act, and every action is the outcome of choice. (Choices do not
always involve conscious thought, and 'not deciding' is choosing not to
decide.) Our choices are our responses to the meaning that our life
and our world has for us.

The difference between my wheel-bearing theory and my theory about
my client's anguish is the difference between the two major scientific
methods. One scientific method aims to discover laws which yield
predictions and display engendering conditions. The other method
develops conceptual systems which make the phenomena intelligible and
display meaning. Despite the claims of Freud and others, no theory of
why people behave as they do fits the first kind of method. All our
psychotherapeutic theories are theories of meaning, theories which aim
to make the phenomena intelligible. (Remember, a reinforcement is only
a reinforcement if the subject chooses to give it that meaning.) Much
of the confusion of therapists arises because they think they are
discovering and applying scientific laws when in fact they are making
the phenomenon intelligible and displaying meaning.

So, when John Heaton set out to examine theory in psychotherapy he
aimed:
>   to show that psychotherapy is best understood as the beginnings of
>   a science of action and its disorders rather than as a cure for
>   disorder of the mind; it is, therefore, to use an old-fashioned
>   word, an ethical science rather than a psychological one.(6)

He went on:
>   Action cannot be imagined outside a society in which there are
>   customs, rules and language. For action is a performance and
>   there are right and wrong, adequate and inadequate performances
>   which have been learned; all actions are embedded in norms and
>   ways of living which enable them to be performed and judged.
>   Actions and their failures are explained in terms of the

actor's intentions, purposes, and the reasons for governing the
society in which he lives. The language of action is used and
shaped in the course of action by the actors so action can only
be identified by concepts and norms familiar to the actor. It
would be impossible for an actor to initiate an act of which he
has no concept.

Thus a disordered act such as a slip of the pen is done
inadvertently, so the agent is not fully behind the act – he did
not mean to do it. Its reasons are explained in terms of the
norms of the society in which the agent lives – fear of exposing
his sexual desires to himself and others, veiled insults, envy
and so on. For the explanation to be effective the agent must
understand the concepts used; he must know what an insult is,
what it is to be envious, etc. and these concepts depend
ultimately on the norms of his society.

Men are responsible for their actions because we hold them
so. An action is the sort of thing that can be commanded,
forbidden, praised, blamed, or thought mad, in contrast to
bahaviour which just happens. So action is not something we
can define by simply pointing at it. Thus I might write my
signature in a moment of idleness or use it to win a fortune
or commit treason. The same movement can in various circumstances constitute any of these actions and many more, so in
itself constitutes none of them. To understand an act we always
need to look beyond physical events into language and society.

The patients that go to psychotherapists and are treated by
them always exemplify disordered action. Things happen to them
like pains, guilt, phobias, obsessions and tics, yet to the agent
there seems to be no cause and no convincing reason either.
Their lives feel empty, they do not know what they want or ought
to do, they cannot get on with people or people cannot get on
with them, they are unhappy and are unable to live and work
satisfactorily. They are usually in a state of conflict which
means that they have no clear sense of agency in their actions.(7)

Heaton recalls the important distinction that Aristotle made
between the productive and the practical sciences:
In the productive sciences the object is to produce a work or
result apart from the doing of making. The important thing is
the product and the technique necessary to produce it and not
the state of mind of the producer; the arts and crafts, medicine
and physiotherapy are examples.

The practical sciences have as their object the manner of
living. They are sciences concerned with human affairs and
try and define the best life and indicate the way to live it.
In these sciences it is the state of mind of the actor that
is crucial for his end is acting in a satisfactory way. Politics
and ethics are examples of such sciences. The important point is
that in the productive sciences the end is known – the physio-
therapist is clear that his aim is to increase mobility and
reduce pain. In the practical sciences on the other hand the end
is not known. It can only be indicated, according to Aristotle,
by a dialectical regress to basic principles from the experiences
of ordinary living.(8)

Thus the various psychotherapists fall into the class of practical sciences. This end is not known in the sense that to aim at relieving the client's anguish, enabling him to choose from a greater range of possibilities, to involve himself more easily in the lives of others and to draw on his creative resources is to reveal an infinite number of ends. Even behaviour therapy which aims at removing a specific symptom or acquiring a specific skill ceases to be a productive science if the therapist carries out his therapy in the belief that such a removal or acquisition will enable the client to lead a fuller, happier life.

It is this end of the practical science of psychotherapy which is a major source of confusion among psychotherapists, as I have been discovering recently. For the last few years I have been examining this question of what we regard as the aim of psychotherapy. In workshops for therapists from a number of disciplines we have been looking at ways of establishing what are our core constructs, the basic dimensions of our construct system on which all other constructs depend. I have also been looking at the core constructs of people who cope with their lives and comparing them with those of people who do not cope.(9) The methods I use could be described as 'a dialectical regress to basic principles from the experience of ordinary living'.

When therapists get together or write their books and articles they usually assume that the general aims of their therapy do not need to be stated. It was refreshing, then, to come across a practical handbook called 'Social Skills and Personal Problem Solving'.(10) The authors began with a statement of their theoretical position (learning theory) and their basic assumption, namely 'We assume that most people would like to learn how to cope with the situations in their lives in ways that are more effective or more congenial to themselves and others'. This is a modest assumption, especially as they say 'most people' and not 'every person'. However, they conclude this chapter with a much broader assumption:

Two final expectations contribute to the atmosphere that permeates successful problem-solving exercises: optimism and cheerfulness. Optimism implies that individuals are far more capable of changing and growing and learning and influencing their environment, than either they or others ever imagine. It asserts, in short, that most people possess unused capabilities which can be mobilized to increase personal competence, both in the ordinary events of everyday life and in some of the extraordinary crises that arise from time to time.

Here this group of therapists are saying that their aim in this practice of the ethical and practical science of psychotherapy is to teach their clients a more adequate performance. They believe that their clients are capable of learning more adequate performances because most people do not ordinarily do the best that they can. I suppose most therapists would agree with them. I know I do. I could not take up the burden of sharing my time and space with such miserable, crabby and difficult people as my clients if I did not have the faith that each of them is capable of behaving better, of living in harmony with themselves and other people. I say 'faith' and not 'radical belief' since I hold to my faith even though I continually meet clients who clutch their suffering to them as a treasure and who have no desire to learn the actions which comprise harmonious living. Therapists err if they think that everyone uses a model of a person as someone who learns and is capable of improving his performance. Such a model implies that a human being is basically good - learning is good, improving is good, wanting to learn and improve is good. But not every person uses such a model. The model of man which has a long history in our society and which is still very popular is that a human being is, in essence, bad, and that the aim of living is to keep this badness in check. Man cannot be the author of his own salvation but must seek help from some outside power. Whether this badness is called original sin or the id, and whether the outside power is seen as God's grace or the wise interpretations of the psychoanalyst, the effect on the actions of the person who perceives himself in this way is the same. He must strive to be good in order to hide his badness, and he must do nothing which might unleash the evil within him. Our depressed clients may not use the concepts of original sin or id, but they certainly experience themselves as essentially bad, evil, unacceptable to themselves and other people. This is the basic belief of the six beliefs that one must hold if one wishes to be depressed,(11) and there are certain great advantages to perceiving oneself in this way.(12) When we act towards our depressed client as if we believe that person to be basically good we threaten that person in two ways. First, he thinks that we are dissembling, that we really despise him and will reject him for his badness, and, second, if we are powerful therapists, we may not use our power to take his pain away but we may destroy his controls and unleash the evil - his murderous anger and jealousy - within him. Our belief in the innate goodness of the person is for many of our clients, not a promise of help but a threat of rejection and destruction.

In the workshops which I run on core constructs I usually pose the question 'Do you see human beings as basically, intrinsically bad or good?' Such a question puzzles some of the psychologists present since they have been taught that the correct model of a person is the non-judgmental one that, with the exception of a few inherited character-istics the person is born a tabula rasa, capable of learning and of continually improving his performance. What they have not noticed in this so-called non-judgmental model is that learning is assumed to be good. (Not everyone regards learning as good. Ignorance can be praised as innocence or regarded as good for the stability of the State and the maintenance of power). If we are born capable of learning we are born good and can, by learning, improve and approach perfection. However, not all the therapists in such workshops believe, or come to realise that they believe, that human beings are basically good. Those therapists who know what it is to be depressed know what it is to experience oneself as bad, and for many of these therapists the idea that human beings are basically bad is not a passing thought in a difficult experience but a persisting belief. Not all therapists share the same model of the person.

Our model of the person influences very greatly how we relate to other people. If we experience ourselves as good, despite some faults

and inadequacies then we find it fairly easy to treat people with trust
and confidence, on the assumption that since we like ourselves other
people must like us and since we are good other people must also be
good. Working on such assumptions we may be unaware that there are
people who fear us because our confidence implies power or who are
jealous of what they see as our good fortune and so hate us.
(Therapists differ very much in the account they take of envy and
jealousy, both in their work and their personal lives. Freud saw envy
and jealousy as central to the experience of neurosis and saw himself
as the focus of the envy and jealousy of others. George Kelly did not
bother to define envy and jealousy(13) and from what I have learned of
Kelly from his wife and students there was nothing to suggest that
Kelly saw jealousy and envy as important in his own life.) Another
danger of assuming that all people are essentially good, though
possessed of some bad habits which could be changed by the appropriate
learning experiences is that we can underestimate the hate and
destructiveness of other people and that we fail to see that there are
people who actually enjoy the suffering of others. When we view the
horrors of El Salvador and Guatemala from this safe distance we can
find explanations in terms of poor education and childhood deprivation,
but when we discover ourselves actually the object of someone who takes
pleasure in destruction then we find, as I have, that the word 'evil'
springs readily to mind. Those of us who believe in the innate
goodness of people and who believe in the methods and precepts of
scientific thought find 'evil' a difficult concept.

Yet many people do believe in evil as a force in the world. Some
people see evil as an outside force, competing with a force of good.
Some people see evil as a force within themselves.(14) Many children
have the 'fact' of their evil nature impressed on them in church and
sunday school. Many children are taught that they are bad along with
the facts about what gender they are ('You're a bad boy! 'What a wicked
little girl you are!') Many children decide that they must be bad, for
why else would their good parents treat them so?(15) Thus many of us
grow up believing that we are bad, evil, unacceptable to ourselves and
others. Believing this we have to work hard to be good, to justify our
existence. We find it hard to be at ease with other people because we
cannot be sure if they are, like us, essentially bad but pretending to
be good, or essentially good and when they find us out will reject us.
In the effort to earn the right to exist many people resolve to do good
to others. Many such people join the helping professions and many do
wonderful work. But sometimes their need to do good impels them to
force their help on people who do not want to be helped or on people
who can be best helped by leaving them alone. Altruistic people can be
very controlling and interfering, and if you protest about their
control and interference and reject the good they wish to do you, you
are shown that you have hurt the altruistic person who does not deserve
to be hurt and so you should feel guilty. God preserve me from my
altruistic friends!

Yet this way of viewing oneself is very common in the helping
professions. In workshops where we do a laddering exercise to discover
the core constructs by which we experience our existence, half or more
of the therapists present a construct of the nature of 'myself as a

member of a group' as against 'isolation'. The rest of the group produce a construct of the nature of 'identity through clarity' as against 'chaos'. Such people have come into the helping professions hoping through the study of psychology and the practice of therapy to gain greater clarity and understanding When we discuss 'myself in relation to others' some of the people having this construct describe it in the reciprocal terms of loving and loved, needing and needed. But some people describe their construct in non-reciprocal terms. They see their very existence as being a member of a group where they are needed. They are loved because they are needed. If they cease to meet the needs of others then they will cease to be loved. Not being needed means isolation and isolation means death.

The dangers of seeing oneself in this way become apparent when, in the workshop, we get on to the question of at what age we each expect to die. Most people give quite a late age - seventies, eighties, nineties even. Some people give a younger age and account for it in terms of the average age at which members of their family die. But some people give an early age and account for it with, 'I cannot bear the thought of being old'. Questioned as to why old age is so terrible, they answer that they could not tolerate being looked after. Now, if you experience yourself as an essentially bad person who is trying to be good, and if you conceive of your existence as seeking identity through clarity and your annihilation as chaos, you have to ward off the chaos of the outside world and the chaos of your badness by being in control. Thus the helplessness of old age is very threatening to you, since you would be in the hands of people whom you do not trust and who would destroy your control and so chaos would overwhelm you. Better a quick, early death. Similarly, if you experience yourself as an essentially bad person who is trying to be good, and if you conceive of your existence as yourself as part of a group and your annihilation as isolation, you have to ward off your rejection and thus isolation by getting the members of your group (your family, colleagues, patients, clients, friends) to need you and to depend on you. You would not make demands on them lest they reject you. Thus the helplessness of old age is very threatening to you since you would have nothing to give and your helpers would despise you. You cannot bear the thought of being a burden. This fear of being a burden often reappears in the workshop when we discuss the question of whether we want to be buried or cremated. This question always provokes quite heated arguments over a number of issues,(16) one of which is whether we should expect our relatives to tend our grave. Some of us feel that we are doing our loving relatives a service by providing our grave as a focus for their grief and mourning, but others feel that they must choose cremation since they could not bear the thought of their grave being a burden to their relatives.

In the workshops, after we have discussed whether we see human beings as basically good or basically bad, I ask everyone to list what they see as the five most important virtues and the five worst vices, in order of importance. What a divergence of opinions this always reveals! How differently we each judge our own actions and the actions of others! The prime virtue can be given as love, empathy, honesty, courage, patience, caring, ability to give and receive, consideration,

optimism, modesty, generosity, forgiveness, unselfishness, tolerance,
and so on. The prime vice (which is not necessarily the opposite of
the prime virtue) can be given as destructiveness, hate, bitterness,
dishonesty, lechery, emotional exploitation, unfeelingness, envy,
jealousy, disloyalty, revenge, sense of despair and so on. As I ask
each member of the group 'Why is your particular virtue/vice important?'
the answers reveal how central this concept is to the person's
judgments and how much it must inform and direct them in the process of
therapy. For instance, I see the prime virtue as courage, since
without courage none of the other virtues is possible. Fear can make
us betray our loved ones, lie, and act intolerantly and destructively.
I am always impressed with how frightened my clients are (before I get
involved in therapy I never knew there were so many things anyone could
be frightened of) and I always encourage them to be brave and so
discover that there is nothing to fear. But other therapists see fear
as no more than a by-product and so concentrate their attention on
other virtues. I have often thought, as I conducted this exercise on
virtues and vices, that it would be possible to construct some sort of
test to reveal whether a therapist and client are well suited, whether
they value the same virtues and therefore are seeking the same goals in
therapy. In one workshop we discovered that one of our number had as
his prime virtue 'intelligence' while another member had as his
'intuition'. As we explored the implications of these it rapidly be
became clear that these two men had approaches to life which were
diametrically opposed. If they were to work together (the first was a
psychologist and the second a psychiatrist) they certainly would not
have worked in harmony. Had they ever become therapist and client the
therapy would certainly have failed, since the psychiatrist despised
cold intellect while the psychologist despised the vagaries of
intuition.

This raises the question of how often do a therapist and client
check that they each have the same goal in therapy? Of course many
therapists do work out with their clients a definable goal - the end of
a depression, the loss of an obsession, the ability to mix easily with
other people and so on. But how often does the therapist ask, 'Why is
it important to cease to be depressed, to be free of an obsessions, to
mix easily with other people and so on?'? You might say that it is not
necessary to ask. Obviously the person wants the pain to end and to be
able to make the most of his life. Why, I would then ask, is it
important to make the most of your life? Again you might feel that the
answer is self-evident. Since this is all the life we have got we
ought to make the most of it. Ah, I say, that is what you think. Not
everyone agrees with you. There is a very good chance that your client
has something else in mind.

When I first began talking with depressed people and trying to make
sense of what they told me I concentrated on the real and immediate -
how they felt, how they got along with their relatives and friends,
what crises and difficulties they had to face. A childhood of being
forced to attend Presbyterian Sunday school and church had left me
with a distaste for religion which fitted well with the behaviourism of
the University of Sydney's Psychology Department and the Freudianism of
my clinical training. It never crossed my mind to ask my clients about

their religious beliefs. But I did become aware of how often death became the topic of our conversation. Sometimes it was the death of someone still loved and grieved over, and sometimes it was my client's own death, something feared and desired. As we talked of death, God kept bobbing up in the conversation, so much so that when I finally wrote a book about depression(17) I had to put God in the index with eleven references to Him. By the time that I had finished that book I had realized that if I was to follow the basic precept of Personal Construct Theory 'First learn your client's language' then if religious belief was part of my client's language, I had to learn how to talk about religious belief.

William James would have found such a statement very strange. He had no difficulty in writing about religious belief,(18) although he never ventured more than a page or two on sex. But Freud had no time for religion, 'the universal neurosis', and psychologists and psychiatrists, determined to make their discipline into science, banished metaphysics and turned religious belief into a symptom of neurosis and psychosis. Such attitudes fitted well with the attitudes of the people wishing to enter psychology and psychiatry. Argyle and Beit-Hallahmi(19) found that medical students who wished to work in psychiatry were more likely to declare no religious application than medical students wishing to enter other specialities, while studies of the religious beliefs of psychologists reveal that 'Psychologists, who show a number of unconventional attitudes, are also generally low on measures of religiosity'.

This is the same result as I always get in workshops and lectures when I ask, 'How do you envisage your death? Do you see it as the end or as a doorway to another life? Hands up those who see death as the end.' And up go the hands. Most of the people in the room see death as the end. They look around in surprise at those people who have their hands down. Then I say 'Well, you're an atypical group'.

I then quote the figures given by surveys of religious belief. The most recent survey in Britain was done by the European Values Study Group who released the first of their results last year. Ted Gordon, who produced a BBC 'Everyman' programme on this, said:
    In Britain ... belief in God is high, at 76 per cent, but regular
    church attendance, at 14 per cent, is the lowest in Europe ... .
    In religious matters, belief in the adjuncts of Christianity is
    low, particularly in the unpleasant areas of faith. Thus 30 per
    cent believe in the devil and in hell. This rises to a 45 per
    cent belief in life after death, and to an optimistic 57 per cent
    for the notion of heaven. One of the most amazing claims is that
    27 per cent of British people believe in reincarnation. Sin is
    accepted as a reality by 69 per cent. Perhaps not surprisingly,
    the highest figure for this is in Northern Ireland (91 per cent).(20)

Surveys of religious belief in the United States give between 94 and 98 per cent of people who believe in God and between 64 and 76 per cent who believe in a life after death.(21) Thus a group of therapists is very much an atypical group.

Why should this matter? The reason that it does matter has to do
with death and therapy has a lot to do with death. Now when we come to
think of death, particularly our own death, we can construe it in one
of two ways. Either death is the end of my identity or it is a doorway
to another life. Once I decide what it is for me - and such a decision
is usually made very early in life - the purpose of my life is
determined. If I see my death as the end of my identity, then I have
to make me life in some way satisfactory. If I see my death as a doorway to another life I have then to live this life in terms of the next
life, to follow the rules laid down by the next life.(22) Since most
therapists believe that life ends at death, they see the purpose of
their therapy as helping their client to create a satisfactory life.
But if the client does not believe that his life ends in death then his
aim in therapy is quite different from that of the therapist. The
client wants to discover how he can become a better person so, when
death comes, he will not be condemned to hell, or to a reincarnation to
a life even worse than this one, or to an eternity of the wanderings of
a lonely ghost. He may not tell the therapist this. All he may say is
'I'm afriad of dying'. Or he may speak of his unending grief at the
death of a loved one without explaining that the way he conceives of
the afterlife makes a re-establishing of the continuity of his present
life an impossibility.

The difference between wanting to make this brief life satifactory
and wanting to meet the standards of the next life came out very
clearly at a workshop I had recently with the students on the MSc
course in clinical psychology at Surrey University. Those students who
saw their life ending in death had written out long lists of what they
must achieve if they were to come to regard their lives as satisfactory.
(Such lists contain things which must be achieved if one is to be
remembered with love and admiration. Few of us want to vanish without
trace.) Then one of the group said that while he had to achieve a
great deal in this life it was not to make this life satisfactory but
to ensure that after his next death he would return to a better life.
This was Atul Vadher whose research work has already made its mark.(24)
He plans, when he finishes his course, to return to Kenya to work with
lepers in order to discover how they come to terms with their illness.
Atul described to us how, as a child, his parents had warned him that
if he was naughty he would return in his next life as an insect whose
life was short and nasty. He felt that through being good in his past
lives he had achieved the status of a man (higher than an animal or a
woman) but that he needed to strive hard in this life in order to
achieve an even higher status (wealth and power) in the next life and
eventual 'moksha', liberation from the round of death and rebirth.

Thus, if Atul ever felt the need of therapy and met up with a
therapist who saw the purpose of life as to make the most of our one
life, Atul and the therapist would not be traversing the same road to
the same goal. Similarly, the client who believes in sin and the four
last things, Death, Judgment, Heaven and Hell is not in the business
of being happy. He is in the business of saving his soul.

Now to talk with a client about sin, God and the Devil,
reincarnation or ghosts, when you do not believe in any of them is very

difficult. You have to find a language. And this is where the
confusion of therapists becomes so great.

In that branch of scientific method where the aim is to discover
laws, make predictions and display the engendering conditions the
scientist is free to make his own language and to expect other people
to learn it. New words are created and old terms are given operational
definitions which limit their meaning and use. The ambiguity of words
is exchanged for the precision of mathematical formulae. But in that
branch of scientific method where the aim is to create conceptual
systems which are intelligible and display meaning all the ambiguity
of language is retained, not just the ambiguity of the scientist's
language but the ambiguity of the language studied. In the practical
sciences of politics, ethics, sociology and therapy we have to take
account of what people say. We have to understand their language and
treat it as an expression of that person's truth. If a client says,
'I know I am damned' and we do not acknowledge the pain that he feels
in that particular way, then we have failed him. If a client says,
'The only thing that keeps me going is my knowledge that God loves me'
and we do not recognize that this is a strength that must be used in
therapy, then we have failed him.

Before we can learn another person's language we need to understand
our own and to recognize that the words and sentences we use do not
always stand in direct relation to reality but are the notations and
myths that we have created in order to make our experience intelligible.
The belief that life ends in death is just as mythical as the belief
that death is a doorway to another life. The belief that every event
has a cause is just as metaphysical a belief as is the belief that all
events are caused by magic or are part of God's Great Design. Myths
and metaphysical beliefs are not irrelevant. They are extremely powerful and we act in accordance with them. The meaning we create _is_ our
purpose and intent.(25) When we ask, 'Why does that person behave as he
he does?' the only intellgible answer must be in terms of an agent and
his action, the meaning he has created, the judgment he has made, the
intention of his action. Knowing these things we can then judge
whether a person's action is right or wrong, adequate or inadequate.
When our intentions, the purposes which are our meaning, are unacceptable to us we can deny them and claim that we have much more noble
motives or that we have no motives at all but are the helpless victim
of unknown forces. We can spring into action to avoid seeing the full
implications of our intention or we can intellectualize our intention
and so drain it of its affect. If we do any of these things to hide
our intentions from ourselves we impair our judgment of our actions.
We may believe we have succeeded when we have not, or failed when we
have actually succeeded.

Each of us needs to be very clear as to just why we go into this
business of helping, for, unless we are, we are in danger of being no
help at all. We know, but we need to know that we know, whether we
are helping so as to make people love us because they need us, or
admire us because we are powerful and have secrets, or because we want
to prove that the world really is a just and fair place, or that
ignorance can be overcome or virtue triumph, whether we are seeking

clarity and understanding, or salvation, or the right to exist, or a
happy rebirth. We need to know why we want our clients to get better,
so that we can put this need aside, for in the paradoxical way that
clients give up their symptoms when they are told to hold on to them,
our wanting our clients to get better ensures that they do not.
Training analysis may have gone out of fashion, but some careful self-
inspection with that powerful question 'Why is it important?' should
never go out of fashion.

So, future applicants beware. I shall be asking, 'Why is it
important to you to become a clinical psychologist?'

NOTES

1   S. B. KOPP, 'Back to One, A Practical Guide for Psychotherapists',
    Palo Alto, Science and Behavior Books, 1977. See also 'If you Meet
    the Buddha on the Road, Kill Him', and 'The End of Innocence', Palo
    Alto, Science and Behavior Books, 1971, 1978.
2   J. HEATON, Theory in psychotherapy, in N. Bolton (ed.),
    'Philosophical Problems in Psychology', London, Methuen, 1979,
    p. 181.
3   Ibid., p. 181.
4   For instance, the medieval historian and Personal Construct
    Theorist, Jeffrey Burton Russell, writes, 'A concept that does not
    respond to human experience will die. But the concept of the
    Devil is very much alive today, in spite of opposition from many
    theologians as well as from those hostile to all metaphysics'
    ('Satan, The Early Christian Tradition', Ithaca and London, Cornell
    University Press, 1981, p. 222). Opponents of the nuclear arms
    race are divided on whether the nuclear holocaust is more likely
    to be caused by malicious intent or simple ineptitude. Russell
    believes in evil; I have faith in human stupidity.
5   The anthropologist Evans-Pritchard was the first to describe how
    the Azande accounted for everything in terms of magic, sorcery and
    witchcraft. A recent ITV programme on the Azande in the series
    'The Vanishing World' showed that, strange though these beliefs
    and rituals may be to us, they provide an effective way of dealing
    with problems of adultery, sickness, jealousy and co-operation,
    although it was hard on the chickens who often die to convey the
    Oracle's message.
6   J. HEATON, op. cit., p. 176.
7   Ibid., pp. 177-8.
8   Ibid., p. 186.
9   D. ROWE, 'The Construction of Life and Death', Chichester and New
    York, Wiley, 1982.
10 P. PRIESTLEY, J. McGUIRE, D. FLEGG, V. HEMSLEY, D. WELHAM, 'Social
    Skills and Personal Problem Solving', London, Tavistock, 1978,
    p. 11, p. 16.
11 The other beliefs are
        (2) Other people are such that I must fear, hate and envy them,
        (3) Life is terrible and death is worse,
        (4) Only bad things have happened to me in the past and only
             bad things will happen in the future,

(5) It is wrong to get angry,

(6) I must never forgive anyone, least of all myself.

From D. ROWE, 'Depression: The Way Out of the Prison', London, Routledge & Kegan Paul, 1983.

12 D. ROWE, Resistance to Change, 'Proceedings of the Annual Merseyside Conference in Clinical Psychology, 1981', London, Plenum Press, 1983 (in press).

13 Fay Fransella, personal communication, 1981.

14 See 'The Construction of Life and Death' for a further discussions of how evil is construed.

15 Ibid., pp. 95-103.

16 Ibid., pp. 127-30.

17 D. ROWE, 'The Experience of Depression', Chichester and New York, Wiley, 1978.

18 W. JAMES, 'The Varieties of Religious Experience', London, Collins, 1977.

19 M. ARGYLE and B. BEIT-HALLAHMI, 'The Social Psychology of Religion', London, Routledge & Kegan Paul, 1975.

20 T. GORTON, Belief in Britain, 'The Listener', London, BBC Publications, 17.12.1981, pp. 741-2.

21 M. ARGYLE and B. BEIT-HALLAHMI, op. cit.

22 For a full discussion of this see 'The Construction of Life and Death', op. cit.

23 See D. ROWE, Construing Life and Death, 'Journal of Death Education', 1982 (in press). Also J. P. CARSE, 'Death and Existence', New York, Wiley, 1980.

24 A. VADHER and D. N. NDETEI, Life events and depression in a Kenyan setting, 'British Journal of Psychiatry', 1981, 139, pp. 134-7.

25 This is another way of saying that constructs are always predictive. See G. KELLY, 'The Psychology of Personal Constructs', New York, Norton, 1955. Also the concept of intentionality, 'the structure that gives meaning to experience', in R. MAY, 'Love and Will', London, Souvenir Press, 1969, pp. 223-68.

Chapter 4

THE CONTEMPORARY RELEVANCE
OF THE PSYCHODYNAMIC TRADITION
Peter Hildebrand

Clinical psychology is regarded as an emerging NHS profession in Great
Britain. It has been estimated that there are some thousand full-time
equivalent clinical psychologists working in the National Health
Service. Yet the development of clinical psychology since the was has
been slow and halting as psychologists have moved themselves from the
role of medical auxillaries towards the status of independent
practitioners. The early clinical psychologists tended to draw on
their academic backgrounds, skills such as research methodology and
statistics as the basis for the work which they were required to do as
testers and providers of normative data for psychiatric investigations.
Naturally enough, the psychodynamic tradition entered very little into
this work so that it is rare to find mention of psychoanalysis in terms
of theory or of practice in their publications. It is probably fair to
say that it was only with the organisation of the Army Psychological
Services during the Second World War that psychodynamics began to play
a significant part in the theory and practice of clinical psychology.

After the end of the war, which was marked by the notable successes
of psychodynamically oriented psychology in the fields of selection and
rehabilitation of members of the Armed Services, many of those who had
been responsible for this work helped to recreate the Tavistock Clinic
and Institute of Human Relations, whilst a more experimental and
statistically based school of clinical psychology gradually formed
around Eysenck and his collaborators at the Maudsley Hospital and the
Institute of Psychiatry. As is well known, Eysenck decried psychoanalysis and psychoanalytic theory and has consistently held that
neither psychodynamic theory nor such developments as the theory of
projective testing were clinically valid or useful. Unfortunately
from the psychodynamic point of view little or no attempt was made to
rebut Eysenck's thesis and the case for the validity of psychoanalytic
psychodynamic theory was allowed to go rather by default. The attitude
of the psychoanalytic world towards Eysenck was well expressed by
Michael Balint who said 'When the caravan moves on, the dogs will bark'.
Even so most psychologists accepted far too uncritically Eysenck's
position. The resulting polarisation remained constant and unchanging
and for many years there seemed little likelihood of change. Clinical
psychology remained experimental and behaviouristic with a great deal

of emphasis on the application of learning theory to psychiatric problems; on the other hand dynamically oriented psychologists interested themselves mainly in the problems of working with neurotic populations and the extension of dynamic theory into work with marriage and the family. The groups remained largely isolated from one another and there was no dialogue to contribute to the profession as a whole.

However, as clinical psychology has expanded in recent years, marked by the publication of the Trethowan Report in 1974, clinical psychologists have begun to develop a view of themselves as independent practitioners of psychological skills which inevitably included psycho-therapy. The psychotherapy which was offered by these psychologists was generally behavioural and based on the work and methodology of the learning theorists. It offered the clinical psychologist a rationale for working with patients suffering from phobias and compulsive disorders of various sorts and permitted him to function independently of the psychiatric establishment. Difficulties quickly arose, however, since onto the initial wave of enthusiasm had passed the limitations of the method and its restricted clinical utility rapidly became clear. Despite repeated efforts such as those of Sloane et al. (1975) to demonstrate that behaviour therapy was superior to other and particularly dynamic forms of therapy, careful methodological studies repeatedly showed that behavioural methods were neither worse nor better than other methods already in the field.

As might be expected two possible solutions to this particular problem soon emerged. The first solution was to become more purist, which seems to have led to the radical behaviourism of Skinner and his followers. An English follower of Skinner, Cullen (1980), has recently discussed the problem that 'private events' i.e. affects, emotions and feelings present to those espousing this therapeutic approach. He says that 'private events' are held to be caused by the environmental contingencies which determine our behaviour. 'The radical behaviourist cannot get away from the existence of private events as Skinner himself has reluctantly had to accept.'
How one knows about the subjective world of another must be faced ... One solution often regarded as behaviouristic is to grant the distinction between public and private events and rule the latter out of scientific consideration ... It is essentially the line taken by logical positivism and physical operationalism ... Yet it is significant that Bridgeman's physical operationalism could not save him from extreme solipsism even within physical science itself. Applied to psychological problems operationalism has been no more successful' (Skinner, 1969 quoted by Cullen 1980). The radical behaviourist then is left with a therapeutic strategy exemplified as follows:
Extinction, high cost and punishment contingencies usually accompany reports with anger and fear ... In all cases affect is related to the contingencies, and is used to teach the patient to uncover such contingencies in their inception and before they become controlling ... A contingency analysis of emotions ... attempts to sensitise people to those emotions so that they can be utilised, analysed and control the contingencies relevant to them and thereby control those emotions. Thus private events are secondary, have no

autonomy but are purely dependent on external events. By
controlling them one can subdue and perhaps even eradicate neurotic
experiences in the individual. But this leaves out of account any
possibility that private events, feelings inside the mind of the
body mind can have any causal effect on the individual, which must
seem to most people working in the field to have rather more to do
with psychological illness than such authors would accept.

A second point which can be made about this approach, can be found
in the account given of the work of Wolpe and Lazarus by Klein et al.
(1969). Klein et al. were impressed by how much use behaviour
therapists made of suggestion and how much they manipulated the expectations and attitudes of their patients. They described 'the explicit,
positive and authoritative manner with which the therapist approaches
the patient destined if not designed to establish the therapist as a
powerful figure to turn the patient's hopes for success into concrete
expectations'. Indeed they remarked that while behaviour therapists
were believed to define clearly and systematically the patient's
problems in terms of manageable hierarchies and select appropriate
responses to be strengthened or weakened, they were frankly surprised
to find that the presenting symptomatic complaint was often side-stepped
for what the therapist intuitively considered to be more basic issues.
Most surprising to them the basis for this selection seemed often to
be what others would call 'dynamic considerations'. So an ultra
behaviouristic solution is a contradiction in terms.

The other possibility is to take an 'eclectic' point of view. There
are nowadays so many forms of psychotherapy which are combinations of
either dynamic or behavioural approaches with other psychological
theories or developments of one of the many psychological theories
available that one can only give these procedures the name of
eclecticism. I recently pointed out that
an eclectic approach which is not based on thorough and long
lasting training, but rather on small workshops of not more than a
few days duration cannot achieve a great deal. At first sight a
judicious and personal choice in the therapeutic shopping basket
or supermarket ought to provide each individual with an excellent
theoretical framework within which he or she could try and understand patients and help them with their problems. Each therapist
could find the type of treatment and modality which suited his or
her personal style the best. The difficulty is that eclecticism
leads to theoretical weakness, to an enormous number of ad hoc
hypotheses, to assertion rather than to careful investigation, to
a constant sliding and movement of hypotheses. However many
training weekends or experiences one gives all that happens is that
one ends up with a mish mash of experience which cannot be regarded
as genuine training. I feel that every therapist needs a process
of mutual feedback within a strong theoretical paradigm and in my
view there is really only one viable theoretical paradigm - that of
the dynamic psychotherapist based on the work of Freud and those
who have succeeded him (Hildebrand, 1980).

If and when a patient walks into my office and begins talking to me
I must have some notion of his motivation, whether he or she is

genuinely committed to a therapeutic encounter of this sort, which I am prepared for on my side. I must ask if we are to work together will this person really endeavour to reveal themselves and talk about their inner worlds, wishes and dreams and fantasies, so that we can see how this is related to their presenting problems. I can, of course, avoid the whole issue if I wish by producing an interview schedule and asking questions, because all that will happen then is that my patient will give many answers and tell me little which will throw any light on the problems with which they are coming. Essentially this is because these will be my questions and they will force answers from the patient. If, on the other hand, I ask the patient what brings him, to tell me about himself and his problems in his own words I will begin to set up the possibility of a dialogue, one which can include communication in the patient's own language which I can try and understand in his terms and where I can offer my understandings back to him.

In my own work and teaching, I use a method of classification first put forward in 1952 by the American psychoanalyst, Edward Bibring. In this paper Bibring describes basic psychotherapeutic concepts which are considered applicable to all methods of psychotherapy whatever their theoretical systems. He makes a distinction between the 'technical' and 'curative' application of the principles involved. The technical factors refer to the techniques employed in the various psychotherapies, the latter the agents which are responsible for changes in the patient.

The term 'therapeutic' comprises both technical and curative aspects of the treatment process. Bibring used the term 'technique' to refer to any more of less typical verbal or non verbal behaviour on the therapist which intends to effect the patient in the direction of the final goals of treatment. He distinguishes five basic techniques, which arise:
   (a)   suggestive
   (b)   abreactive
   (c)   manipulative
   (d)   clarificatiory
   (e)   interpretative
These techniques are supplemented by the processes and procedures which constitute the total course of a treatment process and represent more complex concepts. There are four major types of therapeutic operation, viz.
   (a)   production of material
   (b)   the utilisation of the produced material by the
          therapist and/or the patient
   (c)   assimilation by the patient of the results of such
          a utilisation
   (d)   the processes of re-orientation and readjustment.
It is Bibring's view that these basic principles and procedures give a suitable frame of reference for the examination of psychotherapy and combinations of them can be used to characterise different forms of psychotherapy.

It will further clarify the theory if we discuss the therapeutic principles which underline the five techniques suggested by Bibring. Let me start with suggestion. Bibring defines suggestion as the induction of ideas, impulses, emotions, actions, etc. by the therapist (an individual in an authoritative position) in the patient (an individual in a dependent position) independent of, or to the exclusion of critical or realistic thinking processes. Suggestion aims at the promotion of the treatment process in its various forms as for example asking the patient to fantasize or to dream, or to dream about specific contents or remember specific events. Thus suggestion aims at a direct change induced by the authority of the therapist, either in terms of 'I can cure your phobia' or 'I can show you to become more assertive'. In this view suggestion is frequently used in the service of other therapeutic agents - most of us might perhaps agree that this is particularly so in terms of the behaviour therapist. Suggestion is used to facilitate emotional expression, to help the patient face reality, to produce recollections, to tolerate anxiety or depression. It may well be that the whole transference relationship in the ordinary behavioural therapy situation is based on suggestion and the acceptance by the patient of the therapist as someone endowed with certain technical skills which he will put in the service of the patient's recovering from his symptom. In this sense the therapist may be seen as being in a 'superior' position.

Let us turn now to abreaction. The method of course dates back to the eighteenth century, the underlying theory being that dammed-up tensions which have found abnormal discharge - as in symptoms - must be revived in memory and their normal expression re-established, mainly in the form of emotionally charged verbalisations. There is a clear parallel between the above statement concerning abnormal discharge and the statements made by behaviour therapists who say that symptoms are in fact abnormal processes of learning which have become absorbed into the patient's character structure and that if the patient can re-learn how to carry these activities then he will be cured. In the original Freudian sense, however, abreaction used the following processes to achieve a cure:

(1)   the recollection of split-off experiences, which made them accessible to influence by the conscious personality.
(2)   the transformation of an emotionally strong idea into a weak one through abreaction, i.e. through the discharge in normal ways of displaced emotional tensions, thus making the idea manageable. 'I want to kill my father' - may be transformed into 'kill the ref'.
(3)   the adjustment of the idea which had been deprived of its intensity by learning by counter-suggestion.

What is the curative mechanism of abreaction? By verbalising feelings, thoughts, reactions, impulses, conflicts, etc. one learns to see them more clearly in a more objective perspective. Emotional expression of painful tendencies when met with sympathy results in the gratifying feeling of being accepted and understood, sharing responsibility, and thus being reassured.

The next concept in Bibring's list is manipulation. If we exclude the crude forms of manipulation - advice, guidance, etc., which are the property of all human beings and to which most of those suffering from neurotic disorders actually turn in preference to going to professionally trained psychologists or psychiatrists or social workers, manipulation is defined as the employment of various emotional systems in the patient for the purpose of achieving therapeutic change, whether in the technical sense of promoting the treatment or in a curative sense. Technical manipulation can be employed in a positive or negative form, either to produce favourable attitudes towards the treatment situation or to remove obstructuve trends. For example one can convince, or at least try and convince, the patient that he will be forced to do nothing against his will, on the other hand one can persuade a phobic patient to expose himself to his fears and anxieties. One can also use experiential manipulation, exposing a patient to a new experience, new in the sense of not having been experienced before (or since childhood), either because the opportunity did not arise of because the opportunity was not recognised. A typical, and most useful example of this sort of work would be the sexual therapies developed by Masters and Johnson. When the patient takes responsibility for himself he may indeed have a genuinely new experience. Such experiences when repeated increase his self confidence and thus his capacities. In other words the patient not only has a novel experience in relation to others, but also with regard to himself. There are two types of manipulation, one which uses trends already present in the patient, which have been bound or distorted, and a formative type of manipulation which helps the patient to discover new ideas and thoughts and capacities for himself. It should be noted that suggestion, emotional relief or abreaction and manipulation by themselves do not necessarily promote understanding of the basic problem on the part of the patient and that in this they are fundamentally different from the other two therapeutic principles, clarification and interpretation. Clarification and interpretation constitute the basic factors in what we shall call insight therapy in the sense that the curative factor consists essentially in the extension of self-understanding in the patient. But it is necessary to distinguish between two types of insight which differ not only dynamically, but also in regard to the techniques employed to achieve them and types of material they are dealing with.

Clarification is a term introduced into psychotherapy by Carl Rogers. It is defined as helping the patient to see himself much more clearly. It consists mainly in re-stating feelings in more precise terms by verbalising them in clearer form than the client has put them and then by recognising and stating their meanings clearly and sharply. This re-statement or reflection has to be entirely based on the words of the patient, which implies that it must not transcend the phenomenological or descriptive level. In this sense clarification does not refer to unconscious material, but to conscious and/or pre-conscious processes of which the patient is not sufficiently aware, which escape his attention but which he recognises more or less readily when they are clearly presented to him. Many, if not all, of us are often vague about certain feelings, attitudes, thoughts, impulses, behaviour or perceptions. We cannot recognise or differentiate adequately what troubles us, nor relate matters which are unrelated, we distort reality. In brief there is a lack of awareness where awareness is possible. Clarification in therapy is aimed at such vague and obscure areas in so far as they are relevant from the viewpoint of treatment. Clarification takes place largely on a conscious level, does not meet resistance in the ordinary analytic sense or necessarily arouse negative transference. Bibring considers that as a rule

patients react to successful clarification with surprise and
intellectual satisfaction. Insights resulting from it provide a birds-
eye view of and for the patient with regard to his attitudes, feelings,
character traits and moments of contact so that by seeing his
difficulties more clearly and in a more objective, realistic
perspective he is no longer overwhelmed and frightened by them, is less
identified with them, no longer takes them for granted, nor does he
consider them as constitutional parts of his personality. In brief he
is less intensely involved. In general, neurotic problems are not
resolved by this process of clarification, but are seen in a different,
more detached light. I follow Bibring in considering insights through
clarification as therapeutic though of limited value. Clarification is
employed in nearly all forms of psychotherapy to a varying extent.

Finally, there is insight through interpretation which is dynamically different from that obtained through clarification. Interpretation
in this sense refers exclusively to unconscious material, unconscious
defensive operations, denied instinctual tendencies, to the symbolism
and hidden meanings of the patient's behaviour pattern. Interpretation
by its very nature transgresses clinical data, the descriptive level
and it is solely on the basis of their derivatives that the psychotherapist tries to guess, reconstruct and communicate to the patient
those unconscious processes which are assumed to determine his manifest
behaviour. Interpretation is not a single act, but is a prolonged
process. A period of preparation in the form of clarification
generally precedes it. Insight through interpretation is dynamically
different from insight obtained through clarification since clarification involves detachment while interpretation causes the ego to
become more involved since it requires the re-activation of painful
tendencies, memories and conflicts. Clarification consists in
strengthening the patient's ego through greater objectivity; interpretation initiates a process of re-orientation and re-learning which
results in a more adequate solution of the pathogenic, infantile
conflicts.

Using Bibring's classification we can now spell out the importance
of the dynamic point of view. Without a psychodynamic approach to
therapy we are limited to a surface therapy to 'objective' data, at
best to phenomenology. But with a dynamic approach we can utilise
psychoanalytic theory and its derivatives to provide us with the
possibility of a greatly increased understanding of the phenomena which
we and our patients encounter, which cannot be explained in 'objective
terms'. Certain key notions have to be defined. They are transference,
counter-transference, resistance, defence and interpretation.

First the concept of transference. There are different meanings of
this term but I am using it as first described by Freud to denote the
emergence of infantile feelings and attitudes in a new form as centrally
directed towards the person and the therapist. It is a term which is
also used to encompass all inappropriate thoughts, attitudes, fantasies
and emotions, which are revivals of the past and of past relationships,
which the patient may show whether or not he is conscious of them in
relation to his therapist. They will include such things as the
patient's initial rational anxieties about coming to treatment and

particular attitudes towards people which form part of his personality
structure and which also manifest themselves within the treatment
situation. In classical psychoanalysis the aim is not merely to revive
such feelings but also to assist the patient to structure the whole
treatment around prototypical infantile conflicts, replacing the
original symptoms of the illness with new transference meanings and also
replacing the patient's original neurosis by a transference neurosis
which he can be cured of by therapeutic work. I would follow Sandler
et al. (1973) on whose definitions I have based the above paragraph in
distinguishing between the general tendency we all have to repeat past
relationships in the present, and tranference as a process characterised
by the development of feelings and attitudes towards another person
which represent an over concentration of feeling - inappropriate to the
present - which is therefore seen as the repetition of a relationship
towards important figures in one's past.

If we adopt this definition of transference then the treatment
situation in all forms of psychotherapy may be seen as imbued with more
than one meaning for the patient and the difficulties which inevitably
emerge in most therapies can be understood far more easily than hereto-
fore. No matter how open the patient may be or how easily we may
understand his symptoms, yet transference may interfere with the
situation in such a way that we find ourselves stalemated unless we can
interpret the problem for the patient and ourselves. When for example
I was a member of Michael Balint's team working with FPA doctors, we
found a group of women who came asking for help with sexual difficulties
of a severe nature, often the inability to consummate their marriages.
While some of these women suffered from severe character disorders and
needed long-term treatment, another group who could be fairly clearly
defined in terms of motivation and background could be helped very
quickly provided the therapist was a woman who understood that their
difficulty was based on their need to be given permission to be actively
sexual by a mother surrogate in the transference. Without this understanding, which did not necessarily need to be made explicit to the
patient, we could not have helped these women.

It is, however, necessary to consider other aspects of relationships
as well. The therapist's counter-transference, the sum of his or her
reaction to the patient, is equally important. We are not behavioural
scientists when we take a therapeutic role (even if such a fantasy figure
genuinely exists in psychology proper), but we are involved in a
personal encounter with another individual to which we bring our own
fantasies and unconscious expectations. It is no accident that for
years therapists have preferred the so called YAVIS patients or that for
a long time psychotherapists have maintained with Freud that elderly
patients were untreatable (Hildebrand 1982). As Ella Freeman Sharpe
said, 'to say that an analyst will still have conflicts complexes, blind
spots, limitations is only to say that he remains a human being. When
he ceases to be a human being, he ceases to be a good analyst' (1947,
quoted in Sandler 1973). Without awareness of our own responses to
others we cannot understand what is going on between us and what is
happening in the dialogue. In particular we cannot understand the
patient's strategies, defensive manoeuvres, the way in which he or she
may need to fail or provoke aggression, succeed or manoeuvre their way

into or out of trouble.

Even then there are other factors which interfere with treatment which we must be aware of in any form of therapy. Chief amongst these is resistance, resistance to the awareness of painful or dangerous impulses of memories, particularly in terms of present and past relation- ships as they may have echoed or reappeared in the transference relationship. What psychoanalysts have termed defences are the expressions of resistance, mechanisms such as projection, denial and repression being fairly typical examples of the way in which the individual protects himself against the reactivation of painful memories, experiences and relationships. Thus if one wants to understand all sorts of apparently unconnected phenomena, such as persistant lateness, missed appointments, premature termination of treatment, failure to follow instructions, a concept such as resistance is clearly necessary. Equally much more unobtrusive difficulties, a need to externalise problems, forgetting what the therapist said, turning serious matters into jokes, compulsive smoking during sessions (putting up a smoke screen) are all examples of the sort of behaviour which expresses resistance.

Finally, as I have indicated above, any dynamic therapy, indeed any therapy, demands a theory of interpretation. However, as might be expected, there are many definitions of the process. Sandler et al. suggest four possible meanings of the term. They are:

(1) The therapist's influences and conclusions regarding the unconscious meaning and significance of the patient's communications and behaviour.
(2) The communication by the therapist of his inferences and conclusions to the patient.
(3) All comments made by the therapist, which is a common colloquial usage of the term.
(4) Verbal intervetions which are specifically aimed at bringing about dynamic change through the medium of insight.

From my point of view the most useful of these definitions is that which refers to insight, which takes various forms and I would follow Rycroft (1958) as in his definition of the central element as an interpretation. Rycroft says:

The analyst invites the patient to talk to him, listens and from time to time talks himself. When he talks, he talks neither to himself nor about himself qua himself, but to the patient about the patient. His purpose in doing so is to enlarge the patient's self-awareness by drawing his attention to certain ideas and feelings which the patient has not explicitly communicated but which are nonetheless part of and relevant to his present psycho- logical state. These ideas, which the analyst is able to observe and formulate because they are implicit in what the patient has said or in the way in which he has said it, have either been unconscious, or, if they have been conscious, it has been without any awareness of their present and immediate relevance ... In other words, the analyst seeks to widen the patient's endopsychic perceptual field by informing him of details and relations within the total configuration of his present mental activity which for defensive reasons he is unable to perceive or communicate himself (quoted in Sandler, 1973).

It might be helpful at this point to describe a patient with whom this sort of approach seemed appropriate. The patient is called Barry, he is a writer who has had some professional success. He is 42 with four children, one of whom he and his schoolteacher wife have adopted. He was referred to us complaining of difficulty in writing, depression and fear of dying.

The original interviewer diagnosed him as a very intelligent schizoid character, who was highly defended and would use a great deal of splitting and projective mechanisms. He predicted that Barry would make mincemeat of any therapist because of his wit and his verbal fluency and that he would not really be prepared to involve himself in a transferential relationship. Nevertheless, I took Barry on for a 15-session contract, partly because otherwise he would have had no treatment, partly because I wanted to study this age group.

There seemed to be a possible focus in his material, in so far as his elder brother had been killed in the war. Barry, the youngest of four children, reported that he had been closest to this brother and that his death had come as a shock to him. Barry's father, now dead, had been a manufacturer in the North Country and was described as upright, obsessional and remote. His mother, who was now in a home for the aged, was felt to be warmer, and had spoiled Barry more than she had her other chilren. Barry had trained as a teacher, but soon after his father died, when he was 31, he had given up teaching to become a full-time writer. His work is published, but at little financial gain for himself. They are acidly witty satires on modern life and generally have to do with sadistic attacks on the hero by bureaucracy - and how the hero, an archetypical 'little man' stands up and in the end defeats his enemies. Barry described his marriage as good, but his wife had had two intense affairs with senior members of the staff at the school where she worked. Barry spoke both of his wife and his children warmly and affectionately. The focus of treatment seemed to be very much the question of his identity, although competitiveness and feelings of sexual inadequacy played some part in this as well. We wondered whether Barry might not well be struggling with the recognition of a false solution to the mid-life transition - in Levinson's terms - and it was agreed that the therapist should focus on this and on the links in the transference with his father and lost brother.

The therapy was not easy, although he was well motivated and worked hard. Termination became an issue very early, but the most interesting part of the therapy lay in the confirmation of the clinical hunch about the transference parent link in Barry's life. By the third session, Barry had revealed that he was bi-sexual and that while intercourse with his wife was fairly satisfactory, he got more pleasure out of seeking out lorry drivers at motorway cafes or public lavatories and having intercourse with them, usually fellatio, with Barry as the active partner. His wife knew of this practice and condoned it. He described to me at length how struck he was by the size and magnificence of the genitals of these working-class men (he came from an upper middle-class background) and how impelled he felt to behave in this fashion, even though he knew it to be risky professionally. I interpreted to him that he was projecting his own grandiosity onto the genitals of the lorry drivers, and finding there the magnificent phallus which he dared not display himself because of his fear of the castrating father and the fantasy that the same fate might overtake him as had overtaken his brother. With me he could allow himself to show off at one remove. I thought he was expecting me to punish him, which would put me in the feared and denigrated father role. I felt that he was testing me out to see if it was my intention to take his skills and his potency away from him.

This turned out to be quite a useful interpretation, since he returned returned two sessions later with the following story. He had gone to the opening of a new play, and had seen there an attractive woman whom he wished he could pluck up enough courage to approach and seduce. He thought of asking her out to supper after the play, but she was going on to a party to which he had not been invited. He'd therefore left London, deliberately driven to a motorway cafe - although he knew he was expected at a party his wife was attending - and had picked up a young man aged about 27. To his great surprise, this young man, who had large genitals, had not treated him as an aging queer to be exploited, but had told Barry that he found him attractive and fellated him. He felt moved by this experience, and although he had not told his wife about it, they had made love successfully the next day.

In the weeks remaining to us, quite a lot was worked through concerning Barry's relationship to his father, to me and to his own children. He reported that he was writing again and had finished a book that had hung fire for over two years. His other symptoms seemed to have disappeared, his relationship with his wife improved and was maintained. He did not feel too impelled to go to motorway cafes. You may well object that this result represents a flight into health - but it has been maintained at follow-up, two and five years later.

The therapy seems to have helped him through a mid-life transition in that I think that he was finally able to hold and retain part of his own masculinity which he no longer needed to be projected onto others where it could both be envied and lost and found, but rather acknowledged and used as part of himself in a more mature and productive way. If we set up criteria of change they have been that ideally he should continue to be symptom-free; that he should have given up homosexual practices with both psychological and physical satisfaction; he should continue to take an appropriate parental role with his own children; if his mother died he should mourn for her appropriately; he should achieve satisfaction and productivity in what-ever career he adopts and that relationships with men in superior positions should be good; and finally that he should be responsible for himself and for his actions appropriate supporting evidence should be provided to meet each of these criteria.

Technically speaking, Barry turned out to be a good case for brief dynamic psychotherapy, in so far as his problems could find a focus, and be dealt insightfully with in a relatively circumscribed way, and he could then be left to get on with the work himself.

It is not possible within the scope of a short chapter such as this one to provide evidence in support of the ideas that I have been putting forward. The interested reader is referred to the work of David Malan at the Tavistock Clinic, who has for the past 20 years been attempting to provide the evidence necessary (Malan, 1976). It does seem that with good selection a reasonable number of patients can be helped in ways that permit a validation by other workers in the field.

I have tried to outline the importance of dynamic psychology for the clinical psychologist. I have shown how most therapeutic techniques can be classified and understood and the addition of a dynamic hypothesis adds a qualitatively different factor to our work, one which permits the addition of a new set of personal meanings to the honour mentierium of therapist and patient. Difficulty and failures of therapy can be understood and the encounter between therapist and patient can profit from the extra dimension offered through notions such as transference, resistance and defence. The old split between behaviour therapy and dynamic therapy is breaking down. What is now needed is to work towards the effective combination of the two methods in a way which will underline and fully utilise the merits of both.

REFERENCES

BIBRING, E. (1952), Psychoanalysis and the Dynamic Psychotherapies, J. Am. Psychoanalytic Assoc.', 2, pp. 745-70.
CULLEN, C. (1980), Radical Behaviourism, 'New Forum', 7, no. 2, pp. 35-8.
HILDEBRAND, H.P. (1980), Psychodynamic Therapy, 'New Forum', 7, no. 2, pp. 30-3.
HILDEBRAND, H.P. (1982), Psychotherapy with Older Patients, 'Brit. J. Med. Psychology', 55, pp. 19-28.
KLEIN, M., DITTMAN, A., PARLOFF, M. and GILL, M.M. (1969), Behaviour Therapy - Observations and Reflections, 'J. Consulting Clin. Psych.', 33, pp. 259-66.
MALAN, D.H. (1976), 'Towards a Validation of Brief Psychotherapy', New York, Plenum.
RYCROFT, C. (1958), An enquiry into the function of words in the psychoanalytic situation, 'Int. J. Psycho-Anal.' 39, pp. 408-15.
SANDLER, J., DARE, C. and HOLDER, A. (1973), 'The Patient and the Analyst', London, Allen & Unwin.
SHARPE, E.T. (1947), The psycho-analyst, 'Int. J. Psychoanal.', 28, pp. 1-6.
SLOANE, B., STAPLES, F., CRISTOL, A. (1975), 'Psychotherapy versus Behaviour Therapy', Harvard University Press.

Chapter 5

PERSONAL PSYCHOLOGY AND THE THERAPY OF FAMILIES
Paul O'Reilly

'A Fool can ask more questions than ten wise people can answer'

I want to refelct here on a number of matters. Without apology they
are wide-ranging and complex, but I feel, crucial in the field of
practice which is called Family Therapy. They are: on being an
individual; on being a therapist; on being a family therapist: and on
being a systems thinker. I will discuss each of them making full use
of my knowledge of the reading I have succeeded in doing over many years
now; of my experience of having lived in two families; and of the
learning that I have received, actively and passively as a therapist –
someone who is paid to interfere in other people's lives. At the end
of this chapter I will list a series of reading and articles which are
important with respect to the views I have developed and which may
assist any reader to further explore the questions I pose and the
solutions I propose. They are interim solutions only.

There are three important dimensions along which Family Therapists
vary. They are not the only dimensions but they serve to assist in an
examination of the process of therapy when the 'client' is a family
with a unique history of shared interaction and a shared sense of
future. They also serve to examine the process whereby one person may
arrive at a place so as to be able to say "I am a Family Therapist".
The dimensions are: (i) An ability to be aware of the ME/NOT ME Boundary
and to experience the fluctuations which occur along that Boundary.
(ii) A capacity to Examine Unconscious Processes and to accept the
Essential Uncertainty that is present in such examining, and (iii) An
Acceptance of the Interactional Perspective and the strength to tolerate
the struggle such a perspective demands. Of course they are dimensions
along which all individuals vary and are basic in the personal-political
learning (indoctrination?) to which we are all subjected. It is clear
that people have lived in small 'family' groups for thousands of years
– the decreasing size of the group being the most noticeable change in
the recent past. I suggest that individuation, 'mind-reading' and
inter-relational insight are necessary consequences or properties of
intense group living. However it is not necessary for most people to
examine movement along these dimensions. Therapists ought to do so and
family therapists in particular have little choice in the matter.

Occasionally, painfully, individuals who get to be clients to therapists examine these dimensions, but after a period of time in such examination cease to do so – location in time is sufficient, awareness of movement over time and over place is a matter of more painfulness and can be depowering and deskilling, not the reverse. Location of place on these dimensions and then movement along them with the assistance of a therapist is more of an egocentric, than an exocentric process, and the interactional aspect tends to be unipolar. Individuals may be assisted to define a strong ME through increasing awareness of personal agency but cannot necessarily reconcile the inherent paradoxes which lie in the relationships between each of these dimensions and the other two. There is a process of increasing complexity and uncertainty. The ability to maintain one's own reality, yet acknowledge other people's very different realities is not easily developed and is precarious. 'I know who I am' is much less likely than: 'I am trying to discover who I am' which in turn is less likely than: 'Who cares about who I am – other people will tell me.' And other people to tell we have by being in a family group? or by being a therapist?

ON BEING AN INDIVIDUAL – A CASE STUDY

B is the second of six children. His elder brother is 10 years old when B is born and, in rapid succession there follows a sister, brother, brother and sister. The last is five years younger than B. The family is poor, though B's father is, for the time and place, well educated and highly intelligent. He is a restless man, perhaps somewhat irresponsible, and spends a good deal of time away from the family home – in the Armed Services initially and then in finding employment in other counties (there being little possibility of work locally). B has an early memory of living in a small house and, at the age of three and a half years, of moving to a large one. He and his sister take a walk, on the day of the move, around the new locality (a cul-de-sac of twelve houses). The houses all look the same – B and his sister get lost – they cannot find their house. To them it seems a very long time that they are lost and both get very upset – though B tries not to when his sister first cries. Eventually they are 'found' by a new neighbour and are returned home. The joyfulness of becoming B again in being found quickly wipes away the tears, but the experience is searing – at three and a half years ME is not well developed and when the most important others are not in view and may never be so again then distress and disintegration are rapid consequences. Purposeful action to confirm self is not possible and retreat into total infantile dependency follows. At least B's sister can depend on B: he is NOTHING until found.

When B is six his brother finds a way to leave home. His father, over the next six years, is away for up to nine months of each year, his brother for ten months of each year. B gets to be 'man' of the household, but is frequently 'dethroned' when either father or brother return. B learns to hide feelings, dangerous feelings, about such dethronement. People might get to know and certainly will not like the rage, jealousy, despair and decay of identity that follow each displacement. Anxiety about discovery and anxiety to get it right escalate leading to suppression of feelings and to unconscious experiencing of them through nightmares. And the nightmares are useful

too because nurturance is given by parents on such accoasions. At the
same time though B punishes self for having nightmares in the first
place and for disturbing others. B learns to appear strong and
invulnerable, and develops much skill in the care-taking of others; he
quickly senses other people's needs or displeasure and attempts to
respond as well as possible so as to meet needs or reduce displeasure.

At nine years old B is taller than his peers, physically strong,
silent and literary (encouraged to read widely by his father). It is
at this time that, while father and elder brother are away, his mother
falls off a set of kitchen steps she is using to reach a high shelf.
She is knocked unconscious. All the children rush to her, the youngest
starts crying, B comforts her, the others in turn start crying and
saying that mother is dead. B denies this and reassures them at the
same time as becoming more and more scared. The fear is as much about
not being able to help mother - make her better - as it is about
anything else, but the unknown (unconscious) reasons for the fearfulness
are not then available. They are the fear of losing a sense of self,
of being reduced, of acknowledging personal needs, vulnerability and
mortality and of dependency. Eventually B cries too, having tried to
rouse mother. She eventually recovers, reassures everyone, speaks
wonderingly, and with pleasure of B's display of love for her. He does
love her, but the tears are as much for himself as they are about her.

During most of the three years aged 12-15 B's mother is hospitalised. She had worked in dusty conditions in her early youth and had
become asthmatic, getting close to dying on a number of occasions while
in hospital. B visits her regularly in hospital. He does so twice per
week alone as he is now going to school in the same city in which the
hospital is - that being fourteen miles away from where the family
lives. During that time he sees mother often in the oxygen tent, sits
with her while she is very confused and unrecognising of him and
experiences her being rushed by ambulance to hospital when she relapses
following discharge. Father must live at home now to look after the
family and household. B, in attending school so far away from home (it
seems to him) becomes increasingly independent, especially through peer
relationships within a group of boys and girls. He has a series of
short boyfriend-girlfriend 'loves' and then, when aged 15, falls in
love with a girl whom he dates for a year, loving her a lot, and
occasionally fighting with her about what he and she do to each other.

It is during that year that B's mother gets to be more and more well,
both physically and psychologically, and the whole family moves to a
different county, leaving B behind to complete his education. He
rejoins them after six months. In the moving he stops relating to his
girlfriend, sadly but also feels excited about the moving. The two
seemingly incompatible emotions induce guilt and despair ensues, partly
after the guilty feelings but also because of the deep sense of loss
experienced in the relocation to another county. Familiar things and
places are gone but most of all, familiar people and close friends feel
lost. The rest of the family by this time seem well settled when B
rejoins them and this challenges his reality, his sense of self even
more. Eventually he settles into a new school where he takes advanced
examinations and then goes off to University. The six months not living

with his family has enabled him to be more independent and he now
resists very much being 'entangled' in any disagreements his parents
have or in the usual familial disputes, though he is not able to give up
his problem-solving tendency in that he notices whatever may be happening
in a group of people and then offers solutions. B is sad, and guilty too,
in going off to University. He is excited and has a marked sense of
achievement. But the family has been poor and though not so financially
constricted now his parents have always had to struggle to make ends
meet. Perhaps he should not go to University but find employment
instead? The issue is not resolved for him by family discussion, but
each parent in turn encourages him, tells him their view of the matter
and offers support. Mother would prefer that the children of the family
work as soon as possible so as to bring money into the household but
tells B that he should go to University - that would be best for him.
Father is envious but encourages B, is delighted too and wants B to be
successful. At this age however there is an awkwardness between B and
his father as B has not yet reached that point of being able to be
charitable to his parents as people. He punishes his father for his
(father's) shortcomings, weaknesses, failures ('Shouldn't all parents be
perfect as we love them so much?'). The most effective punishment is
withdrawal of intimacy, of sharing. And as B is secretive anyway being
uncommunicative is a straightforward matter. They still get along well
enough though B's sisters and brothers are encouraging or unconcerned.
B decides to go to University. He finds some old friends, makes some
new friends, falls in love, gets married, while still studying, to a
woman (A) who is training to be a Helping Professional too and they have
a child before they graduate. B loves A, but A is not sure that she
loves B. She likes him a lot, is impressed by him, likes spending time
with him but spends time too with other people, one of whom she very
much likes. But this person, a man, is struggling to get his chosen
business (farming) in order and she is knowing that she does not want
to be married to a farmer. She agonises a good deal. B agonises too
and they both move in and out of intimacy and closeness, feeling inter-
connected in the joint struggling about life and love and in liking each
other. Their marrying is not well received by her family or his, but is
accepted grudgingly. They find somewhere to live and have a mutual
feeling of being in battle against a hostile world or disapproving
adults. Their friends are highly supportive. Both graduate, both
undertake postgraduate training. She in the Social Services; he in the
Health Services. They do so while the daughter they share is growing
and manage to share the care-taking of her. This is possible while they
are students; when they are employed they use a child-minder.

The feeling of mutuality grows and they remain in battle with the
world. It seems as if people expect them to get it wrong somehow. They
seldom disagree, rarely argue and never fight. Positions, viewpoints,
are not adopted by each so as to lead to difference of disagreement.
They are very good together as a couple, are very very good together as
parents but neither has a strong sense of developed personhood. They
work very hard to get it right for each other and over the years a
relationship of mutual liking and trust develops in which B is the
competent, contained problem-solver and A, traditionally, is the feeler,
the person who from time to time is sad, unhappy or concerned for both.
B is a pragmatist and both arrange it so that the other does not change.

Both are powerful people and are very much liked, respected, admired by others, though privately each does not esteem self overly and each knows well how she/he is failing, not succeeding ('I could have/should have got better grades, learnt more, read more, achieved more, been better for others').

When the first daughter they share is four years old, they decide they would like to share another child. They stop using contraception, eventually conceive and a second daughter is born. During the pregnancy they move to a different country because B who is now fully qualified wishes to work elsewhere and A is agreeable, if reluctant, because she feels she would like to be at home full-time with the second daughter, feeling deprived of time with the first because of studying, training and employment.

ON BEING A THERAPIST

They move. B works as a therapist in the Health Service. They find that A must work some too and so she gets a part-time job in a different hospital in the same city. B has been trained eclectically, with a behavioural orientation, but over the next few years he realises that the psychodynamic aspects of peoples' distress/disintegration must be attended to more fully. At the same time he becomes aware that working with individuals in isolation from their context/environment does not feel as if it is the most useful way to be of assistance. He attends self-help groups, therapy groups, goes on training conferences and courses, find people, both locally and nationally, to learn from, reads widely. He has a rare capacity to rapidly incorporate into his therapy and his person concepts and experiences described by others. He becomes aware of his own feelings and of the fact that he has been trained as a male to put feelings away. He is now more personally-politically aware and undergoes a deep personal struggle to understand/integrate all that is happening. How to conceptualise therapy? How to integrate that into everyday living? What to do about the increasing awareness of feeling/emotional oppression? What about personal agency and responsibility in his interactions with others? How to look at and construe the effects of all of this in his relationships with A and the two children they share? What about his increasing belief that the personal is the political? What to do about his feeling now that things between himself and A are not good enough, that he has needs which are not being met? And how to be the person who wants to change what's happening between he and A without that perpetrating the way they relate anyway?

There is such desperation in this struggle. Neediness is painful to experience and is painful for others to be around. Resolving neediness so that needs are acknowledged and a state of being needful is possible and acceptable is an extraordinarily painful matter. The state of being needful as opposed to being full of neediness is one which is difficult to maintain. Making conscious the unconscious (with respect to training and needs) is resisted. Personal consciousness raising, never mind interactional-consciousness raising, is avoided. The state of having needs is maintained with difficulty against the might of cultural-social

expectation and demand. B struggles, sometimes alone, sometimes with
the assistance of others. It becomes clear that there is no end-point
to such personal journeying - the struggle, the journey, is what there
is. How to do things, how to decide, how to act as a therapist, and
as a person, are the key matters for B in the whole process of therapy.
The means of containing self, so as to be able to contain others, must
be explored and awareness of unconscious processes everywhere expanded.
But in all of this, over the next four years, the problem of Power
emerges. B now sees how he is advantaged in the world in being a male
person. Of course there are problems in the expectations that have
been conveyed to him as a male, but he is advantaged in being able to
be more active, competitive, ambitious and powerful in the work compared
to the women he knows. He now sees too that there is a large inequality
of power in a room where he is the therapist and another person is the
client. And increasingly he knows too that how well he hears another
person is very much related to what is happening for him in his world
and to what is not resolved in his relationships with important other
people, both in the past and in the present.

Becoming a therapist is a stressful matter and a number of solutions
to the stress are possible. One way is to get into a therapeutic
relationship with a therapist, either as a client or as a trainee.
Both have advantages and disadvantages. The case for a personal
therapy is strong. The problem is that it can be, for some therapies
at least, an isolating and non-responsible experience. It is a
solution which involves retreat into the self, of the past and, hopefully, awareness of agency in the present. However agency in
interactions with others is not examined other than in a linear fashion
- either the client is wholly responsible or the other/s is/are.
Another solution is to stop the consciousness-raising examination and
develop skills in practice, teaching or management. In this manner it
is possible to be of assistance to others through being competent,
skilful, professional and knowledgeable about theories, constructs,
'the literature'. This solution is a careerist solution in the
helping profession. People who choose this work hard to be promoted
so as to be able to manage, or teach from a position of high status.
Another solution is to put a large amount of energy into family or
personal life. In this solution the professional is divorced from the
personal. The professional is cool and distant, the personal may be
otherwise but is rarely seen by colleagues. People who adopt this
solution live with or marry others who are in a profession or
occupation which does not have a helping component. One more solution
is to live and work in a collective or commune - where there is likely
to be constant examination of personal agency and attribution of
'unconscious' (not known to the person being talked to) needs, desires,
thoughts, actions. There are many other solutions. B had a series of
different ones. He created a network of other therapists who were more
or less in a peer position with respect to him and had similar concerns.
With these, even if seen infrequently, it was possible to examine
agency, become more aware of process not content and be confirmed.
Through this needs get met other than in home or family, or in place of
work, and intimacy with other people grows. Different kinds of
intimacy become possible, even if unreliable. Nothing is clear cut
with respect to therapy and process. Each therapist to individuals

probably has a prime solution and then uses whatever bits of solutions that fit at the time they are necessary. Being a therapist to individuals appears to be a difficult, but possible, task.

ON BEING A FAMILY THERAPIST

Being a therapist to families is a difficult, and hardly possible, task. For some individuals it is a possible, and preferable, solution to the problem of being a therapist. B trains in family therapy over a period of years. He has always tended to work with more than just one other person, with groups of people, but finally started working with groups and families from a system or interactional perspective. Whether or not this is an efficient or effective way of assisting people to change gets to be fairly irrelevant when a solution is being sought. For B it helped with respect to his many difficulties about being in practice as a therapist. B trained himself as a family therapist. Most senior practitioners in this new way of working have done so. B did it in the accepted way - going on (yet more) training courses; video-taping and re-viewing endless hours of therapy with families, this frequently alone, sometimes with others; reading widely in the relevant literature; spending years of seminar time with colleagues, and undertaking a good deal of personal work about family of origin and current relationships. All of which reduces the amount of time available to live in a family!

An ongoing problem for therapists lies, on the one hand, in the paradox of helping people to help themselves and, on the other hand, in the paradox that by helping people whose difficulties frequently derive from political/social/cultural system in to which they are embedded that system is being maintained (so as to produce other individuals who need help!) This apart from the problem of what to do with the enormous power given by those in distress to those who might be of assistance. All of this is somewhat alleviated by the publicity with which a family therapist works. And the family system is being invited to change, rather than stay the same by rendering one member ill, or symptomatic in some way. Power and positioning are more negotiable.

Important issues with respect to personal agency arise in this way of thinking. How one person acts so as to get events to occur; how one person is a producer (direct instigator) of other peoples' behaviour; how one person gets others to be responsible for his/her feelings - all of this must be continually examined. Being a family therapist invites the practitioner to get professional and personal worlds to be congruent - its not possible to stop at the end of the working day. Awareness of personal agency is empowering - it also assists others to be empowered. A most important matter in this way of thinking/ practising is the question of 'coupledom'. B's learning about relationships derived mostly from his experience of being a member of a series of dyads - with his father, his mother, each of his brothers and sisters, that of his teacher, his lovers, A, each of the children he shared with A. At work with each of his colleagues, junior and senior, with each of the clients he worked with over a number of years - some for as long as three or four years. That is not to say that relation-ships in groups did not occur. They did in the early teenage years in particular, in group therapy and other training events and, of course, in the family matrix. But these relationships do not seem to be as important learning areas as those relationships which were dyadic. Dyadic experiences are the building blocks of B's individual development and therefore in therapeutic relationships resonances (counter transferences) occur, both in the individual and family working but especially so in the working with couples. In the family therapy frame the circularities, or patterns of behaviour, which occur, especially in the couple system, are as important as each individual's personal account of the relationship. Patterns develop over time; rules of the relationship are derived - both explicitly and implicitly; and given that intimacy and vulnerability create fear then strong covert rules are frequently developed in couples so that fearful matters, especially with respect to possible loss, are avoided. The pattern of relating that a therapist might develop is a solution but inevitably that pattern affects the way a therapist works. And dyads are different. They remind therapists first of all about their parents' relationship (or lack of it), and then cause them to examine, in some matter, the current solutions they have to difficulties in dyadic relating. This level of awareness, of constant process thinking, can be depleting unless therapists have a sufficiently caring and supporting network. And agency, personal agency, is difficult to maintain. Thus the solution of being a family therapist may be more problematic than anything else.

ON BEING A SYSTEMS THINKER

I want now to examine in more detail the three dimensions along which family therapists vary, both in a static, descriptive way and in a dynamic prescriptive way. I feel they are important concepts with respect to maintaining the systems thinking perspective. I concede that becoming a systems thinker may be nothing more than yet another solution to the problems which occur for therapists who first decide to work more actively with families. I will argue though that the MEANS in working as a therapist are as crucial as the ENDS and that being a systems thinker, with a developed interactional perspective, demands continual awareness of the MEANS.

Most family therapists are socialised as individuals, are trained through one of the accepted helping professions (nursing, medicine, psychology, social work, and the others) to work with individuals, perhaps with groups and then move on to being family therapists. They do so in a more or less decided way and are more or less committed to such a complex way of working. Some family therapists proceed then to work with networks which consist of groups of families, or a whole neighbourhood community, some work in residential settings and some work with large systems or organisations. Each of these - families, networks, residential settings and organisations has a sense of future - they are likely to maintain themselves even if the individuals of which they are made up change and they demand great personal awareness in the systems thinker.

In working with families and other groups with a sense of future (as opposed to 'stranger' groups) the necessity to be able to draw, and maintain, the ME-NOT ME boundary is paramount. The problem is, of course, that each of these work settings assails the boundary in different ways and requires acceptance of movement along it at different times. In everyday living the boundary is unchallenged for the most part and is, for the majority of the time, irrelevant. We know who we are through our history, our possessions, our work, friends and through those with thom we live more intimately. We feel, or not; we think we act in a context-free manner (that we are not determined by what is around us) and we have an established feeling of agency. For all that it is an establishment which is precarious. It is markedly easy for any of us to feel alone, isolated, unconfirmed, unloved. The ME-NOT ME boundary develops for each of us from birth, probably from before birth. For infants everything is ME. Object Relations Theorists describe the process whereby individuation occurs, underlining how total dependency on another requires unconditional love of the other and so the unlikeable, unlovable parts of the other are taken on as part of the ME and then dealt with by being put into a different part of the psyche. Thus the ME-NOT ME awareness arises from bad parts of others being incorporated as bad parts of the self and then split off from the 'good' self. Over time we get to be able, through the love we receive from important others, to be able to reduce the incorporation process and to develop well enough a feeling of ME-NOT ME. I learn to be able to decide what I like and what I do not like. I come under great pressure as a child to like those things that people around me like, to eat those things I am told to eat, to be tired when I am told I am. I struggle to be able to know, regardless of what I am told, that what I feel is sufficient in itself and requires no defence. Of course, enough of the time important people around me must listen to me so that I can develop ME. This listening confirms me - if I am not confirmed enough I have difficulty in knowing whether or not what I feel is acceptable, even to me, and continual lack of sufficient confirmation means that I have difficulty in knowing what I feel, whether acceptable or not.

Group pressure is strong. And in groups we are required, as individuals, to conform. In such a setting, the sense of SELF is precarious. This is generally so in large group settings such as EST events, conferences and, in our development, school assemblies. In such settings pressure to be a good and committed member is experienced by all such that the capacity to act as an individual is very much reduced - so much so that the possibility of leaving is almost non-existent. Similar pressure can occur in families where the members are over-involved in each other, where individual boundaries are hardly developed and where there is consequent fear of loss of others - because everyone is necessary for anyone to experience a sense of SELF and the ME-NOT ME boundary is minimal.

However, most of us, though in a precarious and haphazard fashion, develop enough of a ME-NOT ME boundary so as to act with personal identity in the world. We receive enough messages of personal worth from enough important people so as to be able to do so. However some of us do not - either because of one or two or a series of traumatic events or because over a long period of time we receive few, or no,

messages of personal worth. For those of us who are such, who
frequently experience distress or disintegration, one remedy is to go
to see a therapist. And the therapy of choice would probably be long-
term and, most likely, psychoanalysis or some psychoanalytic psychotherapy. Certainly a form of regression therapy. In these types of
therapy, and in most others, though less acknowledgly, patients or
clients are invited by the therapist to 'relive' previous experiences
and, through the non-impulsive way in which the therapist responds,
discover they are worthwhile people, developing a sense of personal
identity, of personal worth. The individuals pattern, or solution with
respect to relationships (usually a pattern of avoidance) is explored
and the individual's capacity to assimilate, hypothesise and then act
is developed. This change is painful and the essential skill required
of the therapist is that s/he contain the client in distress so that
change can be attempted. Such therapists have been trained to be aware
of the ME-NOT ME boundary so as to contain and will develop ways to
maintain that boundary in a static manner. Once established (generally
in a peronal therapy of some kind) the boundary which is continually
assaulted by clients, who test the therapist to see whether or not s/he
is good enough and who would find it gratifying in the short-term to
discover that the therapist is as worthless as s/he. The simplest
defence, that least demanding of constant re-assessment, is the
building and maintenance of distance - from clients, but, inevitably
from colleagues also. This is one strategy - there are others.

Therapists who work with families find the ME-NOT ME boundary is
continually assailed and the availability of distance-making strategies
is necessarily reduced. The family therapist must be able to enter
into and exit from the families' reality. If s/he cannot exit, change
for the family may still occur, though less efficient and more
haphazard. If s/he cannot enter, families stop attending for therapy.
Family systems are powerful - and most of us have belonged to a family
system of some kind (probably still do). There is likely to be marked
resonance in a therapist with the family, especially with a particular
family member. Then too, therapists are caring people, trained to care
more. And so distress experienced by a family or by a family member
can be painful to a therapist. That it is not painful so as to be
debilitating and that entry into and exit from the families' reality is
possible requires that the therapist continually monitor his/her
position in the ME-NOT ME. But movement occurs and so the therapist is
continually being asked to risk self. Thus strategies to locate and
maintain self are developed. The use of co-therapists, having
supervisors, exploring one's own family of origin and current family
experiences, continually examining self, all of these have been, are
being employed. They are not sufficient in themselves though and the
two other important dimensions need to be utilised so that a therapist
may become a systems thinker.

The examination, and subsequent utilisation of knowledge, of
Unconscious Process is an activity that most are reluctant to indulge
in. In general we do not consider the unconscious in everyday living.
And by unconscious I mean those emotions, motives, drives, awarenesses
which are not usually available to consciousness, but which, with
sufficient and appropriate endeavour can be made available. We all are

part of a continuous communication matrix. It is not possible not to
be part of a communication system, the problem (if such!) is that
communication is a rapid and complex process at verbal, non-verbal and
perceived (attributed) levels. It may be that I would be better
advised using the concept "Subconscious Processes", but I think not.
At any time any one of us has a personal account, usually coherent and
well-built, of actions in the world. But each of us too has mixed
feelings about most matters. And having mixed feelings is not
encouraged - as we grow we are continually expected to 'know one's
mind'. Therefore the personal account, on a verbal level, is not
accompanied by congruent messages on a non-verbal level, or only some
of the time. The receiver of such conflicting messages attributes
meaning to them, with greater or less clarity, at the same time as
having little consciousness of the attribution process - message
received is not necessarily message sent. The solution to this
complexity, especially in groups of people, is for each not to have
personal awareness of the different messages, of the conflicting
experiences. We defend against the complexity by being conscious
(cognitive and rational) and egocentric.

    B received mixed messages from his father. There were verbal
messages of support and encouragement and non-verbal messages of
jealousy and rivalry. It was not possible, at an early age, to
comprehend that both were possible, acceptable, perhaps essential.
All was further complicated, of course, by B's feelings of jealousy
and rivalry, by his different position with respect to power in the
world and by messages given by mother. Best to believe here that one
is acting in a determined, if immature, manner and such acting is goal-
directed. A further degree of complexity occurs when all the feelings
of these participants are taken into account as each affects all the
others. And different messages are given (or received) about the
permissability of different kinds of feelings. From the youngest of
ages we are trained to be in control of ourselves especially with
respect to feelings of fury, anger or rage. It is important that we
be trained not to act on these feelings indiscriminately, the problem
is that a very fine balance of message is required which communicates
on the other hand, that such feelings when present need to be dealt
with, and on the other hand that it is not possible to simply act about
them in a destructive fashion. We are socialised to control such
feelings through the mediating experience of guilt. To minimise guilt
we put away feelings of rage. It is important to note here that men
and women are trained differently about guilt and its expiation. Men
are trained to act to reduce personal feelings of guilt - mostly by
getting out-of-control behaviour to be someone else's fault. Women are
trained that the only way not to be guilty is to act so as to please
others (especially men) as often and as well as possible. And guilt
gets to be present if a woman fails to do this.

    Freudian or analytical psychology describes the different parts of
the psyche as they are developed to cope with this complexity. Other
thinkers have different views but my concern here is to reach some
understanding of the way in which 'Unconscious Processes' are present
for therapists, not to describe the complexities of the mechanisms by
which they are mediated. It is important to know that fearfulness

(following inability to have a ME-NOT ME boundary) derives from
confusion and refusal of the paradox. And, increasingly, the
resources available for any person alone to solve problems in a real
and changing world are reduced. Vision is blinkered, that different
people have different realities is denied, and the capacity to act in
a determining and realisable way is eroded. To do so the language used
by individuals gets more and more limited, therefore limiting.
Transformational grammarians have assisted us in describing how the
ability to be aware of Unconscious Processes is decreased by the
reductions in the way language can be used symbolically or not.

But therapists who work with clients may not act impulsively, though
can act intuitively. It is necessary for a therapist to be aware of
personal motives and needs so as not to attribute (project?) to the
client thoughts and feelings of the therapist. This is an ongoing
requirement which is draining and feelings of personal depletion are
endemic among therapists. Taking care so as to be able to take care in
a useful and growth-inducing manner for clients is very costly.
Various strategies to cope with these kinds of demands are possible.
One is to rigidly adopt a particular theoretical position and to defend
that position strenuously so that it is no longer merely a tool but
gets to be the way in which the whole world is viewed - in a highly
evaluative manner. Another strategy is to insist that all pathology in
the dyad, therapist-client, lies in the client. It is the fantastical
ideas of the client which are addressed, directly of indirectly - the
fantastical material of the therapist is not present because s/he has
already dealt with that in personal therapy! A third strategy would
be to combine both of these because then we have a fixed theoretical
position and a belief that all pathology is in the client which allows
for a range of different level explanatory concepts to be developed.

It is not possible for therapists with families to employ any of
these. Family therapists must continually be aware of conscious and
unconscious processes in the family and family plus therapist systems.
The dance, the movements, the patterns which are continuously present
amongst family members confront the therapist with problems that may
only be solved, in part, by continual self awareness and examination
of personal as well as familial unconscious material. The explicit and
implicit rules, communication and expectations which occur in family
systems make particular demands of the therapist who needs to be able
to contain the systems in distress, and fearful of change. The family
has a shared fantasy of catastrophe following any change and that
fantasy will be maintained by the mixed messages circulating in the
system. And the motives, the needs, the fantasies, the experience of
the family therapist are all changing too. This crucible of possible
chaos requires that the therapist maintain personal equilibrium in a
moving and uncertain state and know that monitoring all of this affects
that state too. Accepting this 'Uncertainty' is not easy and continuous
exposure of Unconsciousness may be extraordinarily depleting. Thus,
most frequently, family therapists work together in teams - to support
and assist each other, though such a solution may lead to stuckness,
not growth and capacity.

The third dimension - An Acceptance of the Interactional Perspective

- is more difficult than the other two to describe, or conceptualise, using a language which is primarily linear. The Interactional Perspective is concerned with circular causality and pattern repetition, and the concepts used have an 'Action Imperative' - they require clear decision-making by therapists in both their professional and personal worlds.

The socialisation we undergo is concerned to enable us to be functioning, albeit not independent, adults. In a consumer-spectator society we are trained to be selfish and acquisitive. We are trained to feel helpless in the face of large events and in the face of large suppositions by those in power. The way to proceed then so as to minimise the stress created by such training is to focus on personal comfort and to attribute motives, meanings and most importantly, responsibility for actions to others. Consideration of the interactive is therefore unlikely and a capacity to examine personal agency unlikely. And examination of the usefulness to self, and to systems to which we belong, of our feelings and actions is difficult. Focus on process, not content is hardly possible. We are all trained to be linear thinkers - to continually employ notions of cause and effect. The political usefulness of such training (to maintain the system) is not a matter I shall discuss here. Suffice to say that on both a micropolitical and macropolitical level changes between generations must be rendered minimal. Attributive punctuation assists in minimising change. The following is an example of such punctuation:-

Two people live together for some time. They go to see a therapist to get some help with their feeling of disease, manifested by the drinking behaviour of one of them. The first says 'he drinks too much'. The second says 'I only drink because she nags'. Thus:

| First | Nagging | | Nagging | |
| Second | | Drinking | | Drinking |

and so on. Each has a highly individual, linear account. The circularity is not aknowledged. And the usefulness of the circularity to keep both together perhaps, cannot be investigated. Change occurs of course, when another circularity which is less distressing can be employed to perform the same task, or when they separate.

Linear thinking, the lack of an Interactional Perspective, leads couples to take polar opposite positions. One member may attribute all responsibility for actions (of both) to the other. The other may take on all responsibility for changing so that both change. A clinical example is the couple which arrives in therapy because one of them is being physically violent to the other. The first hits the other because of 'what she says, does or doesn't do'. The second works to change to make it better. The second thinks 'If I can change then she will not hit me any more.' Therapy is the final attempt to change.

Therapists who are systems thinkers can perceive how actions are both cause and effect and can contain themselves in a communication matrix able to address the circular patterns which occur; and examine the personal and systematic usefulness of such patterns. But an ability to examine circular processes is continually undermined by inability to maintain the ME-NOT ME boundary and lack of awareness of

Unconscious Processes. Apart from the understandable inertia of the family system and the socio-cultural pressure insisting that a member of the family is symptomatic through personal fault (!) or that (with enlightenment) it is the family which is the patient.

OVERVIEW OF THE DIMENSIONS

By now the interconnectedness of the three dimensions will be apparent, and the systems thinker maintains all three in balance, knowing that movement on one demands movement on the others and that not enough of any reduces capacity. It may be clear too that intimacy becomes a matter of concern to the systems thinker. Apart from the intimate knowledge of self there is the intimacy which is created in the systems working and the responsibility of the therapist to evolve distance – regulating mechanisms which are containing of the system at the same time as enabling closeness to be possible. Each therapist solves these problems differently – and solutions are obvious given enough attention to the three dimensions described.

Which are you – a wise person or a fool?

BIBLIOGRAPHY

BANDLER, R. and GRINDER, J. (1975), 'The Structure of Magic', Palo Alto, Calif., Science and Behaviour Books.
BATESON, G. (1973), 'Steps to an Ecology of Mind', London, Paladin.
BATESON, G. (1980), 'Mind and Nature: A Necessary Unity', London, Fontana.
BOSZORMENYI-NAGY, J. and SPARK, G.M. (1973), 'Invisible Loyalties: Reciprocity in Intergenerational Family Therapy', New York, Harper & Row.
GRINDER, J. and BANDLER, R. (1976), 'The Structure of Magic', II, Palo Alto, Calif., Science and Behavior Books.
GUNTRIP, H. (1968), 'Schizoid Phenomena, Object Relations and the Self', London, Hogarth Press.
GURMAN, A. and KNISKERN, D. (eds) (1981), 'Handbook of Family Therapy', New York, Brunner Mazel.
HALEY, J. (1973), 'Uncommon Therapy: The Psychiatric Techniques of Milton H. Erickson', New York, W.W. Norton.
HALEY, J. (1976), 'Problem-Solving Therapy', San Francisco, Jossey-Bass.
HINDE, R.A. (1979), 'Towards Understanding Relationships', London, Academic Press.
HOFFMAN, L. (1981), 'Foundations of Family Therapy. A conceptual Framework for Systems Change', New York, Basic Books.
LIEBERMAN, S. (1980), 'Transgenerational Family Therapy', London, Croom Helm.
LOMAS, P. (1981), 'The Case for a Personal Psychotherapy', London, Oxford University Press.
MAHLER, M.S., PINE, F. and BERGMAN, A. (1975), 'The Psychological Birth of the Human Infant: Sybiosis and Individuation', London, Hutchinson.

MALAN, D. (1979), 'Individual Psychotherapy and the Science of Psychodynamics', London, Butterworth.

MINUCHIN, S. (1977), 'Families and Family Therapy: A Structural Approach', Cambridge, Mass., and London, Harvard University Press.

OPEN SYSTEMS GROUP (1981), 'Systems Behaviour', London, Harper & Row in association with the Open University Press.

POSTER, M. (1978), 'Critical Theory of the Family', New York, Seabury Press.

ROSENBERG, M. and TURNER, R.H. (eds) (1981), 'Social Psychology: Sociological Perspectives', New York, Basic Books.

SMAIL, D. (1978), 'Psychotherapy: A Personal Approach', London, J.M. Dent.

WATZLAWICK, P., BEAVIN, J. and JACKSON, D. (1967), 'The Pragmatics of Human Communication: A Study of Interactional Patterns, Pathologies and Paradoxes', New York, W.N. Norton.

WHIFFEN, R. and BYNG-HALL, J. (1982), 'Family Therapy Supervision: Recent Developments in Practice', London, Academic Press.

WYCHOFF, H. (1976), 'Love, Therapy and Politics: Issues in Radical Therapy', New York, Grove Press.

YALOM, I.D. (1981), 'Existential Psychotherapy', New York, Basic Books.

Chapter 6

A PERSONAL APPROACH TO TEACHING PSYCHOLOGY
Phillida Salmon

In this chapter, I want to consider what it means to teach academic psychology at the tertiary level of education. My own institutional context will serve as a starting-point, since it is neither particularly reactionary nor particularly progressive and is probably fairly typical. The major commitment of the Department is to a one-year postgraduate course in developmental psychology. Teaching methods are traditional, with a heavy predominance of lectures. Assessment is through course-work, an empirical dissertation and written examinations. The syllabus is intended to cover the whole course of human development, from conception to early adulthood. It is structured into six separate areas including Psycho-biological Development, Social-Psychological Development and Intellectual and Linguistic Development. Essentially, this course details the presentation of a body of knowledge to each successive generation of students and the certification of the degree to which, by the end of the year, they have assimilated it.

As one of the course tutors, I am expected to offer one part of this body of knowledge - the course of human socio-psychological development, as depicted in the standard texts which represent the currently received view in academic psychology. These texts, which are quite homogenous, portray young human life in certain characteristic ways. Typically, change and development are considered in terms of particular spheres such as aggression, sex-typing, moral development and peer group relations. In each sphere, the course of normal development is depicted for particular age levels, and factors accounting for deviance are considered. Throughout the account, statements are justified by reference to evidence from research.

To offer such a body of knowledge to students is to engage in an extraordinary activity. There stands one human being, pronouncing, to other human beings, upon what it means to be human. In doing so, she presumes to tell them what life is and, by implication, what her own and their lives are. And the account she offers is, by any reckoning, a strange one. Whole dimensions are missing. All that gives life its vitality and its poignancy is absent from this picture. Nowhere does one find hope, joy, love, faith, nor the dark side of human feeling - anguish and loss, guilt, hate and despair. Instead, the picture is

flat, bleached, sanitized. Nor is the course of life depicted one
which, for many people, would be easily recognizable. As a generalized
portrait of the life-style of one particular section of Western society
it could hardly approximate to the experience of minority group
students, let alone those from the Third World. The credibility of the
account is still further undermined by the whole explanatory framework
in which it is couched. In place of our human capacities for agency
and creation, external events and given attributes are seen as governing the forms that life takes. In this account, too, situations are
defined without reference to the meanings which they may have for those
who experience them. This is all part of a very static picture of life,
in which the great historical movements and the conflicts and struggles
of human groups play no part, and there is no sense of the interconnectedness of people across time.

The presentation of this kind of account must put even more at risk
then the possibility of student alienation. Surely lecturers risk
becoming alienated too. How is it possible to expound as truth a view
of human life which has so little resonance in one's own personal
experience without a sense of bad faith and inner protest?

Those who endorse the approach I have described sometimes define
their academic activities in terms of a particular metaphor. They see
themselves as offering students a map. The map is an inter-connected
series of guidelines through the huge territory represented by the
mass of research findings published over the last ten years or so.
People who use this image see themselves as enabled to create their own
map by virute of the time they have spent within the territory, reading
new texts, keeping up with the journals and maintaining contact with
the work of academic colleagues. What is most significant about this
image of mapping a territory is that it carries the assumption that the
landscape itself is given, and not at issue.

How is this landscape actually constituted? It is, of course,
constructed out of the findings of research. Not just any research,
but 'good' research. And what does good research consist of? It is
research which addresses itself to 'relevant' and 'important' questions.
It is research which is 'sound' in its methodology. It is research
which produces 'meaningful' findings. I should like to consider what
each of these aspects mean. First, the questions that are defined as
being relevant and important. It is significant, I think, that there
is seldom much debate about the questions to which research is
addressed, although it is these, more than anything else, which
govern the nature of the research. Perhaps this is because the people
who staff academic institutions and funding bodies share a broadly
similar situation in human society and adopt broadly similar
perspectives towards human life. Yet for other kinds of people these
may hardly be questions at all, while other, very different, questions
may urgently need asking.

Research is also judged to be good if it follows certain methodological procedures. These amount, I think, to the adoption of two interlinked assumptions - about cause-effect relationships and about
generalizability. Many of the rules about research have to do with

controlling extraneous sources of variance – that is, making sure that the results obtained are not an artifact of 'other variables'. These 'other variables' characteristically turn out to be such things as age, gender, race, social class. These are, of course, the very same categories which, in academic psychological texts, are credited with causal functions in human life. Yet perhaps the functions they possess represent nothing more than the power our particular society gives them – the modes through which it operates in the ways it does.

The second assumption governing judgments about the soundness of research methodology is that any conclusions drawn should be generalized beyond the particular sample studied. What this generally means is that the researchers should be able to make statements about large groups of people – statements as to the factors which make people behave in particular ways. The groups of people to be included in these generalizations are typically limited by the same categories – age, gender and so on. Within these limits, broad statements of cause and effect are expected. The underlying logic is that people basically differ only in the social categories to which they belong. Again, if this is a meaningful statement at all, it can only represent a statement about prevailing social attitudes.

Good research is supposed to produce meaningful results. Just as with the questions to which research is addressed, any particular research findings are likely to be more meaningful to some people than to others. Experiencing things as meaningful means being able to assimilate them into one's existing assumptions. In turn, those assumptions are governed by a particular experience and position in life. If there is general agreement in academic circles as to which recent research ventures have produced the most meaningful, the most significant results, this may again be no more than a reflection of the broadly similar outlook on life of those who staff academic institutions.

Fundamentally, the findings of any research venture can never do more than confirm its own starting-point. It is that starting-point itself which is really crucial. Yet this fact is implicitly denied in the way research findings are used to support the official view of human life. A student's challenge is habitually met with the same, supposedly incontrovertible, response. The lecturer cites the literature, pointing to research evidence which 'proves' the statement. By this means, a highly particular, yet altogether unexamined, outlook on life is reified into universal human reality.

Most academics, if asked what they hoped to achieve in teaching psychology to students, would, I think, describe goals not altogether unlike those of most psychotherapists. Probably they would talk about enhancing the ability to deal with personal difficulties and conflicts, about developing a fuller and richer understanding of life, and about widening the sphere of personal agency so that individuals could begin to tackle social problems and injustices. But to ask most under-graduates or postgraduate students about their experience of studying psychology would, I am afraid, elicit a very different account. It is now almost a truism that, for most students of psychology, the excitement, curiosity and urgency which they brought to their quest have turned, by the end of their academic studies, into boredom, if not actually disillusionment. Any interest or enthusiasm experienced in academic courses typically happens incidentally, outside the official curriculum, through chancing upon a particular book, meeting an interesting fellow-student or, sometimes, encountering a member of the academic staff as a person, outside the academic role. The stuff itself of academic courses is at best purely instrumental – a means to entering professional work. It almost always remains externalized, rather than intermeshing with vital personal convictions or creating new possibilities in how to live.

I think it is generally true that most psychotherapy clients would have a less sorry story than this to tell. It may also be true that, in its history, psychotherapy has traversed some of the paths that academic psychology is now treading. At any rate, there has been a general movement among psychotherapists away from a didactic and authoritarian approach towards a much more personal one. From Rogerians to Gestaltists, personal construct to women's movement therapists, the practice of therapy seems increasingly grounded in a concern for the individual person, within a particular personal-social context, and with particularized experiences, beliefs and expectations. The assumption that human life could be generalized, and that therapists possessed its secrets, has been widely abandoned.

This shift in orientation has had two major implications, each of which, if taken by academic psychology, would revolutionize its practice. One concerns the relationship between learner and teacher and the other concerns the nature of knowledge. In psychotherapy it is now widely assumed that deeply meaningful learning can occur only in the context of a genuinely personal relationship. This means not only that clients should be acknowledged and affirmed as the unique persons they are. It also means the genuine presence of the therapist as a particular human being. In academic psychology the creation of this kind of highly personal context for learning goes against some of its most fundamental traditions. The idea of scientific detachment, which marked the beginnings of psychology, is still generally endorsed. It informs such practices as the rejection of applicants suspected of having personal motives for studying psychology. It applies also to academic staff, who are expected to achieve their areas of expertise without reference to their life experience, and to propound views of human functioning regardless of whether of not they actually believe them. An impersonal and didactic character also pervades typical academic learning contexts, with lectures and laboratory work predominating over seminars and tutorials. More importantly, where staff meet students or students meet each other, talk is not expected to be personal.

This ignoring of the personal is often, in practice, quite disastrous. As I suggested earlier, the generalized account of human life which makes up the body of knowledge in academic psychology is one one which passes over many students and contains a highly offensive view of others. The life-styles of working-class people, homosexuals, or one-parent families are patronizingly defined, the potentialities of black children, or of girls, are denigrated, the intellectual powers of rural Third World people are contemptuously dismissed. By failing to take into account the persons to whom their courses are addressed, academic psychologists must often, unwittingly, ride rough-shod over many students.

For all those involved in trying to understand human life, the enquiry must be rooted in their own personal context, their own personal convictions and their own personal questions. Inescapably, this must mean that learning starts with the explanation and articulation of personal understandings. As most psychotherapists know, such explanations cannot occur within the context of an authoritarian relationship.

Although meaningful learning in academic psychology demands a context which is genuinely personal, this context is necessarily not quite that of psychotherapy. The contact between students and fellow-students or staff is less intensive than the contact between clients with each other and with therapists. The scope of students' concerns is also likely to be broader, less closely focussed and more variable than that of psychotherapy clients. This means that a greater proportion of the work done in academic study, as against psycho-therapy, will probably be done privately. But that does not alter the fundamental need that the context of academic learning should be a personal one. Its personal character must, I think, consist in two standpoints: towards others in the learning situation, and towards what is learned.

In most academic psychology contexts now, if students talk personally to each other, it is likely to be outside the official lectures and seminars or at least outside the official business of these. Personal interchanges with academic staff may never happen at all. Both students and staff are busy, in their dealings with each other, keeping the rules of the game. If the topic of discussion is adolescence, they refer to recent textbooks, to theories, to research evidence; everyone scrupulously avoids any mention of their own experience of being adolescent, of their own adolescent children, of a particularly moving film or novel about an adolescent. In their writings both students and staff similarly abjure personal references of any kind. The origins of concern in students' research projects, like the topics for academic discourse generally, are drawn from existing literature - never from personal contexts of personally crucial issues. Yet it is when - through the mutual trust of a small student group or the passionate concern of one member - the rules are broken and someone comes out from behind the literature, that the tepid converse of academic seminars becomes a vital and engaged inter-change. It is not just that genuinely personal statements have a life and vividness totally lacking in stale second-hand accounts. Talking personally also puts the ideas at issue within their proper framework. To speak to others in the first person allows - in fact demands - that what is said reflects the particular situation, experience, under-standings and dilemmas of the speaker. It is ultimately those which govern the meaning, or the lack of meaning, that any academic material will have.

Speaking in the first person also fundamentally alters the character of learning relationships. As I have argued elsewhere (Salmon, 1980), we all learn through modes which involve other people, whether through face-to-face contact or more indirectly. Current academic psychology does, I think, make the social encounters of learning very difficult indeed. The literature which constitutes the official body of knowledge is, with rare exceptions, very lifeless, dessicated and hard to engage with; there is seldom any sense of an encounter with the writer. The same traditions render most laboratory work and empirical dissertations alienating and depersonalizing. The student is not expected to engage personally with the adults and seminars where students meet academic staff and fellow-students, those involved trypically experience each other only through the screen of references to published work which may have little real meaning for any of them.

Of course, most students doing academic psychology courses manage, at least at times, to break through the constraints and inhibitions of scientific objectivity and to establish some genuinely personal encounters with others. But often, perhaps, personal aspects, through being denied, present themselves very subtly and deviously, in ways which disturb and undermine, rather than facilitate, learning. I am thinking particularly of what happens when academic staff expound views which have no personal significance for them, may even, in fact, run quite counter to what they believe. It must be that, in such situations, the sense arises of a lack of conviction; the message is unclear, contradictory and uncomfortable. This, I am sure, is often the case, because in academic psychology, teachers are not expected to take a personal stance towards what they teach.

It seems to me that it is only through the preparedness to take a personal stance towards psychology that anyone could possibly have the right to teach it. To teach should mean to offer what is personally meaningful. And psychology comes to have personal meaning only if one has reflected deeply on one's own journey so far through life. That entails struggling to see how one's own experience is encompassed in what one understands life to be. It means trying to be aware of the extent to which what seems personally meaningful reflects a very particular standpoint or is more broadly accessible. It involves keeping alive and treasuring the themes and convictions which resonate deeply in one's own experience, as well as holding in awareness the issues, the conflicts, the anxieties that haunt one's life. It means the constant effort to be aware of all the areas of human life about which one knows nothing.

What I have been describing is, I think, the activity which a teacher of psychology needs to engage in, not just privately in the course of living, but in the standpoint which he or she constantly takes towards the body of academic psychology. To approach the academic literature, actively and personally, to examine it from the viewpoint of one's own contexts, one's own questions, one's own lived and known experience – this makes it possible both to enrich and develop one's own personal understandings and to create a structure of meaning within which academic material can be viewed.

One of the consequences of doing this is that any aspect of academic psychology which one presents to students comes already framed in terms of personal meanings. This is so, I think, even if one does not actually spell out what the personal ramifications of it are. And in fact it is seldom appropriate to do this, although the readiness to share personal experience and reflections with students seems very important. More often to be made explicit, I think, are the themes and the sources which, as a person, one has found specially rich in meaning. For me, certain ideas in pscyhology seem full of deep significance in my own experience. One of these is the idea of reference figures and reference groups – that is, of other people, other lives, as a source of reference and inspiration in one's own life. Most poignantly, it is expressed in Thoreau's comment 'If a man does not keep step with his companions, perhaps it is because he hears a more distant drummer.' The richness and meaning of this concept, for me personally, make certain lines of work in psychological research stand out as salient and significant. For example, Lifton's study (1961) of brain-washing and techniques of psychological interrogation seems particularly important. As Lifton found, the strange collection of people – Turkish infantrymen, English army officers; and American Jehovah's Witnesses – who have generally been found to resist this kind of psychological assault, have all shared a common heritage; identification with a clearly defined reference group. The firmness of this social identity, and the strength and support of invisible others, evidently proved sufficient to withstand even brain-washing. Schachter's studies (Schachter and Singer 1962) of how people interpret the effects of psychotropic drugs seems to be equally significant in showing, from a different perspective, how crucial is the reference function which people hold for each other. In these studies, as Schachter found, people based their interpretations of the drug effects they were experiencing, not on the actual chemistry of the injected substance, but on the feelings and reactions of their supposed fellow-subjects. I take this to mean that, even in the most intimate and private areas of our experience, we look to others to help us define, and to confirm, what we feel.

Sources in academic psychology are also far from being neutral, or much-of-a-muchness. Again, I think it is appropriate to be quite explicit about books and writers who carry for oneself a real sense of personal conviction and enrichment. There must be, for anyone, a number of these. Among writers whose work I have personally found exciting and significant are George Kelly (Maher (ed.) 1979), Oliver Sachs (1971) and Ernest Becker (1973). Kelly's ideas, at first encountered through working with Don Bannister, have proved important for me over a long period. Their first impact was in confirming my own long-held but articulate feeling that different people inhabit different worlds. Later I came to experience for myself the real, sometimes frightening, openness of life that, as I read him, Kelly was describing; this made my work as a clinical psychologist something altogether different from what it had been before. The same sense of possibility has, I think, informed my experience of education and educational psychology, and has been one of the reasons for feelings of discontent with these areas as they currently are.

I came across Sach's book, 'Awakenings', quite by chance; but, again, it seemed to speak of deeply important things. It is difficult to define exactly the significance of this book, which is the story of one man's spiritual voyage into the bizarre and often terrifying inner worlds of brain-damaged and deeply troubled people. I think, for me, its meaning lies in the possibility of the communion of feeling and experience across huge gulfs of horror and confusion, and ultimately, in the possibility of full humanity in even the most outwardly degrading circumstances. Becker's 'Denial of Death' also encompasses the depths, as well as the heights, of human experience. To me, Becker's concept of life as a project to be undertaken in faith, courageously, in the absence of certainty, as a gift to be offered back to life - that concept is both moving and inspiring.

In teaching psychology meaningfully, an essential goal must surely be to help students become present to themselves, so that they are able to engage with the material from their own personal standpoint. Whereas in psychotherapy this usually means an intimate joint explor- ation, academic psychological study is likely, I think, to involve work of a more private kind. But as a teacher of psychology, one's concern ought to be with enabling this to happen, through strong and sustained encouragement of students continually to reflect upon and dwell in their own personal experience, their own concerns, their own questions. One route into this kind of personal explanation is through autobiography. Developmental psychology, for instance, certainly looks very different if it is approached from the viewpoint of one's own progess through childhood and adolescence into adulthood. In such personal experience, the chapters which seem to have divided the journey may not at all coincide with the conventionally accepted stages. Nor may the concerns, the themes, in one's own personal development reflect those which form the focuses of official psychology. The contexts of living may, too, seem to have been very different from those conventionally portrayed.

I think it is crucially important for anyone who is studying psychology to reflect on things in this way. It is not just that doing so may enable a student to question the universality of the conventional accounts given by psychology. Even more importantly, it means becoming increasingly aware of one's own framework of experience and meaning - which is the framework within which one's studies need casting. As things are now in academic psychology, this personal framework is characteristically ignored; instead, external definitions, focuses and assumptions are uncritically adopted. The result is that the material of learning remains superficial and devoid of any real meaning. The personal standpoint which should have informed the study of psychology is treated with disrespect, but takes its revenge in sabotaging the attempt to assimilate ideas that are personally alien.

People also study psychology for future purposes. Whether or not the academic degree leads to professional psychological work, those who are now engaged in the study of psychology will be leading lives, as adults, in human society. For most students, I think, concerns and questions about their future roles, at least in work and sometimes more broadly, are salient in the original decision to study psychology.

Again, all too often such real and urgent personal concerns fail to intermesh with academic study, which either bypasses them altogether, or reduces them to the instrumental goal of getting a ticket into professional work.

A personal approach to psychology whould make one's own present and future contexts central, and put at issue one's own potential social role and practice. An obvious example in developmental psychology is the work of professional educational psychologists, which many students are preparing to enter. Really to engage in study from the perspective of one's future personal involvement in such work would lead to something very different from the induction into standard perspectives, standard practices, typical now. It would mean the development of as full and intimate an understanding as possible of the personal meanings involved and potentially involved in the role. What does that position in society, towards educational success and failure, actually mean? What are the political and social implications of taking that role? How far is the role consonant with other roles that one has taken in one's life so far, and that one wishes to take? What does that professional position mean to oneself personally and to others with whom one is personally and professionally involved? It perhaps hardly needs saying that it is impossible to begin to answer these questions without extensive first-hand exploration of educational psychological practice - not merely academically, but from the conscious standpoint of one's own values, concerns, and potential agency.

Ultimately, these questions can be answered only through a sustained and serious study of the lives of the other human beings who are involved in the work that educational psychologists do. Conventional psychology does scant justice in particular to just those kinds of people who are most centrally affected by educational psychological practice. Because it is rooted in the standpoint of those who have power in society, it characteristically bypasses the situations, and the experience, of those who do not. Economic and social security and stability, a positive experience of schooling, an expectation of an occupational career and good life-chances - all these things are built into the portrait of life offered in mainstream academic psychology.

It is because the outlook and concerns of the privileged minority in our society are reflected in its conventional psychology - just as they are in its official media - that certain unrepresentative yet unquestioned perspectives are habitually taken towards social insitutions. For most inner-city working class people, particularly those from ethnic minorities, the wholly benign image incorporated in the texts, of education, housing, employment, police and the judiciary would be rare indeed. The frustration, humiliation, misunderstanding and discrimination experienced by many such people in our society is nowhere to be found in the writings of psychologists regarded as authorities.

These considerations seem especially important when the situations of educational psychology clients are at issue. The context is, of course, that of school - an institution which has very different significance for different groups of people. In practice, the events leading to referral to educational psychologists are already overladen with very particular, official meanings - meanings which need to be closely examined. In school a congenial place, happily interlinked with life at home, a place in which one daily experiences a sense of worth, and in the process acquires the ticket for entry to larger and more exciting opportunities? If school is like this, then truancy, disruptiveness, poor attainment, can only signify failure, inate perversity. But suppose schools are experienced very differently. For a black teenager, living in poverty, in crowded delapidated housing, life in the classroom can hardly mean the same thing. Where schools seem merely to perpetuate the inequalities of the out-of-school world, one may not automatically accord respect to teachers. To someone all too conscious of the prospect of imminent employment, the ostensible offer of certification for work, to every child, must, to say the least, have a hollow ring.

To the extent to which, in their study of psychology, students are enabled to reflect deeply and personally on their own future practice and what it may mean - to that extent, their studies can provide a leverage for social change. I believe that our psychology, and real psychology, underlies what we do in our everyday lives and, therefore, ultimately, how we construct our society. It is only by examining, honestly and intimately, the personal standpoint from which, as individuals, we act in our lives, that we can begin to question some of our social practices, and start, together, to remedy inequalities and injustices.

As long as psychology remains a body of knowledge to be passed down to each new generation of students, it will continue, unwittingly, to perpetuate the social status quo. By its present exposition of one particular viewpoint, one particular life-style, it legitimizes and serves the privileged minority in our society. Through its incorporating of the perspectives of that minority, it maintains demeaning stereotypes and ignorance of other groups. Because it refuses to examine the standpoint of the research which constitutes its accepted wisdom, it reifies all the assumptions and practices of our present-day society.

In place of an academic psychology which closes down personal and social possibilities, we have to build one which opens up human imagination, creativeness and agency. This, I am sure, can only be done by an approach which sees psychology, not as a body of knowledge to be transmitted, but as something which has to be created anew by everyone who studies it. Only a psychology which is rooted in our own experience, our own contexts, our own real concerns, can inform the standpoint from which we speak and act in the world.

REFERENCES

BECKER, E. (1973), 'The Denial of Death', New York, Free Press.
LIFTON, R.J. (1961), 'Thought Reform and the Psychology of Totalism', New York, McGraw-Hill Book Company.

MAHER, B. (ed.) (1979), 'Clinical Psychology and Personality: The Selected Papers of George Kelly', New York, John Wiley.
SACHS, O. (1971), 'Awakenings', Penguin Books, Harmondsworth, Middlesex.
SALMON, P. (ed.) (1980), 'Coming to Know', London, Routledge & Kegan Paul.
SCHACHTER, S. and SINGER, J.E. (1962), Cognitive, social and physiological determinants of emotional state, 'Psychological Review', 69, 379-99.

Chapter 7

ON THE UTILITY OR OTHERWISE OF PSYCHOTHERAPY RESEARCH
Andrew Treacher

During the last several years, I have had to rely heavily on various members of the mental health establishment. I have encountered over twenty different therapists, been in two mental hospitals, had countless medications thrown at me, and amassed a staggering number of bills. I have been diagnosed schizophrenic, manic-depressive, cyclothymic personality, borderline psychotic, agitated depressive, hysterical, and just plain neurotic - to name a few of the labels this broad brush of scientific endeavour has pasted on me. I have been overmedicated, overanalyzed and underanalyzed. I have been given suicidal advice. But somehow along the way I have met a few wise and tender people. Too few.

All this is to say that psychiatry, because it probes the dark recesses of the human psyche, is a fragile science. And it is terrible to make the discovery, after a series of unfortunate circumstances, that you have also been a victim of the individual and collective ignorance of a profession that, because it is essentially unmonitored, attracts into its ranks a brand of charlatan that wouldn't dare practice in other branches of the medical establishment. A person with no more than everyday neurotic symptoms can handle the greed, the stupidity, the immaturity and the outright mistakes - including wrong diagnoses and prescriptions for inappropriate medications - of these inept pratitioners. Although he shouldn't have to. But when you are ill, relying on them is like trying to read a book by the light of a firefly.

I managed to survive. But I'm not generous enough of spirit to forgive or to forget the brutality of such a system. The road to recovery from mental illness is so interminable, so fraught with its own ups and downs, that fighting incompetence en route is intolerable excess baggage.

BARBARA GORDON, 'I'm Dancing as Fast as I can' (1979).

Barbara Gordon's fully justified lament about her harrowing experiences
of various forms of psychiatric treatment, which included psychotherapy,
may at first sight seem to be a strange starting point for a review of
psychotherapy research, but I would justify it simply on the grounds
that such impassioned statements draw our attention to the urgency of
taking psychotherapy research seriously. Barbara Gordon was lucky in
discovering a committed psychotherapist who helped her heal her deep
psychological wounds but her suffering at the hands of incompetent
therapists raises a number of crucial issues which need to be addressed
by all practising psychotherapists.

If Barbara Gordon's experiences had concerned publicly supported
services then perhaps there would be little surprise at the way she was
treated but she was in fact a fee paying client living not in the
backwoods (where services might be expected to be poor) but in New
York where the availability of private services is probably second to
none.

Some commentators, including Szasz (1961), have assumed that private
contractual therapy solves many of the problems associated with the
'institutionalized' therapy carried out in publicly funded settings but
clearly this assumption is both naive and false. Private practitioners'
activities are in fact accepted as being beyond scrutiny provided
certain minimal ethical and competency rules are observed. Given the
vulnerability of clients seeking help for their psychological problems
there is no reason to assume that they will easily escape exploitation
at the hands of ineffective therapists or indeed charlatans.

Malcolm's recent book 'Psychoanalysis: the Impossible Profession'
(Malcolm, 1982) provides some rich insights into why there is no reason
for assuming that psychoanalytic psychotherapy is above suspicion as
far as efficacy is concerned. Her journalistic investigation of the
state of psychoanalysis in New York may seem insignificant when compared
to the volume of research published in academic books and journals, but
nevertheless she makes a crucial point about the scientistic nature of
psychoanalysis which has been all too readily overlooked. In the course
of her investigations she met Hartvig Dahl whom she describes in the
following terms:
Dahl is an analyst without patients. He is a psychoanalytic
researcher - a member of a small, scattered group of analysts who
work mostly alone and mostly without the respect or interest of
their patient-seeking colleagues. The reason for their inferior
status derives from the nature (and history) of psychoanalysis
itself. Its therapeutic and scientific functions have traditionally
been viewed as inseparable; the therapeutic encounter is seen as the
laboratory of the science of psychoanalysis. Accordingly each
practising analyst is a scientific investigator, each case an
experiment yielding corroboration or elaboration or interesting
refutation of established theory, each patient a sort of unwitting
laboratory animal. The non-practising analytic researcher doesn't
fit into this self contained dual purpose scheme of things, and is
felt to be superfluous and a little declasse. Hartvig is the New
York Psychoanalytic Institute's grudging concession to the claims of
'pure research'; he is a sort of shabbas goy to the orthodox membership.

Obviously not all psychoanalysts are hostile to research. The
existence of the meticulous if disappointing 20-year Menninger study
(Kernberg et al., 1972; Voth and Orth, 1973) is a tribute to those
psychoanalysts who are sensitive to the criticisms of the ineffective-
ness of psychoanalysis which have been common currency since Eysenck
first attacked psychoanalysis in 1952 (Eysenck, 1952). However, the
cabalistic nature of psychoanalysts which is so clearly documented by
Malcolm undoubtedly makes them less open to research. And they take
this tradition straight from Freud as Malcolm demonstrates in her
quotation from Freud's Introductory Lectures: 'You cannot be present
as an audience at a psycho-analytic treatment. You can only be told
about it and, in the strictest sense of the word, it is only by hearsay
that you will get to know psychoanalysis .'

Such a position serves, of course, to preserve the sanctity of the
therapist-relationship but in my eyes it confirms the psychoanalyst as
a secular priest who wishes to keep his activities as mysterious as
possible. The essential lack of accountability contained in this
position is also very striking but it is debatable whether other schools
of psychotherapy are open to investigation either. Some innovators
such as Carl Rogers undoubtedly encouraged and inspired such investigations but this does not necessarily mean that psychoanalysts are to be
singled out for particular criticism although there is a strong tendency
for psychoanalysts to assume that their 'scientific' approach places
them in a unique position vis-a-vis research. Malcolm is very useful
source for making this point - she explains the lack of interest in
the efficacy of psychotherapy by referring to work of Waelder whose
influential book 'Basic Theory of Psychoanalysis' is something of a
bible to orthodox analysts. Classical analysts' failure to take an
interest in new techniques, even in the face of their own lack of
success with a whole range of clients, is explained in the following
terms:

> It so happens that the therapeutic variations of the 'classical'
> setting usually make it much more difficult to <u>learn more about the</u>
> <u>patient; whatever their therapeutic merits may be they are</u>
> <u>scientifically sterile.</u> The real difference between 'orthodox' and
> 'liberal' analysts is therefore not that the former cling to
> tradition while the latter are open to innovation, but, rather, that
> 'liberals' seem to assume that all problems are already fundamentally
> solved, so that the structure of a case can, at least in its
> outlines, be understood in a relatively short time, and all that
> remains is the task of influencing a condition already properly
> understood; while the 'orthodox' analyst looks upon a new case as
> a new enigma that will yield its secrets only very slowly and
> hardly ever entirely. In short, the 'orthodox' analyst stands <u>more</u>
> <u>in awe of the unconscious.</u> (Emphasis in the original.) (Waelder,
> 1960.)

This passage I find most revealing as it presents psychoanalysis
primarily as a science of human behaviour and only secondarily as a
therapeutic procedure. Such a position also performs the latent
function of enabling psychoanalysts to look disdainfully at empirical
research as the outcome of psychotherapy - clearly outcome is a crudity
that the true scientist will not consider important in his pursuit of

truth!

It is arguments like these that unfortunately lead me to wonder whether psychotherapists should be considered as being indistinguishable from other workers in what Magaro and his colleagues (Magaro et al., 1978) have called the 'mental health industry'. In his scathing attack on the current state of the psychiatric services in the USA Magaro makes some challenging points about the generally accepted finding that research has had a minimal impact on practice (Bergin and Strupp, Malan 1973):

> Our thesis is that practitioners of therapy, especially those who deliver publicly supported services to primarily lower class, psychologically disturbed clients, have not demanded better knowledge from researchers. We argue that because the mental health industry is financially dependent on 'mental illness' there is no real reason to treat effectively. (My emphasis – A.T.) More specifically, large numbers of professionals and non-professionals, and a huge amount of capital, are employed in public mental facilities whose raison d'etre is mental patients. That this client group receives a minimum of effective care ... is in our view a function of the industry's need to maintain this group in a client status. Thus although we start by asking why (psychotherapy) researchers do not provide the answers that most practitioners claim they need to work more effectively, we suggest that practitioners covertly maintain the status quo out of self-interest. Especially important in such an analysis are the functions of professional groups, the ethic of professionalism, the bureaucratic organization of the mental health delivery systems, and, most important, the actual record systems of institutional treaters.'

For the reasons already given in my discussion of psychoanalysis, I see no reason why Magaro whould single out practitioners in public institutions as being more hostile to research. Indeed, I suspect that partly because of the way that research in funded more outcome studies have been carried out with the co-operation of publicly employed practitioners than with the co-operation of private practitioners. It can, of course, be argued that orthodox psychoanalysts are particularly efficient at keeping clients in a dependent state and indeed, as Malcolm points out, they expect their clients to work with them for six to eight years as opposed to one to two years which used to be the norm at the time of the first World War. But nevertheless I would support Magaro's emphasis on the fact that research has little impact on the work of such practitioners (although I would, of course, hasten to add that research has little impact on private practitioners either!).

It should, of course, be added (and Magaro does not bring this out sharply enough) that researchers have often opted for undertaking studies which are superficial and do not answer questions that therapists are interested in. For example, Bergin and Lambert (1978) in their extensive review of the outcome literature (which will be considered in greater detail later in this chapter) point out that the enthusiasm which greeted the introduction of behaviour therapy with its allegedly more favourable outcome study could be partly attributed to the fact that the studies cited were often analogue studies not based upon patient samples. The needs of professional researchers to produce

a product, a publication, can therefore be seen as primary in determining much of the inconsequential papers that are published. The
competitive nature of academic circles can also be seen as important in
determining the lack of collaboration which has been a marked feature
of the field of psychotherapy research.

The split between researchers and practitioners is typical of the
division of labour within capitalist societies which has been clearly
documented by Braverman (1974). Attempts to bridge the gap on an
individual or group basis, of course, are common but it is naive to
assume that such initiatives have any long term effects given the
professional boundaries that exist between researchers and therapists.

My criticism of Magaro's position does not, however, detract from
my acceptance of his major thesis which is similar to Illich's attacks
on the medical profession (Illich, 1975, 1977) which he views as the
main barrier to health. Other writers, notably Powles (1973) and
McKewon and Lowe (1966), have similarly questioned the medical
profession's claims to have contributed to major shifts in the health
status of the populations of industrialized countries during the last
hundred years. They see such factors as impaired living standards,
sanitation, housing and diet as contributing much more fundamentally to
any positive shifts that have occurred. Magaro's work therefore needs
to be understood within a broader approach which assumes that the
claims that any professional group makes in relation to their 'product'
will necessarily be problematic and contradictory. Although far from
espousing a consistently Marxist position, Magaro assumes that it is
impersonal and structural factors which explain why mental health
workers have a vested interest in maintaining the status quo. As Caine
and Smail (1969) have argued in their important book 'The Treatment of
Mental Illness: Science, Faith and the Therapeutic Personality', the
helping professions have unsurprisingly always reflected basic cultural
assumptions and values help by certain elite sections of society. The
rise of psychiatry as a so-called 'scientific' discipline is nothing
less that another example of this phenomenon despite attempts by
Whiggish historians to present the reality in a different light.
(Comparison of the work of Jones (1970) which is so popular with
medical audiences, with the more critical recent work of Scull (1978,
1981) is valuable in illuminating this point.) It is equally true
that treatments themselves, as Magaro argues, are primarily social
phenomenon, reflecting specific historial trends and based on values
and assumptions that are subject to change. Brodkin (1980) has
explored the establishment of family therapy as a major mode of treatment from this point of view. He argues that family therapy must be
viewed as 'the product of an ongoing interplay between macrosocial
conditions and micropsychological experiences of Americans during the
last half of the twentieth century'. Needless to say, this interplay
is complex and Brodkin is quick to point out that it is precisely at a
period when the traditional nuclear family is under so much threat that
family therapy makes its appearance as a coherent discipline.

Portes's (1971a, 1971b) thoughtful criticisms of behaviour therapy
are also of interest in this context. Portes argued that behaviouristic theories were inadequate for understanding behaviour because they

lacked (a) a systematic understanding of meanings, and (b) an explicit recognition of self-reflectiveness in human beings. The strength of Portes's position hinges around his ability to relate these well known and well recognised deficiencies in the behaviourist paradigm to phenomena occuring in society as a whole. According to Portes, the crucial question to ask is 'what changes in the relationships and roles of man in the modern world, what transformations in the prevailing beliefs and values, have brought about the increasing acceptance of behaviouristic theory and its applications?' Portes, basing his views on the work of Weber (1958, 1965) and Sorokin (1937), carried out in the inter-war period, assumes that the main characteristic of the contemporary era is its inexorable trend toward rationalism. Against this background it is possible to see the behaviour therapy's claims to 'objective' success are not the only reasons for its emergence. From the standpoint of the sociology of knowledge, the crucial question to ask is what factors in the surrounding cultural context have made the image of man conveyed by behaviourism so attractive to therapists and patients. Portes insists that 'its better fit' into existing social structural arrangements seems a function of its rational simplicity (the person as a consequence of a few logically consistent principles) and its greater claim to scientific status (its principles as derived from experimental research).' In other words, in a period of rapid technological advance in which there is an unrelenting rationalization of both individual life and the life of society, a form of highly technical therapy which dismisses humanistic psychology as 'unscientific' is likely to gain wide currency.

Yates's careful documentation of the development of behaviour therapy is of interest in this context (Yates 1970). He shows that there was at least 30 years of 'behaviour therapy' with clients before Lindsley actually coined the term in a relatively obscure paper published in 1954. Behaviour therapy's very rapid emergence to become a dominant form of therapy would thus be explained by Portes's argument. Clearly the cultural context for the emergence of behaviour therapy was absent in the 1920s and 1930s but the disjuncture produced by the Second World War and the opening of the Cold War created a new climate in which behaviourist ideas thrived.

This digression to examine Portes's work may seem to detract from my argument but I would insist that the obverse is true. It is impossible to examine the field of psychotherapy research without being sensitive to the wider issues involved. This rise of behaviour therapy cannot simply be explained as yet another example of inexorable scientific progress as some behaviour therapists (notably Eysenck (1971)) would have us believe. It is again to Portes what I turn to make this point clear since in a memorable passage he makes the following observation about the way that empirical observations are used to justify different intellectual positions:

> Attempting to use empirical research to lend permanent objectivity to intellectual productions is somewhat futile. If a behaviourist presents us with a rat that follows automatically S-R patterns, a gestaltist can lead us to a most insightful Tenerife monkey. The question of why experimental psychologists have stressed one line of study rather than the other cannot be answered on the basis of their

relative merits. The needs of men, their points of view, and even
their mental disorders follow different culturally and structurally
influenced channels. Changes in these underlying elements point
today to the growth of one approach and to the decadence of another.
True, many contemporary experimental techniques and results are
likely to be preserved in future times, but again they will be interpreted and applied within a significantly different framework.

The work of Brodkin, Portes, Illich and Magaro is crucial to my
argument since such critics refuse to accept at face value the claims
that members of the healing professions make in regard to the efficacy
of the particular forms of treatment they practise. In my book
'Psychiatry Observed' (co-authored by Geoff Baruch) I have argued that
major changes in psychiatric treatment have typically occurred without
any major efficacy study being carried out (Baruch and Treacher, 1978).
The introduction of new psychotropic drugs is perhaps an exception to
this general rule. Controlled studies are undertaken but the
researchers usually have a notorious tendency to underestimate the side-
effects and the dependency inducing effects of long term prescribing
(Klass, 1975).

It is, of course, of crucial significance that efficacy studies of
drugs are so prominent. The explanation is quite simple – there are
enormous profits to be reaped if the battle for the doctor's
prescription pad is won by one drug company at the expense of others.
The impact of the market on psychotherapy is much more complex since it
is the personal skills of the psychotherapist that are being marketed
and not a nicely encapsulated agency. The study of the efficacy of
psychotherapy is therefore in fact the study of the efficacy of psychotherapists – a truism which is very easy to overlook. But since
psychotherapists rely on psychotherapy for their livelihood, they will
predictably be very wary of having their work minutely examined by
independent observers because the results could be potentially damaging
to them both at a personal and an economic level. Of course, there are
notable exceptions to this rule – psychotherapy research does after all
get undertaken but the practitioners are safely guarded by anonymity
and one can safely assume that there is little chance that any of their
clients will ever be informed as to whether the results of the study
showed them to be effective or not.

My initial remarks have, I hope, served to draw attention to the
obvious fact that psychotherapy outcome research cannot be considered
in a vacuum. If my arguments are correct it is necessary to approach
such research with extreme circumspection – why on, a priori grounds,
should we expect such research to be valid or influential if psychotherapy is literally an industry – a form of entrepreneurial activity
controlled by well paid professionals who really have no interest in
changing the status quo? Perhaps I overstate my case but it is
important to bear these issues in mind as I begin my brief summary of
the current state of the field of outcome research.

Comparative studies of different forms of therapy have been carried
out and Luborsky, Singer and Luborsky (1975) have provided an extensive
review of such work but there is little discussion of whether such work

has had any noticeable effect on practice. Indeed, commentators such
as Malan (1973) have pointed out that there is little evidence that any
outcome research has had an effect on practice although he cites the
Menninger study and his own studies at the Tavistock as notable
exceptions to this rule. It is, therefore, important to examine both
the recent history and current state of the field of psychotherapy
research to discover whether there is any valid reason for psychotherapists to take the research seriously. Such a task, if to be undertaken definitively, would require a book length presentation, so I will
have to adopt a less trustworthy procedure - namely to examine the views
of firstly David Malan (who is perhaps the best respected British
psychotherapy researcher) and then his more famous American counterpart,
Allen Bergin. My assumption is that both are important opinion makers
in the area of psychotherapy research and that they have been important
in influencing the historical development of the field.

It is perhaps no surprise that given the youthfulness of the field of
psychotherapy research no adequate history has yet been written but an
article by Malan (1973) has provided the beginnings of such a history.
It is perhaps no surprise that Malan begins by dissecting Eysenck's
famous paper 'the effects of psychotherapy, an evaluation' first
published in 1952. Eysenck claimed to show that roughly two thirds of
neurotic patients improve irrespective of whether they are treated or
not. Eysenck's iconoclastic paper was surprisingly not effectively
rebutted until Cartwright (1956) published a paper which demonstrated
that greater variation could occur in treated patients as opposed to
waiting-list controls. This meant that while some patients showed
greater improvement, others showed greater deterioration than the
controls. Eysenck's concentration on averaged results effectively
obscured this possibility. Surprisingly, the biased nature of Eysenck's
position was not fully exposed until 1965 when he once again repeated
his attack on psychoanalysis (Eysenck, 1965). But this time he was
taken to task by Kellner (1965, 1967) who, in acting as discussant of
his paper in the 'International Journal of Psychiatry", pointed out that
(i) Eysenck had manipulated the use of the drop-out rate from therapy
when calculating the efficacy rate of behaviour therapy as compared
with psychoanalysis. Needless to say, he accepted Wolpe's figure of a
90 per cent improvement rate (which excludes patients who broke off
treatment prematurely) while for the psychoanalytic results he placed
patients who dropped out in the same class as those who did not improve.
(ii) Eysenck's review of the literature was incomplete since he had overlooked a number of studies which recorded positive outcomes for psychoanalytic approaches. When Bergin and Garfield assembled their key book
'Handbook of Psychotherapy and Behaviour Change', Bergin undertook a
further exhaustive review of the literature which once again took
Eysenck to task (Bergin, 1971). Malan (op. cit.) stresses that the
following conclusions arrived at by Bergin are of particular importance:
(1) Bergin calculates that across diagnoses a spontaneous remission
rate of about 30 per cent is realistic. In doing so he exposes yet
another statistical trick by Eysenck to inflate the spontaneous
remission rate of neurotics. The technique he used is summarised by
Malan as follows:

   Throughout the review ... Eysenck dichotomized therapeutic results
   into 'improved' and 'unimproved'. Where the author concerned had

four categories of improvement this was easy; where he had only three, Eysenck halved the middle group, assigning one half to 'improved' and one to 'unimproved'. Now it so happens that in one of the two important studies ... (of) 'spontaneous remission' ... there are three categories. Did Eysenck divide the middle into two as he had done for the treated series? No, he classed the whole of the middle category as 'improved' giving an inflated value of 72 per cent improved instead of 52 per cent.

(It should be noted that more recent work by Bergin (Bergin and Lambert, 1978) has subsequently exposed other flaws in Eysenck's work although paradoxically Bergin has come to accept 43 per cent as an acceptable spontaneous remission figure although even this figure is considered unsatisfactory as the state of the published research is methodologically very dubious. It would, of course, be invidious to accuse Eysenck of consciously manipulating his figures to favour his position - historians of science would probably see the issue differently, i.e. as yet another example of a scientist's conceptual framework influencing the way that reality is actually preceived.)

(2) By accepting that 'slightly improved' and 'improved' categories can nevertheless be taken as improved, and by not including early drop-outs as failures, Bergin is able to suggest far higher figures for improvement rate than Eysenck, i.e. 65 per cent for all forms of psychotherapy other then psychoanalysis, and 83 per cent for psychoanalysis itself.

(3) When these latter figures are put together with the strong cumulative evidence for the deterioration effect, then the conclusion that under the right conditions psychotherapy has a positive effect is considerably reinforced.

Needless to say, Bergin's conclusions have themselves come under attack, notably from one of Eysenck's disciples (Rachman, 1971) and also by May (1971). Malan concluded that Bergin's stance on spontaneous remission is no more securely based than Eysenck's and that his position on deterioration is equally shaky. However, the reviewing of psychotherapy research received a new twist with the publication of Meltzoff and Kornreich's book 'Research in Psychotherapy' in 1970. This blockbuster study listed no less than 101 controlled studies of psychotherapy. The authors' positive conclusion was that 'the better the quality of the research, the more positive the results obtained' (Meltzoff and Kornreich, 1970).

Malan in reviewing their work is similarly positive since he says that 'it needs to be said that if we choose to meet Eysenck on his own ground, that is by accepting cumulative marginal evidence, then there is no question that there is an overwhelming proportion of positive results. No one can say any longer that there is, on average, no difference between treated patients and controls.' But having affirmed (somewhat paradoxically) this statement which is based on the overall findings of Meltzoff and Kornreich, he then exposes the weaknesses of their data as far as adult, non-psychotic patient groups are concerned by showing that only eleven of their studies with such populations survive if the basically inadequate (but necessary) criterion of a follow up of a minimum of six months is accepted before the study is accepted as valid. (The vast majority of their studies publish results for changes at termination and not at follow-up.) But if the requirement that treated

subjects should be both patients (as opposed to volunteers) and adult
and non-psychotic, then only four studies survive. These prove to be a
motley collection involving the use of didactic lectures with peptic
ulcer patients (Chappell and Stevenson, 1936); dynamically oriented
individual therapy with ulcerative colitis patients (Berle et al. (1954)
and Grace et al. (1959)); three kinds of group therapy with alcoholic
patients (End and Page, 1957), and group desensitization with phobic
patients (Lazarus, 1961).

I personally find these results desultory and disappointing. Malan
himself stresses that studies of dynamic psychotherapy on adult psychoneurotic outpatients are entirely absent. Rather than debating the
significance of these findings he comforts himself by reviewing five
studies which apparently validate the use of psychotherapy with psychosomatic disorders. But his own methods of arguing do not stand up to
any scrutiny. Of the five studies he cites - one, the Chappell and
Stevenson study already cited above used not psychotherapy but didactic
lectures as its form of treatment, while another study by Orgel (1958)
is on Malan's own admission 'not a properly controlled study' which was
'justifiably omitted' by Meltzoff and Kornreich. In fact it was
essentially a clinical case study report of his own work provided by
the practising psychoanalyst himself. So, on the basis of three
defensible studies (one of which combined physical treatments with
psychoanalysis) Malan is prepared to state that 'there is considerable
evidence that dynamic psychotherapy is effective in psychosomatic
conditions'. This surprising statement is all the more remarkable given
his much more objective statement, in the same breath, that 'the
evidence in favour of dynamic psychotherapy in the ordinary run of
neuroses and character disorders - for which, after all, this form of
psychotherapy was developed - is weak in the extreme'.

Given Malan's psychodynamic orientation it is no doubt perfectly
understandable why he should wish to salvage something from the wreckage
of psychotherapy research but his partisanship is clearly revealed in
his method of constructing his evidence. Strangely rather than talking
about his own disillusionment with psychotherapy research he immediately
changes course in his article to discuss the disillusionment of others.
He notes that after the euphoria generated by the first and second
Research in Psychotherapy conferences (held in 1958 and 1961)
disillusionment with outcome research was noticeable in the literature
in a marked form at the third major conference held at Chicago in 1966.
A similar disillusionment with dynamic psychotherapy research began to
crystallize in the work of Strupp and Bergin (1969) in this same period
but by the time they came to publish their important work 'Changing
Frontiers in the Science of Psychotherapy'(Bergin and Strupp, 1972) a
deeper disillusionment had occurred. Bergin and Strupp now presented a
general mood of disillusionment with psychotherapy research in general.
One of the main planks of this disillusionment concerned the failure of
research to have any impact on therapy. Strikingly, one researcher
(Luborsky) interviewed by Strupp and Bergin let the cat out of the bag
by reporting, in a circuitous way, that it was the general opinion of
most psychotherapy researchers that their own therapy was not
influenced by research. Luborsky even cited Rogers (albeit anonymously)
as supporting this position and yet Rogers had, at that time at least,

probably contributed more to psychotherapy research than anybody else.

As Malan implies Strupp and Bergin's book can be seen as a nadir in the history of psychotherapy research – it contains some profoundly pessimistic statements including Truax's suspicion that Q-sort techniques (most commonly used by researchers investigating client-centred therapy) are invalid and that isolated statistical findings at the .05 and .01 levels are unimportant and should be ignored by practitioners since they are not powerful enough. In a similar vein Bergin himself concluded that traditional experimental designs and inferential statistics have little relevance to the study of clinical problems and that the demand for controls was too great and too advanced for most studies of clinical intervention.

The outstanding irony of Strupp and Bergin's work, as Malan points out, is that having set out convinced that the field of psychotherapy was ready for large scale collaborative studies, they end up by saying the reverse. They conclude that it is difficult to isolate the effects of any given variable, that such studies have minimal effect on clinical practice, and that above all there was a lack of motivation amongst research workers. As an aside it is also worth adding that Strupp and Bergin's conclusions as far as psychoanalytic work is concerned were even gloomier. They talked of psychoanalytic workers abdicating serious research interests and debated whether the approach has anything to offer in terms of viable future research.

The picture of gloom painted by Strupp and Bergin was not without chinks of light however. Malan, adopting a more optimistic stance, insists that 'the position is not hopeless, because Bergin states that during the course of these interviews he has become convinced that some dynamic psychotherapists do get important therapeutic results but that it is difficult to show this with conventional means of outcome'. Then somewhat emotionally he adds 'the fact that Bergin, the seeker after truth – whose background has nothing to do with our field – should come to this conclusion, is one of the most hopeful things that has happened in this area during the last 20 years'.

That Bergin should support the idea that dynamic psychotherapists can be effective seems only just as it was clearly in step with the consensus of researchers at that time – or to put it another way – there was agreement (despite Eysenck's position to the contrary) that it was not possible to claim that one school of psychotherapy was superior to any other. Meltzoff and Kornreich (1970) summarised the situation succinctly when they stated that
> There is hardly any evidence that one traditional school of psycho-
> therapy yields a better outcome than another. In fact, the question
> has hardly been put to a fair test. The whole issue remains at the
> level of polemic, professional public opinion and whatever weight
> that can be brought to bear by authoritative prevention of
> illustrative cases ... there is no current evidence that one
> traditional method is more successful than another (cited by Bergin
> and Lambert, 1978).

Similar reviews by Roback (1971), Lambert and Bergin (1973), and Bergin and Suinn (1975) arrived at essentially the same conclusion but it was perhaps a paper by Luborsky, Singer and Luborsky (1975) which best caught the mood of this period. The paper's subtitle (taken from a statement by the Dodo in Alice in Wonderland) asked whether it was true that 'Everyone has won and all must have prizes'. Unsurprisingly the authors declared that in fact their careful study did show that everybody had won since most comparative studies of different forms of psychotherapy found insignificant differences in proportions of patients who improved by the end of psychotherapy. A further blockbuster analysis of no less than 375 outcome studies by Smith and Glass (1977) also arrived at a similar conclusion which Bergin and Lambert (1978) also agreed with in writing their chapter on the evaluation of therapeutic outcomes for the second edition of the Handbook of Psychotherapy and Behaviour Change (Garfield and Bergin, 1978).

Their review includes an examination of two recent well controlled outcome studies which confirm the 'no win' outcome. Thus the two studies involving the comparison of behaviour therapy either with short-term analytically oriented psychotherapy (Sloane et al. 1975) or either rational emotive therapy or client-centred therapy (Di Loreto, 1971) produced equivocal results in which no single form of therapy could be taken to be more effective. Bergin and Lambert (1978) also briefly review both the famous 20 year Menninger study and the influential studies of brief psychoanalytic therapy carried out by Malan (1976a, 1976b) himself at the Tavistock Clinic. Their summary of these studies is worth citing - if only to contrast their lack of enthusiasm for their significance which contrasts markedly with that of Malan in the paper cited earlier in this chapter (Malan, 1973):

It seems fair to say that psychoanalysis and psychoanalytically oriented psychotherapy appear to be effective forms of treatment with some psychoneurotics and a variety of psychophysical reactions. These therapies seem to be as effective in this regard as others. Because of the time required its otherwise expensive nature and its failure to show success exceeding other briefer forms of psychotherapy, psychoanalysis can hardly be considered the treatment of choice for particular clients or types of psychological disturbance.

Interestingly, in a recent interview Malan himself has taken up an essentially similar position as the following sombre statement demonstrates:

I'm becoming convinced that the truth of dynamic psychotherapy is that it is effective but only in a very small proportion of patients. This is a very gloomy truth really. Every now and then you meet a patient who obviously has been profoundly helped by it and in controlled studies these people are there hidden among the statistics but there aren't enough of them to make it significant. We expend such enormous effort in doing psychotherapy and seeing patients in long term therapy over years and yet, I think, in the majority of patients the rewards for our efforts are pretty small. So one doesn't know what to do about dynamic psychotherapy as a therapeutic method because I'm not at all convinced that the amount of effort that's put in is proportional to the results achieved. At the same time it is the only method that offers the hope of a radical solution to the majority of neurotic problems' (Barnes, 1980).

Bergin and Lambert, being I suspect amongst the most dispassionate observers of the psychotherapy scene, also deliver something of a coup de grace to the client-centred school by summarising the Arkansas study (Mitchel (1973), Mitchel et al. (1977)) which attempted to test the client-centred hypothesis that facilitative therapist attitudes are necessary and sufficient conditions. Genuineness was found to have a modest relationship to client change but strikingly no less than nine other studies cited by Bergin and Lambert failed to find any relation-ship between client improvement and therapist interpersonal skills. These findings are all the more depressing as previous work by Truax and Mitchel (1971) had created the impression that there was a direct link between these variables and outcome. If there is such a link then it is substantially more ambiguous than at first thought. (And, needless-to-say Rogers's scepticism about research findings seems fully justified! Although it should be stressed that Bergin himself (Bergin 1966) has argued in the past that client-centred therapy was the only interview-oriented method that had been validated by research.) The final study reviewed by Bergin and Garfield, the Vanderbilt University Study (Strupp, 1977, Strupp and Hadley, 1978) is equally iconoclastic albeit in a different way. The study compares the effectiveness of professionally trained therapists with a group of college lecturers. Neurotic students were assigned to both groups on a matched pair basis. The results revealed that the professionally trained therapists were no more effective than their lay colleagues.

These discomforting results are perplexing enough as far as psycho-therapists are concerned but it is equally true that behaviour therapists cannot take much comfort from Bergin and Lambert's review as they state that 'the early dramatic results that overwhelmingly favoured behaviour therapy and its broad generalization are fading. This is probably because many positive results came from analogue studies instead of from clinical populations.' It would be wrong however to end a review of Bergin and Lambert's work on an entirely negative note since in comparing their review with Bergin's review in the first edition of the handbook, it is possible to generate some cautious optimism about psychotherapy research. Indeed it looks as though the pessimism of the early 1970s has changed to a modest positive mood by the late 1970s. Bergin and Lambert therefore state that recent outcome data look more favourable than the work they reviewed in 1971:
    a growing number of controlled outcome studies are analyzing a wide variety of therapies. These findings generally yield positive results when compared with no-treatment, wait-list and placebo or pseudo therapies. This may be the result of improvements in designs but we believe that a major contributor to these newer findings is that more experienced and competent therapists have been used in recent studies. Our review of the empirical assessment of the broad range of verbal psychotherapies lead us to conclude that these methods are worthwhile when practised by wise and stable therapists.

This summary is intriguing as it carries with it the assumption that previous research tended to evaluate the work of less experienced and less competent therapists! On a more sombre note they also point out that since differences in outcome between various forms of intervention are rare it has not proved possible to study the relationship between specific treatments and specific problems in such a way that useful information about assigning different clients to different treatments could be generated.

Such a finding dovetails to some extent with related findings, reviewed by Gurman and Razin (1977), which stress that personal factors are crucial to the success of even the more technical therapies. Technique is crucial since it provides a credible rationale and modus operandi for the therapist but without the necessary personal dimensions provided by the therapist therapy flounders. Bergin and Lambert (1971) also stress the importance of <u>client characteristics</u>. Indeed they hypothesize that the largest proportion of variation in therapy outcome is accounted for by client factors (e.g. motivation to change). The personality characteristics of the therapist come second with technique variables coming in a distant third.

If the validity of their hypothesis is accepted then it follows that as the interpersonal dimensions of therapy interactions are more carefully explored it will become possible to match therapists and clients in more meaningful ways. This in turn will mean, according to Bergin and Lambert, that there should be more emphasis on therapist selection and interpersonal skill development. But such an emphasis will inevitably re-open the question of whether (to quote Bergin and Lambert) the role of the 'indigenous, non-professional helper' should be given a prominence which is normally taken by the professional helper.

It is to Bergin and Lambert's credit that they raise this issue directly - in many ways this is the 64,000 dollar question which raises the issue of spontaneous remission rates once again. Earlier in their review they tackle the spontaneous remission issue deciding that as far as any evidence is valid it is best to assume a rate of approximately 43 per cent across all disorders (hence revising their 1971 estimate upwards by 13 per cent). However, they very interestingly tackle the issue of whether 'spontaneous remissions' can be taken at face value. To label a phenomenon 'spontaneous' usually means that we just do not understand what is causing a phenomenon but previous work by Bergin (1963, 1966, 1971) suggests that many people experiencing psychological disturbance quite naturally obtain help from their spouses, friends, teachers, doctors and clergy rather than trained professionals. It is salutory in this context to recall that the thorough nationwide survey of the USA carried out by Gurin, Veroff and Feld (1960) for the Joint Commission on Mental Illness and Health, revealed that the vast majority of people seeking help for personal problems not only avoided contacting mental health professionals but generally reported that they were more satisfied with the help they received than those who contacted psychiatrists and psychologists. This dismal (or positive according to how you look at it) finding was confirmed according to Bergin and Lambert by a study by Christensen and Magoon (1974) of students seeking help for emotional problems. They rated friends as being the first source of help with psychiatrists coming last.

Bergin and Lambert conclude from studies like these that the so-called 'sponateous remission' of control groups may well be due to active non-professional care-seeking by them. 'Perhaps psychotherapists

are not unique. Perhaps selected helping persons in the 'natural'
social environment provide adequate of better coping conditions for
neurosis than do trained mental health experts.' Obviously until some
research is carried out in this area, it is only possible to speculate
about the processes involved but Bergin and Lambert themselves provide
an interesting example of a process of natural healing which they came
across in the course of undertaking a survey of 'normal' people for a
government agency. They came across an exceptionally effective, popular
college graduate who came from a chaotic pathology-inducing family background. (All other family members had been hospitalised for severe
mental illness.) It turned out that he had survived because he had
become unofficially adopted by a well functioning neighbourhood family
with whom he spent most of his time. The mother of this family was
exceptionally nurturant and yet fostered independence and self-
dependence.

Discoveries like these are well known to family and network
therapists (e.g. Speck and Altreave, 1973), but it is easy for
professionally trained therapists to overlook them. In America some
attempt has been made to draw upon the strengths of local communities by
giving minimal training to carefully selected volunteers. Bergin and
Lambert cite at least a dozen studies as examples of this approach –
initial results are encouraging and clearly this is an important growth
area which overlaps with other work involving the construction of self-
directed change packages or kits. The latter may well prove to be just
another fad but the popularity of Gordon's best-selling Parent
Effectiveness Training Manual (Gordon, 1975) indicates that there is a
very real public demand for guidance and counselling in parenthood and
other areas of personal life.

Bergin and Lambert concluded their review on an optimistic note –
they are acutely aware of the methodological difficulties involved in
designing valid studies but they 'continue to be optimistic that
research is leading us toward becoming more and more helpful to the
many suffering people who seek relief from psychological distress.
There are few feelings more gratifying than the satisfaction of
collaborating with the community of researchers and clinicians in an
enterprise that may benefit those who need help.'

My prolonged excursion into the recent history of psychotherapy
outcome research has for reasons of space (and time and resources)
necessarily been superficial since to review psychotherapy research
properly needs research funding as Malan (1973) has commented. However,
I feel my summary is in step with the current mood of psychotherapy
research. As Shapiro (1979) has commented in his review of a recent
conference organised by the Society for Psychotherapy Research, there is
a mood of optimism amongst psychotherapy researchers and yet to the
dispassionate outsider such optimism might well seem misplaced. It is
almost as though Shapiro is arguing Dodo fashion that the researchers
have all done well and must have their prizes too. But are there any
water-tight reasons for psychotherapists to take outcome research
seriously? Should they seek to change the way they do therapy given
the contorted and contradictory history of outcome research?

Perhaps a personal example will serve to illustrate this point - in the mid-1970s my department started to discuss the possibility of launching a psychotherapy training programme. Naively I suggested, basing myself on the work of Truax and Mitchel (1971) and Bergin (1966), that such a course would do best to adopt a Rogerian standpoint as it seemed to be the only approach backed up by research. My suggestion was treated with polite amusement by my more experienced psychiatrist colleagues who were not prepared to accept that a training programme could just be established on the basis of scientific research. Of course, their scepticism about such procedure has turned out to be fully justified as subsequent research has shown that the original claims in support of the Rogerian school must be treated with great caution.

It is also important to consider the other side of the coin - supposing a particular form of psychotherapy was shown to be effective - would such findings be influential or not?

I have already suggested some of the reasons why psychoanalysts would not be disposed to take such research seriously and I have used Magaro's arguments to support the idea that therapists of all hues may not have any interest in taking such research seriously either but perhaps the issue can best be focussed by considering the issue of the National Institute of Mental Health collaborative project on the treatment of depression. Bergin and Strupp's dream of a collaborative study (Bergin and Strupp, 1972) has at least come true but will it turn out to be a nigthmare? If we leave aside disputes over methodology which caused some concern at the 1979 SPR Conference (Shapiro, op. cit.), we are left with the perplexing issue of what would happen if this study, which compares two forms of psychotherapy, Beck's cognitive therapy and Weissman's interpersonal therapy with drug therapy (imipramine), came up with a substantial positive finding in favour of the drug?

It would be scarcely credible that committed psychotherapists (of whatever hue) who have spent many arduous years developing their skills would accept such findings and direct their patients to doctors who would prescribe imipramine. A more likely course of events would be that psychotherapy might be designated 'non-reimbursable' so that American patients receiving treatment funded by health insurance would be unable to claim their fees.

Fortunately such an outcome is probably unlikely as there is already some evidence that Beck's approach has already been shown to be superior to drug treatments (Rush et al., 1977), but supposing Beck's method was also shown to be superior to Weissman's IPT? Would clinicians actually change their methods to be in step with such empirical findings? Obviously hypothetical questions like these tend to lead nowhere so we are left wondering whether there is any possible way out of the impasse. Strangely by examining an extreme solution to the problem it becomes possible - through the process of thesis and anti-thesis - to construct a workable solution. One way out of the outcome research dilemma is to dismiss it as positivistic nonsense which is of no value to the psychotherapist.

Such a position has been spelt out by Bannister in a paper entitled
'The nonsense of "effectiveness"'. Although very brief, this paper
contains important ideas which contribute to an understanding of why
psychotherapists may be so uninfluenced by research. Bannister's
argument is deeply radical and in effect takes psychologists to task for
introducing into psychological discourse terms and ideas which emanate
from the medical model:

> (One) of many guises in which the medical model still dominates our
> thinking is the ever flowing tide of research into the 'effectiveness'
> of psychotherapy ... Psychotherapy is a particular formalisation of
> human relationship - just as human relationship can be formalised by
> marriage, by a business partnership, by a rule-bound game, by
> kinship, by legal procedures and so forth. To start from the
> premise that psychotherapy may not be effective is in essence to
> start from the premise that human relationship may not be effective
> and this is an absurdity. Are you really prepared to contend that
> your relationships, your love affairs, your enmities, your long-
> standing dialogue with your Uncle Albert - whether the effect is
> good, bad or chaotic - have been, in some strange sense,
> 'ineffective'? (Bannister, 1981).

For a construct theorist to argue this way is particularly bizarre
as in order to refute his dogmatic position it is only necessary to
treat 'effectiveness' as a superordinate construct and begin to
substitute subordinate constructs such as 'damaging' vs. 'non-damaging'
or 'life-enhancing' vs. 'life-destroying' or 'positive' vs. 'negative'.
If these far more concrete constructs are utilised rather than the more
abstract rubric 'effectiveness', then it is perfectly possible to
evaluate psychotherapeutic relationships in the same spirit as any
other form of human relationship. And, of course, this is precisely
what we do in everyday life - we are continually assessing the quality
of our relationships and often deciding to opt out of them if the
assessment proves negative - how else do divorces occur or lovers break
up or children decide to avoid their parents?

The vulnerability of Bannister's position can also be brought out by
examining the literature on deterioration in psychotherapy. Bergin and
Lambert (1978) review many such studies but the study by Ricks (1974)
is particularly striking. The caseloads of two therapists (dubbed
'supershrink' and 'pseudoshrink') working in a child guidance clinic
were followed up several years later when the adolescent boys in
question (who had received treatment previously) had become adults.
Twenty-seven per cent of supershrink's caseload were judged to have
become schizophrenic while 84 per cent of pseudoshrink's cases
deteriorated to some extent. Clearly psychotherapy can be damaging
despite Bannister's passionate plea to the contrary!

Bannister's position is particularly startling if it is juxtaposed
to the methodical, dispassionate arguments of, say, Bergin and Lambert.
The gulf between them seems totally unbridgeable and yet it is
impossible to escape attempting to come to terms with their rival
positions. In essence Bannister seems to accept Magaro's position that
psychotherapy is a cultural phenomenon which for historical reasons is
deeply embedded in the way some people live their lives but he then

develops his own conclusion that it cannot be considered open to the
type of positivistic 'objectivising' that is the hallmark of Bergin's
work. And yet this is not entirely true since Bannister is prepared to
accept that psychological research into the process of psychotherapy is
necessary while at the same time arguing against outcome research. He
justifies his position in the following terms which I quote at length:
> A moral ground is frequently offered to legitimate the question 'is
> psychotherapy effective?'. We are paid to do psychotherapy ... (so)
> there is a moral onus on us to check that it is of value. Such an
> argument has a nice righteous ring to it but it ignores three
> aspects of the situation. Firstly, psychological therapy has an
> intrinsic moral base in that it is a way of <u>paying heed</u> to the person.
> Most of our ways of responding to psychological distress are
> institutional. They are standardised and factory processed ...
> Psychological therapies, however falteringly, at least struggle to
> make the person's own vision of the world the starting point.
> Secondly, psychological therapies ... are still our best hope of
> arriving at some kind of understanding of personal situations and
> thereby they may inspire us to change institutions so that they make
> more sense when they become the <u>personal situation</u> of the client.
> Thirdly, the idea that we will involve ourselves in or discontinue
> the practice of psychological therapy makes sense to us, that is to
> say we can see reasons why we have been of no help to this person or
> some help to that person, and we find that we can develop and
> elaborate our understanding through our work, then we are likely to
> continue to work in this way <u>whatever the literature may say</u>.
> Equally, if our experience of psychotherapy is that it is a
> depressing confusion then we are unlikely to continue again
> <u>regardless of what the literature may say</u>.

Unfortunately I have no space in which to debate the first two points
(which are clearly contentious in their own right) but obviously the
third point is of crucial interest to my present argument. Bannister
is, I think, absolutely right in making this point but it is paradoxical
that in his very next paragraph he stresses the necessity for process
research:
> Research should be concerned with the issue of what is going on in
> psychotherapy. If we had a developed, thoughtful and imaginatively
> researched psychology of interpersonal interacting group processes,
> the effect of two phenomenologies meeting, the relationship between
> the experiment that is the psychotherapy session and the experiment
> that is the client's life outside, then we would be professionally
> blessed in offering psychological aid to the psychologically
> distressed.

It seems truly quixotic to me that Bannister can argue that process
research is valuable but that to be involved in outcome research is to
behave as a 'psychic paramedic' (to use his quaint term). Surely there
can be no objection to combined process and outcome research? Are
psychologists really to be invited to be so grandiose that they are to
deny their interest in finding out whether their therapies help their
clients?

But I need to return to the central plank of Bannister's position -

the crucial point about his position is its utopianism. Outcome
research that is unrelated to process research is correctly rejected as
being largely meaningless but we are offered pious hopes instead. The
project that Bannister proposes - of discovering what happens when 'two
phenomenologies meet' - may be laudable but the sheer pragmatics of the
average therapy situation militate against such a time-consuming
approach. So what in practice can be done to change this dismal
situation? As my comments so far have been largely both critical and
negative I wish to end this chapter on a more positive approach by
drawing on my work as a family therapist. My own personal view is that
family therapists have much to offer all therapists who seek to take
the issue of efficacy seriously. This may at first sight seem paradoxical as family therapy is no better researched than any other dimension
of therapy but it is largely social nature of family therapy which
contains the seeds which can germinate a richer approach to therapy and
the place of research in enhancing therapy.

Bannister argues that we need to research the meeting of 'two
phenomenologies meeting' but he fails to explain how this can be carried
out. Within his personal construct model it can be assumed that it is
the therapist who will take the lion's share of the task. But how can
the therapist maintain the independent stance of a researcher as well
as being involved directly as well? Bannister will no doubt reject
this point as alien 'medical thinking', of positivistic nonsense, or
both, but I can reply with some justification that his position is one
of enmeshment with his clients. To solve this particular conundrum it
is essential to start from the assumption that the therapist is
incapable of evaluation his or her own efficacy. This in turn means
that colleagues must be involved as direct observers of the process of
therapy if any progress is to be made. And it is precisely in this
dimension that certain schools of family therapy have made very valid
contributions to the development of efficacy. The public nature of
family therapy, the use of co-therapy (Dowling, 1979), of live
supervision in the room (Smith and Kingston, 1978), or live supervision
from behind the one way screen (Montalvo, 1973), has a salutory effect
on the way therapists work. The alienated, privatized way in which
individual therapists work is strikingly different to the work of a
family therapy team manning a clinic. Individual therapy can, of
course, be supervised in vivo but it rarely is - instead post hoc
supervision takes place and the data used for the supervision is the
therapist's verbal account of what happened. Audiotapes or videotapes
of sessions are now also being used by individual therapists for
supervision purposes but this of course does not deal with the vexing
problem that therapists are often out of touch with essential features
of the therapeutic process occurring during the session. Colleagues
observing a session but not participating in it may at times also lose
touch with essential features of the session but they usually
can retain some independence from the process and therefore are able to
guide the therapist's work.

Clearly these innovations by family therapists have important
implications for improving efficiency. Within such a system the
therapist's weaknesses and strengths are open to examinations - they
cannot remain hidden unless the whole team is involved in a collusion

to do so. No doubt this can and does happen at times but there is no reason to assume that this is generally so. The crucial point about the social nature of family therapy is that it readily allows a research component to be built into the work of the team participating in the clinic. The trusting relationships between therapists that are built up in such clinics facilitate the introduction of research tools rating both the behaviour of the family and the therapist. At present the only factors that hold back such research is firstly the lack of easily used research tools and secondly the inadequate funding of research. Once therapists move out of the closet and start sharing what they actually do to their clients then there is no logical (or emotional) reason why they cannot take the next step which is to study their own efficacy more directly. But it should be noted at this point that they, of course, are not invited to study their 'own' efficacy in any real sense – what they are studying is the efficacy of the team. In other words they are studying a social product to which several people have contributed. So there is no question of putting one's own ability on the line in the way that an unsupervised individual therapist would have to. In my view this creates a new freedom as far as the therapist is concerned – if the therapy is shown to be effective then everybody can be satisfied but if the therapy is shown to be ineffective then there can be a joint struggle to make the necessary changes. Or to put it more cryptically, unity is strength.

REFERENCES

BANNISTER, D. (1980), The Nonsense of 'Effectiveness', 'New Forum, Journal of the Psychology and Psychotherapy Association', Autumn, p. 13.
BARNES, B. (1980), David Malan: Psychodynamic Scientist, 'New Forum, Journal of the Psychology and Psychotherapy Association', Autumn, pp. 3-5.
BARUCH, G. and TREACHER, A. (1978), 'Psychiatry Observed', London, Routledge & Kegan Paul.
BERGIN, A.E. (1963), The effects of psychotherapy: Negative results revisited, 'Journal of Counselling Psychology', 10, pp. 244-50.
BERGIN, A.E. (1966), Some implications of psychotherapy research for therapeutic practice, 'Journal of Abnormal Psychology', 71, pp. 235-46.
BERGIN, A.E. (1971), An evaluation of therapeutic outcomes, in A.E. Bergin and Garfield, S.L. (eds), 'Handbook of Psychotherapy and Behavior Change: An Empirical Analysis', New York, Wiley.
BERGIN, A.E. and LAMBERT, M.J. (1978), An evaluation of therapeutic outcomes, in Garfield S.L. and Bergin A.E. (eds), 'Handbook of Psychotherapy and Behavior Change: An Empirical Analysis', New York, Wiley.
BERGIN, A.E. and STRUPP, H.H. (1972), 'Changing Frontiers in the Science of Psychotherapy', Chicago, Aldine Atherton.
BERGIN, A.E. and SUINN, R.M. (1975), Individual psychotherapy and behavior therapy, 'Annual Review of Psychology', 26, pp. 509-56.
BERLE, B.B. et al. (1953), Appraisal of the results of treatments in stress disorders, 'Res. Publ. Assoc. Nerv. Ment. Dis.', 31, pp. 167-77.
BRAVERMAN, H. (1974), 'Labor and Monopoly Capital. The Degradation of Work in the 20th Century', New York, Monthly Press Review.

BRODKIN, A.M. (1980), Family Therapy: the making of a mental health movement, 'Amer. J. Orthopsychiat.', 50, pp. 4-17.
CARTWRIGHT, D.S. (1956), note of 'Changes in psychoneurotic patients with and without psychotherapy', 'J. Consult. Psychol.', 20, pp. 403-4.
CHAPPELL, M.N. and STEVENSON, T.I. (1936), Group psychological training in some organic conditions, 'Ment. Hyg.', 20, pp. 588-97.
CHRISTENSEN, K.C. and MAGOON, R.M. (1974), Perceived hierarchy of help-giving sources for two categories of student problems, 'J. of Counseling Psychology', 21, pp. 311-14.
DiLORETO, A.O. (1971), 'Comparative Psychotherapy: An Experimental Analysis', Chicago, Aldine Atherton.
DOWLING, E. (1979), Co-therapy: a clinical researcher's view, in S. WALROND-SKINNER (ed.), 'Family and Marital Psychotherapy - A Critical Approach ', London, Routledge & Kegan Paul.
ENDS, E.J. and PAGE, C.W. (1957), A study of three types of group therapy with hospitalized male inebriates, 'Quart. J. Stud. Alcohol', 18, pp. 263-77.
EYSENCK, H.J. (1952), The effects of psychotherapy: an evaluation, 'J. Consult. Psychol.', 16, pp. 319-24.
EYSENCK, H.J. (1965), The effects of psychotherapy, 'International J. of Psychiatry', 1, pp. 99-144.
EYSENCK, H.J. (1971), Behavior therapy as a scientific discipline, 'J. of Consulting and Clinical Psychology', 36, pp. 314-19.
GARFIELD, S.L. and BERGIN, A.E. (1978), 'Handbook of Psychotherapy and Behavior Change: an Empirical Analysis', 2nd ed, New York, Wiley.
GORDON, B. (1979), 'I'm Dancing as Fast as I Can', New York, Harper & Row.
GORDON, T. (1975), 'Parent Effectiveness Training', New York, Plume Books.
GRACE, W.J. et al. (1959), The treatment of ulcerative colitis II, 'Gastroenterology',26, pp. 462-8.
GURIN, G. et al. (1960),'Americans View their Mental Health', New York, Basic Books.
GURMAN, A.S. and RAZIN, A.M. (1977), 'Effective Psychotherapy: A Handbook of Research', New York, Pergamon Press.
ILLICH, I. (1975), 'Medical Nemesis', London, Calder & Boyars.
ILLICH, I. et al. (1977), 'Disabling Professions', London, Marion Boyars.
JONES, K. (1970), 'The History of the Mental Health Services', London, Routledge & Kegan Paul.
KELLNER, R. (1965), Discussion in H.J. Eysenck, The effects of psychotherapy, 'International J. of Psychiatry', 1, pp. 322-8.
KELLNER, R. (1967), 'The Evidence in Favour of Psychotherapy', New York, Atherton Press.
KERNBERG, O.F. et al. (1972), Psychotherapy and psychoanalysis, 'Bull. Menninger Clin.', 36, nos 1 and 2.
KLASS. A. (1975), 'Thar's Gold in them there Pills', Harmondsworth, Penguin.
LAZARUS, A.A. (1961), Group therapy of phobic disorders by systematic desensitization, 'J. Abnorm. & Soc. Psychol.', 63, pp. 504-10.
LUBORSKY, L., SINGER, B. and LUBORSKY, L. (1975), Comparative studies of psychotherapies, 'Archives of General Psychiatry', 32, pp. 995-1008.
MALAN, D.H. (1973), The outcome problem in psychotherapy research, 'Arch. Gen. Psychiat.', 29, pp. 719-29.

MALAN, D.H. (1976a), 'The Frontier of Brief Psychotherapy', New York, Plenum Press.

MALAN, D.H. (1976b), 'Toward the validation of dynamic psychotherapy: A Replication.'

MALCOLM, J. (1982), 'Psychoanalysis: the Impossible Profession', London, Pan Books.

MAGARO, P.A. et al. (1978), 'The Mental Health Industry - a Cultural Phenomenon', New York, Wiley.

MAY, P.R.A. (1971), For better or for worse? Psychotherapy and variance change: A critical review of the literature, 'J. Nerv. Ment. Dis.', 152, pp. 184-92.

McKEOWN, T. (1979), 'The Role of Medicine', Oxford, Blackwell.

MITCHELL, K.M. (1973), 'Effective therapist interpersonal skills: the research goes on', invited address, Michigan State University, East Lansing, Michigan.

MITCHELL, K.M. et al. (1977), A reappraisal of the therapeutic effectiveness of accurate empathy, non-possessive warmth and genuineness, in A.S. Gurman and A.M. Razin (eds), 'Effective Psychotherapy: A Handook of Research', New York, Pergamon Press.

MONTALVO, B. (1973), Aspects of live supervision, 'Family Process', 12, pp. 343-59.

ORGEL, S. (1958), Effects of psychoanalysis on the course of peptic ulcers, 'Psychosom. Med.', 20, pp. 117-25.

PORTES, A. (1971a), On the emergence of behavior therapy in modern society, 'J. of Consulting and Clinical Psychology', 36, pp. 303-13.

PORTES, A. (1971b), Behaviour therapy and critical speculation, 'J. of Consulting and Clinical Psychology', 36, pp. 320-4.

POWLES, J. (1973), On the limitations of modern medicine, 'Sci. Med. & Man', 1, pp. 1-30.

RACHMAN, S. (1971), 'The Effects of Psychotherapy', Oxford, Pergamon Press.

RICKS, D.F. (1974), Supershrink: Methods of a therapist judged successful on the basis of adult outcomes of adolescent patients, in D.F. Ricks et al, (eds), 'Life History Research in Psychopathology', Minneapolis, University of Minnesota.

RUSH, A.J. et al. (1977), Comparative efficacy of cognitive therapy and pharmacotherapy in the treatment of depressed outpatients, 'Cognitive Therapy & Research', 1, pp. 17-37.

SCULL, A. (1979), 'Museums of Madness', London, Allen Lane.

SCULL, A. (1981), 'Madhouses, Mad-doctors and Madmen - the Social HIstory of Psychiatry in the Victorian Era', London, Athlone Press.

SHAPIRO, D. (1979), Society for Psychotherapy Research, 'New Forum, Journal of the Psychology and Psychotherapy Association', Autumn, pp. 36-7.

SLOANE, R.B. et al. (1975), 'Psychotherapy versus Behavior Therapy', Cambridge, Harvard University Press.

SMITH, D. and KINGSTON, P. (1980), Live supervision without a one-way screen, 'J. of Family Therapy', 2, pp. 379-87.

SMITH, M.L. and GLASS, G.V. (1977), Meta-analysis of psychotherapy outcome studies, 'American Psychologist', 132, pp. 152-70.

SOROKIN, P.A. (1937), 'Social and Cultural Dynamics', vol. 2, New York, America Books.

SPECK, R.V. and ALTREAVE, C.L. (1973), 'Family Networks', New York, Vintage Books.

STRUPP, H.H. (1977), 'The Vanderbilt psychotherapy process – outcome project', paper presented at the 8th Annual Meeting, Society for Psychotherapy Research, Madison, Wisc.

STRUPP, H.H and BERGIN, A.E. (1969), Some empirical and conceptual bases for coordinated research in psychotherapy, 'International Journal of Psychiatry', 7, pp. 18–90.

STRUPP H.H. and HADLEY, S.W. (1978), Specific vs. non-specific factors in psychotherapy: a controlled study of outcome, 'Archives of General Psychiatry', 36, pp. 1125–36.

SZASZ, T. (1961), 'The Myth of Mental Illness', New York, Harper & Row.

TRUAX, C.B. amd MITCHELL, K.M. (1971), Research on certain therapist interpersonal skills in relation to process and outcome, in A.E. Bergin and S.L. Garfield (eds), 'Handbook of Psychotherapy and Behavior Change', New York, Wiley.

VOTH, H.M. and ORTH, M.H. (1973), 'Psychotherapy and the Role of the Environment', New York, Behavioural Press.

WAELDER, R. (1960), 'Basic Theory of Psychoanalysis', New York, International Universities Press.

WEBER, M. (1958), Bureaucracy, in H.H. Gerth and C.W. Mills (eds), 'From Max Weber: Essays in Sociology', New York, Oxford University Press.

WEBER, M. (1965), 'The Theory of Social and Economic Organisation', New York, The Free Press.

YATES, A.J. (1970), 'Behaviour Therapy', New York, Wiley.

Part two
POLITICS

Chapter 8

POLITICS, PSYCHOLOGY AND PSYCHIATRY
David Pilgrim

This chapter will sketch those aspects of psychiatry, particularly its core model and social function, which conflict with the assumptions and aspirations of psychological practice in the NHS. Additionally, the specific institutional politics of the two professions will be scrutinised, with particular reference to the practice of psychotherapy by non-medical personnel, in a work setting dominated by the medical model.

Some psychiatrists are fully committed psychotherapists, though they are marginal to their medical culture in terms of numbers and influence in Britain. To advocate psychotherapy in the NHS is not necessarily an anti-psychiatric posture therefore, although such an advocacy, if held in the absence of duplicity, is pro-personal and anti-reductionist. What divides psychotherapists of different professional backgrounds in these circumstances is basically money and power.

With the exception of my present place of work, all of my career to date has been spent in workplaces where these differentials are not the only characteristics which are politically problematic. In the NHS most psychiatric establishments are characterised by the medical model as a guiding form of theory and practice. When this is the case, psychotherapy can survive but at a high cost to its efficiency. At a personal level, practising psychotherapy becomes an enervating project and the work setting is experienced as unsupportive at best and openly hostile at worst.

The medical, organic, illness or faulty machine model (Russel-Davies 1970) is recognised more enthusiastically by critics than advocates. Practitioners who peddle the model, diagnose mental illness and employ chemicals, electricity or the scalpel for their patients' conditions, are loathe to acknowledge that this style of conceptualising and intervening constitutes a modus operandi to be viewed and critised. The commonest defence against such a recognition is along the lines that a therapeutic armamentarium exists, including a number of treatment approaches, psychotherapy being one, which can be used in turn to treat patients. In this rationale, the core notion of illness is notably untarnished, in terms of epistemological validity. Baruch and Treacher (1978) describe this as a portmanteau type of model and point to Clare (1977) as one of its more articulate apologists. Clare attempts to disable opposition to the medical model by integrating criticisms made of it, thereby turning a potential defeat into a victory.

MEDICINE AND SOCIAL CONTROL

The unfettered operation of the medical model involves certain forms of deviance being classified, controlled and contained. These social procedures are defined medically as diagnosis, treatment and hospital-isation. The social control function of psychiatry has been explored at length by both liberal and marxist writers (See Szasz 1970; and Foucault 1965 and Ingleby 1981 respectively). Organic psychiatry holds sway presently over the consciousness not only of its own practitioners and fellow travellers (mainly nurses) but also policy makers in health care. As such, organic theory and practice represent not simply ideology but hegemony.

Figure 7.1 outlines the reciprocal interactions of three key areas of social reproduction with subsume elements of structure, super-structure, production, exchange and consumption. Each area has been characterised historically by coexisting progressive and reactionary poles. The family nurtures children and gives them a good enough start to cope with the stresses of the life cycle but also typically encourages conformity and a respect for respectability. Science generates humanly useful ideas and technology but produces objecti-fication, reductionism and nuclear weapons. Medicine has offered an asylum and care function for the distressed and dying but has deflected scrutiny away from society and towards the individual. Illich (1976) has brought into question the cure function proudly boasted by medical zealots. The major shifts in the population's health have been a function of social, not medical, advance. If people are given nutritious food, decent housing, sanitation, clean water, an unpolluted environment and work, which is productive, safe and stress-free they will typically live their three score years and ten reasonably healthily without the need for medical interference for common, benign, self-limiting forms of sickness. On the other hand, populations denied these healthy environmental factors will become sick and tired. In unhealthy social conditions, medicine mystifyingly attempts to offer a repair response to sickening social processes. Unemployment, pollution, poverty and alienated labour are political phenomena mystified and their linkages to sickness dislocated if medical practitioners and health care planners look no further than biochemistry and human plumbing. Such an approach only tackles the skin-encapsulated end point of a pathogenic society. (In an improved society distress will still be there, for life is intrinsically tragic and painful. Birth, death, sickness, separation and all manner of psychological dramas will exist as long as mankind. It is historically relative though to call these human activities illness and give powers of control over them and language describing them to medicine.)

The psychiatric version of medicine involves: the deprivation of

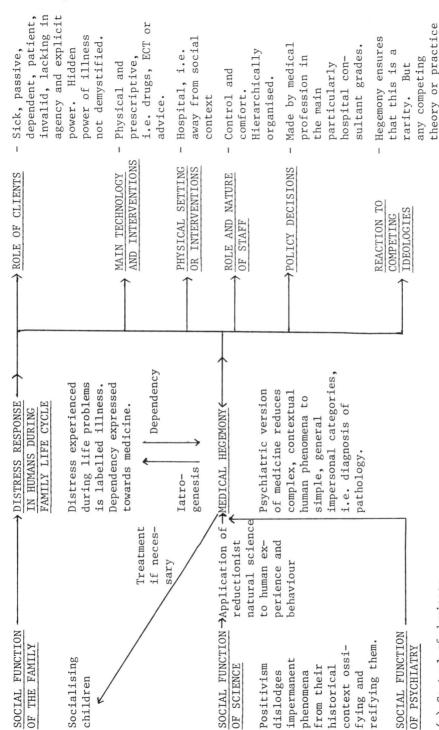

FIGURE 7.1

liberty; the invalidation of protest; the expropriation of self-help;
the mystification of problems in living; and the unwillingness of
therapists to facilitate personal meaning seeking in suffering. Psychotherapy at least holds the potential for a reversal of these trends,
as do other humanising lobbies such as various self-help groups, the
hospice movement and the natural childbirth movement in other medical
areas. It is significant that illness at present constitutes grounds
for the indefinite deprivation of liberty without trial under sections
of the Mental Health Act and National Assistance Act. These powers are
matched only by the Prevention of Terrorism Act and Immigration Act.
Taken together these pieces of legislation put into context the policing
function of medicine.

LIMITS TO LIMITS TO MEDICINE

In the first draft of his seminal critique of medicine, Illich (1975)
attacks medicine for being sickening on three counts, which he calls
clinical, social and structural iatrogenesis. In turn these refer to
people being made worse rather than better by medical interventions;
people becoming addicted to therapy as a panacea for problems in living;
and people giving up their capacity and responsibility for self-care.
Whilst acknowledging that capitalist medicine takes the greatest toll
in this regard, he maintains that industrialisation itself is the
problem to be solved. His economic referrant is therefore weak and
ambiguous. His utopian call for action stemming from this analysis
involves dismantling the trappings of our industrial age: medicine,
schooling, fast transport, etc.

The drawbacks of this analysis have been described by Doyal (1980)
and Navarro (1975). Illich assumes that industrialised forms of
organisation are intrinsically undemocratic and dehumanising. His
critics argue that the genuine ownership and control of health care by
workers and consumers would reverse these characteristics. Presently
the NHS is not socialised but nationalised health care and power
distribution within it mirrors the class and gender relations in wider
capitalist society. Illich would throw the baby out with the bath water
as far as concern, human contact and protection from an inhospitable
world are concerned, if health care systems were dismantled. A more
realistic programme for health care, realisable via the labour movement,
is on offer by these critics: democratic control of the NHS; a shift of
resources away from the hospitals to the community; increased funding
for research into prevention; the abolition of private medicine; and
the political opposition to identified sickening social factors.

Illich and critics would concur that at present medicine functions
conservatively as an obstacle against or a substitute for social
change. Capitalism benefits from medicine by the latter: offering a
social control function to remove and contain one aspect of deviance,
which handicaps the productive process; focussing on illness and thereby
defusing protest against a sickening society; protecting capital's debt
to its sickened victims; and offering its hardware up for production
and therefore profit. The skin-encapsulated view of illness suits
medicine, as well as the ruling class, as doctors receive the largest

crumbs for not asking awkward questions.

The natural science branch of positivism, employed by medicine, seeks to offer an ideology based on dispassionate value-free neutrality. Szasz (1972) disputes this rationale when applied to psychiatric illnesses, which he describes as mythological. Physical illnesses in this revised scheme are legitimised, however, so that social processes antecedent to and resulting from these phenomena are ignored. Illich, Scheff(1966) and Sedgwick (1972) counter the dualism sustained by Szasz and offer a socially contextual epistemology with deviance as the super-ordinate construct in this new, monistic scheme. This places values back into the discourse surrounding sickness. Sedgwick argues that, 'All descriptions of illness express a social judgement' and Illich, 'All disease is a socially created reality'.

The so called facts that a positivistic view of illness discovers, called a plethora of syndromes and diseases,are socially contextual. They are a function of a set of questions being asked and answered. The framing of these questions takes place in peculiar social conditions at a particular historical juncture.

SOCIAL AGNOSIA: A COMMON MEDICAL MALADY

Jacoby (1975) describes the psychological left since Freud as suffering from 'social amnesia'. If this is true, the medical right (i.e. medical majority) has not merely forgotten the social; it has never known it. Being socially ignorant, medical hegemony employs reduct-ionist reasoning. Medicine, as a result, is a mystified and mystifying attempt at applied science. The organic psychiatrist, like the policeman and soldier, enjoys social respectability without being able or willing to acknowledge and own the political role involved. As far as psychiatry is concerned this is evident in its tendency to look downwards at its organic roots. This is illustrated in Figure 7.2.

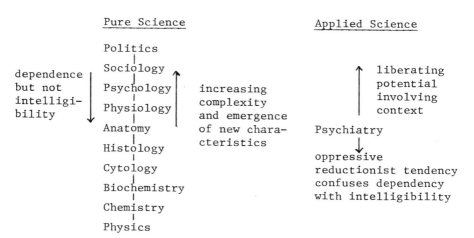

FIGURE 7.2

The medical model attempts to make higher levels of phenomena intelligible in terms of lower orders of material organisation. Where this cannot be proved, as is the case with the largest group of mental illnesses, the neuroses and functional psychoses, it is blindly asserted. This hoped-for-reductionism merely gilds the lily of error. Moreover a unidirection downward looking view neglects the psycho-social phenomena associated with physical complaints (See Nicols, ch. 12 in this volume).

Since British physicians secured legal control over emotional deviance via acts of parliament in 1828 and 1845, the majority of them have expressed this specious rationale. With the ascendancy of bacteriology later that century came the deification of germ theory and its concomitant search for the magic bullet. In the 1920s and 1930s under the influence of Lewis and Meyer the psycho-social context received some temporary respite. With this exception, most psychiatrists this century have been tempted down the organic garden path of physical reductionism. The political character facilitatively interacting with this form of reasoning has been elitist and doggedly conservative. When the NHS was in the offing, post-war, the majority of medical practitioners wanted to abort the embryonic social reform. Outside the owners of capital, the medical profession has no equal as a power lobby and Bevan integrated his medical opponents at a high price. Their twin preoccupations with money (clinical freedom) and power (clinical responsibility) are evident even now. Truly socialised health care has been chronically stifled by those having most to lose by democratic reorganisation (see Foot 1973 and Lindsey 1963).

The links made earlier between social conditions and health have been partially integrated into Labour policy. This is evident in the 1976 document 'Prevention and Health: everybody's business' (HMSO). No political and financial commitments were offered following this publication. Individual responsibility for prevention was emphasised, without criticising the political phenomena which facilitate unhealthy behaviour. More recently a DHSS report (Black 1980) advocates: greater preventative research; the abolition of child poverty; greater community funding for health care projects; and an attack on tobacco profits. Patrick Jenkin enclosed a disclaiming preface, in which he refuses to implement any of the report's proposals. Moreover, the report's availability has been restricted along with its message that the rich get healthier as well as richer at the expense of the poor. This is taking place against a backdrop of public sector cuts and more consultants seeking out fatter salaries on the commercial market. These private practitioners were of course trained at public expense.

THE POLITICAL NATURE OF PSYCHOTHERAPY

From a humanistic viewpoint all forms of psychotherapy represent a progressive step away from the medical model. This is not to say, however, that the various psychotherapeutic methodologies are a political monolith. In terms of theoretical aspirations, all the therapies offer some form of liberation, though they vary in the degree of their claims. The more socially aware a therapy the more the social

context is deferred to. The more psychologically oriented a therapy is
the more ambitious its claim for liberation in the absence of social
change.

The values encouraged by the 'growth' or 'human potential' movement
centre on the resolution or endurance of problems within the individual.
Spring from the rich soils of Californian consumerism this movement
emphasises the growth, joy and self-actualisation on offer to those
prepared to pay the bill and put on the blinkers. The humanistic step
taken away from the medical model goes no further than psychology.
This paralysis of praxis derives, itself, from a form of reductionism;
psychologising politics.   This tendency is especially evident in the
conservative wing of depth psychology, where psychology is attributed
with qualities of primacy rather than mediation. As a result political
activity may be seen from the viewpoint as nothing but conformity to or
reactions against parental political values, or antagonism to oppressive
leadership is nothing but transferred anger from parents or the
introjected bad part of them projected onto social institutions.
Clearly these dynamics do play a role in energising an individual into
political activity but they cannot explain away the content or meaning
of political phenomena, which are rooted in the economic organisation
of society, with its peculiar forms of production and class ownership
and control.

The psychodynamic left is mainly characterised by the various
attempts to marry Freud and Marx: sex-politics; the Frankfurt School;
and British and French anti-psychiatry. (For a comparative view of
these variations see Mitchell (1973), Jacoby (1975), Fromm (1974) and
Turkle (1978).) Despite real enough theoretical differences between
these positions, a common distillation is the view that the family
mediates and reproduces prevailing oppressive social relations. Unless
social conditions have significantly progressed since social relations
were interiorised in childhood, it becomes problematic to differentiate
between projection and reality perception in the psychological phenomena
manifested by contemporary adults. What evolves from the left
clustering is an inversion of the psychodynamic right's pathologising
of political militancy. Fromm speaks of the 'pathology of normalcy'.
Cooper maintains that sanity and madness are juxtaposed and together
equidistantly opposite to normality. Laing notes that chemotherapy and
lobotomies are only necessary after the 'normal social lobotomy' has
failed. What is being grappled with now is not why a few riot, rebel,
revolt, steal or go mad but why the majority avoid these detours from
conformity, in an oppressive society on the brink of a nuclear holocaust.

The political complications evident at a theoretical level in
psychology become more complex at a practical level. Psychoanalysis
and humanistic therapies have often functioned conservatively by being
hijacked by individualism, so that social change is judged irrelevant,
dangerous or a substitute for a more valuable change of heart. Applied
behaviourism such as behaviour modification in the classroom and
behaviour therapy as drugless tranquilliser, has fared poorly as a
humane human science. It has invariable colluded with social norms in
an unthinking manner. The practical projects of conservative applied
psychology have sought to individualise what is social or, more crassly,
enforce social conformity.

Realistically, psychotherapy can be helpful in a number of ways,
however, including: decoding mystification; providing caring human
contact; taking the sting out of earlier insults; and providing an
experiment in authenticity. The practical obstacles to psychotherapy
being efficiently employed however include:
(a) Internal limit setting is unrealistically high, when psychology is
    offered as a vehicle for liberation without social change.
(b) Psychotherapy availability is not always free when needed. Buying
    power still determines accessibility to some degree.
(c) Medical hegemony has ensured that psychotherapeutic resources
    remain scarce via protectionism and legitimisation of the medical
    model.
(d) Consumer uptake of psychotherapy services is impeded by the cultural
    view of mental illness conflicting with psychotherapeutic
    assumptions.

CLINICAL PSYCHOLOGY AND THE ROD IT HAS MADE FOR ITS BACK

Psychologists' own professional roots are inauspicious, themselves, and
it is inaccurate to view this profession as a sort of pure and honourable counteractive to the degradation inflicted on humanity by organic
reasoning and practice. The nomothetic-psychometric ticket, that the
profession used to insinuate its way into the NHS, treated the human
spirit neither tenderly nor with respect. In the 1930s, psychologists
measured moral fibre for the Armed Services and tried to screen
malingerers who might avoid conscription to the ranks of cannon fodder.
The labelling tradition persevered in a health setting, so that testing
psychic urine samples colluded with and reinforced the validity of
psychiatric nosography and diagnosis. As it became clearer during the
1950s that problems of validity, reliability, base rates and cut-offs
brought the scientific status of psychometrics into question, psychologists collectively hit an identity crisis. (To this day though some
psychologists take shelter in this anachronistic pursuit.)
Increasingly, the advantages of helping rather than labelling people
offered new hope for the profession. The therapeutic challenge that
was then embraced by psychologists, initially was not received
badly by their psychiatric colleagues. Symptom-oriented behaviour
therapy, particularly, did not conflict with the practice of the
medical model. What proved offensive to psychiatrists were the
criticisms levelled at the conceptual validity of the faulty-machine
view and the hostility expressed towards hospitalisation and the other
trappings of the medicalisation of deviance. Those who preside over
hegemony are not used to being criticised and doctors understandably
became distrustful of psychologists for their alternative theories and,
more often than not, alternative politics (See Pallis and Stoffelmayr,
1973).

    Presently, all concerned experience an inevitable pride if relation-
ships between psychologists and psychiatrists are contrived to be
harmonious. Contrived they inevitably are though because inter-
personal compatibility cannot solve basic theoretical contradictions.
My own experience of multi-disciplinary meetings has been that
psychologists are still more likely, than any others present, to

challenge medical assumptions or take flight psychologically (day-dreaming) or physically (not attending). In contrast most others present express dependence on the personification of the medical model, which varies from automatic quiet acceptance to sycophantic head-nodding agreement. The inter-personal phenomena common to these relationships are leader oriented. The consultant thinks and often speaks of 'his' (or much less often 'her') staff patients etc., the use of personal, possessive pronouns directly pronouncing politics. The meetings fail to take place if the consultant fails to arrive.

Bion (1959) described group behaviour like this as a fight-flight and dependency culture respectively. His study of groups was in terms of low structure and shadowy and ambiguous leadership. In contrast the political reality of health service organisation is one of high structure and a quasi-military style leadership. The individual valencies, which Bion described for different cultures, were family derived, primitive and unconscious. Explicit political issues overlay and coexist with these individual tendencies, setting up a set of secondary valencies, which may coincide with or conflict with individual temperament. When nurses fight and resist the rules of the medical game or psychologists meekly accept the adjunct role encouraged by psychiatry, Bion's primary valencies are subordinating the political tendencies within professional groupings. However, conflicts of interests between professional groups are as important as personality differences, within and between these groups, in understanding the political phenomena that distill out in everyday organisational life. It is utopian to merely psychologise these difficulties and hope that a group therapist could resolve inter-professional disputes, for this confounds and erroneously conflates part of a problem with its totality. This was evident in the experiment, doomed to failure, set up by the BBC's 'Panorama' a couple of years ago, when trade unionists and managers were brought together in the presence of group analysts. The material realities of ownership and control do not disappear because the representatives of labour and capital take off their ties, roll up their sleeves, and struggle to communicate honestly and with feelings with one another. The search for inner harmony and the struggle for political justice are twin tasks facing humanity. One cannot substitute for the other, no matter how hard the evangelists of either cause persuade us otherwise. However, by keeping in mind their social context, a synthesis rather than a mutual substitution is possible in theory and practice.

THE PSYCHIATRIC PATIENT: VICTIM AND AGENT

Engels contended that 'men make their history themselves but in a given social environment which conditions them'. Ingleby (1973) and Laing and Esterson (1970) employ Sartre's concept of praxis which describing the dehumanising theory and practice of impersonal psychology and clinical psychiatry. Praxis subsumes the same dialectical components described by Engels: material constraints (field of possibilities) are the back-drop for the individual agents choice (project). This human condition is denied by impersonal theories, be they psychological of psychiatric. When these theories are applied, they take on practical political significance. Psychiatric patients are a common target for these applications, which seek to reduce praxis to process (action without agency). As such, the successful application of the medical model coincidentally represents the political control of deviance and the spiritual degradation of some part of humanity. When a patient presents to a psychiatrist and is dutifully diagnosed and treated in hospital a number of social processes are taking place in the guise of medical procedure. The first process is one of mystification and has two components; the reified conceptual frame in operation and the physical siting of the events. The conceptual frame, the medical model, converts personal and inter-personal phenomena into signs and symptoms. A smoke-screen is thereby generated by the doctor. Because the screen is erected in hospital, the immediate inter-personal dynamics antecedent to diagnosis are geographically removed and psychologically ignored by those with socially and legally legitimised authority for managing deviance. The conscientious application of medical procedures to social situations involves what Laing (1975) has described as 'putting dark glasses on in an already darkened room'.

The second process is one of invalidation and has been described at length by Goffman (1968) and Cooper (1970). The latter writer calls this process the negation of the negation and describes it as follows:
first there is a negative act, an act of invalidation of a person by others; this may involve diagnostic labelling, passing sentence, physically removing the person from his social context: second (concurrently, rather than chronologically after), this negative act is denied in various ways; it is held that the person has invalidated himself or has been invalidated by his inherent weaknesses or disease process, other persons have nothing much to do with the matter. By means of this double negation, the social group conceals its praxis from itself.

Mystification and invalidation victimise the patient. The patient responds and a circular interaction is set up, resulting in chronicity (both for doctors and patients), unless the patient escapes from the psychiatric mill or the psychiatrist inverts his or her traditional practice. Rosenham (1973) reports how insinuation into the patient role as experimenter involved 'writing behaviour' being construed as part of psychopathology. If the communications of invalids are invalid, then their personal isolation will increase, as will their indignation about the isolation.

Braginsky and Braginsky (1974), in another role playing experiment, found that rudeness and hostility during the diagnostic interview on the part of subjects correlated with the degree of pathology attributed to them. If subjects once labelled mentally ill then ingratiated themselves, flattering and thanking their diagnosticians, then they were pronounced normal. In the same study, it was found that the severity of pathology attributed was also a function of the extremity of the manifest political ideology on the part of subjects.

Braginsky et al. (1969) found that early in their careers, patients would typically strive to improve and escape from the psychiatric system. A similar exploration of chronic patients revealed, in contrast, that they took no interest in their psychiatric problems or their discharge

and invested their energies into maintaining and extending the material
perks and entertainments of the institution that sheltered them. These
patients explicitly preferred the sick role, and the material pay-offs
it brought, compared to social isolation and economic poverty in the
outside world.

These studies illustrate something of the incessant tension between
psychiatric degradation and wavering patient agency. Hospitalisation
and the practical application of mechanistic principles may make patients
unpersons but the end-point of existential death is staved off by the
patients themselves rescuing some egotic but paltry prizes. The
immediate pay-off of entering the psychiatric sick role involves an
inauthentic collusive project which may serve to protect individual egos,
protect family functioning in the present or a pledge to an interiorised
historical family, and protect the jobs and theory and practice of
hospital oriented psychiatric workers. Systems theory and psychoanalysis
have described these stabilising processes well. The work of R.D. Scott
and his colleagues (Scott 1973 and Scott and Starr 1981) has creatively
explored the top layer of this tangle labelled the 'Treatment Barrier'.
The barrier itself conceptually and practically precedes confronting
defence mechanisms and is therefore a pervasive primary obstacle to
psychotherapy. The cultural assumption underpinning the barrier is that
staff, patients and relatives believe that at the centre of an inter-
personal (psycho-social) drama or crisis is an individual who is ill
and lacks agency. As a result the patient's communications are mystified
and invalidated and the patient is split off from their social context
and sealed off in an alienated psychiatric space. The inter-personal
dynamics preceding this process become obscured and therefore not
honestly acknowledged and worked with. The implications of this are
that the hospital sector is unnecessarily over-used and its therapeutic
potential over-valued by all parties in the collusion.

The use of the treatment barrier as a conceptual paradigm illustrates
the additive effects of social and structural iatrogenesis. (If the
patient remains enmeshed in the psychiatric mill clinical iatrogenesis
takes the form of institutionalisation.) Scott advocates a crisis
intervention service as an alternative to most hospitalisations. This
advocacy is naturally threatening to the hospital oriented psychiatrist,
whose salary, status and model is sustained by beds. Not surprisingly,
Scott's attempts to effect his crisis policy met with extreme
psychiatric animosity. Attempts to negate via integration have been
evident practically and conceptually, adding to this type of active
opposition. Dinsdale et al. (1979) found that staff attitudes in a
psychiatric unit gave the impression that psychotherapeutic insights
were being negotiated with patients. When staff behaviour was recorded,
however, this insight facilitating was absent. What was present was
beds, meals, pills and electricity. To confirm the collusive aspect of
the treatment barrier, the discrepancy between attitude and behaviour
was mirrored in the patient's own responses. From the staff's point of
view though, the cultural mystique that psychiatry works psychologically
is maintained, and the kudos of psychosocial models is stolen and their
oppositional impact defused. Similarly chemical treatments are
increasingly being conceptualised as psychological projects (See e.g.
Usdin and Forrest 1976, 'Psychotherapeutic Drugs').

A MEDICAL DEGREE AS A VALID FIRST-CLASS TICKET OF ENTRY TO HEALTH CARE
POLICY MAKING

For Scott to negotiate his crisis service, or Cooper his Villa 21,
medical credentials had to be shown. This is an example of irrational
authority primarily employed to self-maintain at the expense of those
subordinated to it. Thus Illich and Kennedy, in his Reith lectures,
can be attacked first and foremost for not being physicians. Szasz and
Laing are protected from this superficial line of criticism. However, a
complement of this is that physicians not toeing the party line should
expel themselves. Siegler et al. (1969) argue that Laing should give up
his medical qualifications, if he proposed notions which are offensive
to the conventional wisdom of his profession. These examples conflate
medical identity with health care legitimacy. London (1964) notes that
the American Psychoanalytic Association recommended that only medical
practitioners should be allowed entry to analytical ranks. The Bright
Bill recently before Parliament concerning the registration of psychotherapists would mean if made law that a pathologist or surgeon could
automatically practice psychotherapy but a clinical psychologist may
not be able to (see Hansard, 15 April 1981).

    Despite the contributions that psychologists and social scientists
have made to the field of psychotherapy, their authority is extremely
shaky in a health care setting. Freud advised his students to study
medicine, not for its help to the theory and practice of psychoanalysis
(for the most part medicine eschewed its aims) but to overcome career
obstacles placed before 'lay', i.e. non-medical psychotherapists.

    Presently in the NHS it is difficult all the time and impossible
some of the time to criticise or influence what is held to be the
possession of medicine. Hospital consultants habitually form an uneasy
alliance with senior medical administrators to maintain, and if possible
extend, their own entrenched power in health care. Important but weak
lobbys exist (Community Health Councils), likewise with lay members on
employing authorities. Even these are not democratically elected and
the salaried management teams hold pretty tightly onto purse strings
and power reins. These characteristics militate conservatively against
democratisation within health care staff set ups and attempts by the
patient-consumer lobby to monitor and modify the values and practices
of medicine (see Burns and Doyle 1981).

    With specific regard to medical protectionism in relation to psycho-
therapy, Freud would be saddened by the destiny of his own legacy. In
'The Question of Lay Analysis' he commented:
    We do not consider it at all desirable for psychoanalysis to be
    swallowed up by medicine and to find its last resting place in a
    textbook of psychiatry under the heading 'Methods of Treatment' ...
    It deserves a better fate and it may be hoped, will meet one (1959,
    p. 248).

    The ascendency of armamentarium consciousness has sought to engineer
the very fate that Freud feared. This along with other integrations has
blocked an explicit dialectical antagonism and converted it to a covert
contradiction.

THE PSYCHIATRIC OBSTACLE COURSE: A CHECKLIST

The obstacles that the medical model puts up before non-medical psychotherapists involve the medicalisation of problems in living and the
retaliation against methodologies, which compete with, and bring this
process into question. The first set of impediments results from the
conscientious application of the medical model and includes collusion
with the treatment barrier and symptom resistance, as well as the
chemical, electrical and occasional surgical interference with the
emotional life of its client population. These procedures take place
in an artless state of ignorance about their implications for psychotherapeutic work. In contrast, the second set of impediments involves
a variety of pre-meditated strategies on the part of organic mandarins.
My own experience of working in a variety of psychiatric settings has
taught me that the first set of problems are pervasively present,
whereas the second set varies with the existence of hawkish defenders
of medicine. As a psychotherapist faced with these two hostile sets
of political processes, I have lived, for most of my career, between
the intolerable and the unobtainable and have met the following
specific difficulties:

1   Hospitalisation

The problems surrounding hospitalisation have already been discussed
in relation to the treatment barrier. As one example, I saw a woman
inpatient labelled as suffering from a depressive illness and being
treated with anti-depressants. Quite quickly she disclosed that her
husband was cruel to her and her son by a previous marriage. During
her stay in hospital the husband visited her regularly and acted
protectively towards her (because she was ill), demeanor approved of
by the ward staff. He was dissuaded from upsetting her by raising
any problem of the marriage in his visiting conversations. The
patient welcomed this quiet interlude. After discharge marital therapy
was impossible to negotiate because the husband saw no point in
attending, for it was his wife who was ill. Their problems persevered.

2   Concurrent competing interventions

These are problematic to psychotherapists because they interfere with
the emotional life of clients and the meanings attached to it become
disturbed. Additionally, they encourage the recent transference of
the attitude that the therapist is going to do something to or
prescribe something for clients. I was seeing a man whose medication
led to him repeatedly interrupting the sessions for water for his dry
mouth. Such a communication could have been significant but the
chemical induction made it difficult to use. Later, the man saw the
consultant who told him that his progress was inadequate and that he
would be better agreeing to ECT. We had been exploring, in the
sessions, the issue of his passivity in relation to authority and more
specifically his father in childhood. The contemporary possible re-
enactment could not be explored because of the extensive reality base
of the passivity encouraged generally in doctor-patient relating. My

low profile stance had little chance of survival when the man was being
offered the devil he knew. He kept asking me if I had found the answer
to his problems yet and whether I had decided what to do with him, a
stance as intelligible in terms of the expectations generated by the
consultant's attitude and behaviour as in terms of transferred feelings
from childhood. When emotional life is being turned up, turned down or
turned off its natural flow and psychological significance is masked or
lost. The prescription of advice compounds these difficulties.

3   Concurrent competing interventions (second type)

Occasionally psychotherapeutic endeavours are deliberately undermined
by the referral agent if the medical model is being strained too much
by attempts at integration. I saw a family along with a social worker.
The responsible consultant espoused a sympathy with family work but in
practice rarely worked with others using this approach and opted far
more habitually for traditional chemical and electrical interventions.
Attempts during the sessions to break through the treatment barrier
and start to work with the intelligibility of the identified patient's
behaviour were scuttled by the consultant. Without telling the family
therapists he arranged with another social worker for the patient to
be transferred to a charity hostel. The parents of the identified
patient accepted this willingly as a communication that their son was
being sent to an appropriate place for the mentally ill. Our efforts
to put illness on hold were to no avail.

4   Team leadership and pseudo-democratic decision making

In team meetings consultants speak the longest with apparent sagacity
about patients. Frequently they do not know the patient's circumstances
in depth, compared to junior doctors, nurses and para-medics. Rarely
or never do they offer themselves up as a role model in psychotherapy.
Contractual commitments, often strained by private practice, mean their
contact with patients or other staff members is superficial, sporadic
and fleeting. Despite this, they have the right, which they exercise,
to arbitrarily start certain procedures of intervention and stop others.
This autocracy varies from benevolent diplomacy to authoritarian
directiveness, but autocracy it inescapably is. As mentioned earlier,
where a dependency culture exists things run smoothly, albeit
uncreatively. Opposition to views and decision is rare and is sometimes
stifled by fear. Junior doctors, particularly, are pressured into
sycophancy as their future depends on their superiors' references.
Nurses, since Florence Nightingale, have been disuaded from acting in
the absence of medical directives by their own hierarcy. The legal
reality that the bogey of consultant clinical responsibility is
contrasted with is striking. The leader of the team cannot be held
responsible for negligence on the part of other team members. It is
they themselves who are liable. So obeisance in reponse to consultant
presence offers team members no immunity from hostile litigation (see
Nodder 1980). However the medical model itself is the religion behind
the priest, so those who basically believe rarely sustain a critique
and it is only the occasional outburst of non-conformity or theological

quibbling that is indulged in by non-consultants.

Consultants themselves reserve the right (based on the armamentarium principle) to regulate the conduct of practitioners of any approach or skill deployed within the team. As far as psychotherapy is concerned, intellectual and experiential exposure to psychological approaches during an average psychiatric training is neither wide nor deep. Any natural capacity doctors might have for exploratory encounters with patients is well outweighed if the practical role expectations of the medical model are dutifully employed. This model demands doctor behaviour which is directive, and interrogatory. Doctors who become good psychotherapists, despite their training, have achieved no mean feat in unlearning these role expectations.

Haley (1975) picks up some of these contradictions and iniquities in his paper wisely and prophetically entitled 'Why a Mental Health Clinic Should Avoid Family Therapy'. If rationally pursued family work involves: role flexibility; a flattening of the staff hierarchy; a suspension of assumptions about the importance of individual pathology; and the acknowledgment that no core professional group has any inherent expertise from tradition, so leadership and wage differentials are unnecessary. Thus the team leader has most status and money to lose by policy guided by a family approach. Also family work and beds do not mix well so again psychiatrists' traditional hospital linkages are under threat. Haley notes that these threats provoke institutional resistance, typified by team leaders manifesting the following pattern:
(a) The family approach is initially welcomed (as are all new ideas!)
(b) The programme is delayed for as long as possible until the staff
    lose interest.
(c) If the advocates persist, they are sent no referrals, on the
    grounds that no suitable cases exist.
(d) If the advocates are still undaunted, they are sent a very
    difficult family, referred usually to a therapist 'with a good
    heart and little experience'.
(e) The family work goes badly and is closed down on the grounds that
    it has been tried and found lacking.

5   A psychological veneer to case discussions

A relic of dynamic psychiatry, which has been introjected and fossilised in the medical model, is that of a psychological slant in history taking. There is a disjunction between what is explored by the traditional diagnostic interview and what is then utilised therapeutically. Case notes typically give doctors 'clerking' patients important psychological guidelines for therapeutic amplification: details of childhood; present relationships; mood, etc. These are carefully recorded and then, by and large, ditched. What is sifted out are a narrow band of details to justify diagnostic pigeon holing, prognosis and prescription. The first phase in the procedure, however, leads to a disarming feeling that everything is being rationally utilised, including psychological material (see Dinsdale et al. mentioned earlier). Attempts to offer a psychological form of exploration of the case are often not accepted as needed, as it is claimed by medical practitioners that this has already

taken place and judged of limited utility, for the person is suffering
from an illness best dealt with using pills and electricity.

6   In-patient emphasis

The medical model is hospital oriented. Nowhere is this more apparent
than in the structures the cadres of medical hegemony choose to employ.
My experience is that out-patient case conferences are non-existent,
day-patient conferences are rare but ward rounds are given pride of
place in medical and, therefore, multi-disciplinary activity. Inpatients receive careful and sometimes intense scrutiny vis-à-vis the
other patient types, and as a result are ignored when leaving hospital.
In the final chapter of 'Asylums', sub-titled 'Some notes on the
vicissitudes of the tinkering trades', Goffman (1970) describes, with
chilling clarity, how doctors try to turn patients into serviceable
objects and the hospital is the focus for mechanistic interventions and
approximates, therefore, to a garage. More commonly, since this
description was made, community nurses export their spanners like
insecure AA men adrift from their well oiled workshops. Maybe this
arrangement would be acceptable if people were cars but they are not.

   Faced with this spectacle, psychotherapists find themselves speaking
a foreign language in a xenophobic culture. When asked to join in the
tinkering occasionally, the psychotherapist is being asked to work with
those most entangled in the treatment barrier. Attendance at important
ward rounds inevitably provokes alternating boredom and exasperation.
Non-attendance induces attributions of laziness and insularity from
others in the team. One consequence of this mutual disaffection can be
punitive referral control, which can be demoralising if it generalises
to restricting preferred out-patient work.

7   Referral control

The medical model assumes that the basic function of psychologists is
diagnostic assessment.   As a result some referral agents may only
refer in this manner and object if therapeutic contact is made and
amplified. A variation on this is that diagnostic assessment is seen
as the main function of psychologists, so that time is taken up test
bashing, which could be used in therapy. As mentioned earlier,
psychologists historically colluded with this role, and training courses
today still teach assessment early in the curriculum (as the procedures
are relatively simple and non-threatening). This has the effect of
legitimising psychometrics in teaching areas. One consultant I knew
was understandably perplexed about why probationers gobbled up
assessment referrals with gusto yet he met resistance from supervisors
when he asked them to pursue similar work.

   A second form of referral control is the punitive type. When
psychiatric referral agents are displeased, for whatever reason, with
the style of working of 'their' psychologist they stop referring. This
is a relatively common strategy, which in the extreme can lead to what
is known as 'constructive dismissal' in industrial relations terms.

Where job-description of psychologists pre-empt them receiving anything
but psychiatric referrals, this may damage the morale of the psychologist and certainly curtails the accessibility patients have to a
psychology service.

7   Administrative restrictions on training

When non-medical staff offer to provide a training resource in psychotherapy or attend for training themselves, the medical model loses out
in terms of ideological allegiance, worktime lost from diagnostic
procedures and the impact of alternative propaganda. Armamentarium
consciousness is not offended so much by these threats if medical
practitioners retain their traditional leadership role in the
training events. Medical school training has ensured that power and
leadership are assumed to be the 'natural' property of doctors. These
assumptions are so entrenched, that words of deeds creating any
dissonance around them are the stimulus for frenetic political
activity. At a grander level Bevan encountered this in his fight with
the BMA, but anyone having the audacity to challenge medical authority,
at any level, meets a certain talion reaction. I have known
administrators pressured to restrict room space, and nursing or social
service managers pressured to dissuade attendance of their subordinates
at training events not blessed by consultant approval and leadership.

   There is little wonder that psychologists have struggled with such
passion, for so long, to free themselves from organic psychiatric
chains. Unfortunately, the price often paid in the struggle includes
recurring waves of anger and desperation, which mar both efficiency and
motivation.

REFERENCES

BARUCH, G. and TREACHER, A. (1978), 'Psychiatry Observed', London,
Routledge & Kegan Paul.
BION, W.R. (1959), 'Experiences in Groups', New York, Basic Books.
BLACK, D. (1980), 'Inequalities in Health: Report of a Research Working
Group', DHSS.
BRAGINSKY, B.M., BRAGINSKY, D.D. and RING, K. (1969), 'Methods of
Madness. The Mental Hospital as a Last Resort', New York, Holt.
BRAGINSKY, B.M. and BRAGINSKY, D.D. (1974), 'Mainstream Psychology',
New York, Holt.
BURNS, P. and DOYLE, M. (1981), 'Democracy at Work', London, Pan.
CLARE, A. (1976), 'Psychiatry in Dissent', London, Tavistock.
COOPER, D. (1967), 'Psychiatry and Anti-Psychiatry', London,
Tavistock.
DINSDALE, J., KLERMAN, G. and SHERSHOW, J.C. (1979), Conflicts in
Treatment Goals Between Patients and Staff, 'Soc. Psychiat.', 14, 1-4.
DOYAL, L. (1980), 'The Political Economy of Health', London, Pluto
Press.
FOOT, M. (1972), 'Aneurin Bevan', London, MacGibbon & Kee.
FOUCAULT, M. (1967), 'Madness and Civilisation', London, Tavistock.
FREUD, S. (1959), 'Complete Works', vol. 20, London, Hogarth.

FROMM, E. (1970), 'The Sane Society', New York, Fawcett.
FROMM, E. (1974), 'The Crisis of Psychoanalysis', Harmondsworth, Penguin.
GOFFMAN, E. (1970), 'Asylums', Harmondsworth, Penguin.
HALEY, J. (1975), Why a Mental Health Clinic Should Avoid Family Therapy, 'J. Marr. Fam. Coun.', January.
ILLICH, I. (1975), 'Medical Nemesis', London, Boyars.
ILLICH, I. (1978), 'Limits to Medicine', London, Boyars.
INGLEBY, D. (1973), 'Counter Course', Harmondsworth, Penguin.
INGLEBY, D. (1981), 'Critical Psychiatry. The Politics of Mental Health', Harmondsworth, Penguin.
JACOBY, R. (1975), 'Social Amnesia: A Critique of Contemporary Psychology from Adler to Laing', New York, Beacon Press.
LAING, R.D. (1975), 'The Politics of the Family', Harmondsworth, Penguin.
LAING, R.D. and ESTERSON, A. (1970), 'Sanity, Madness and the Family', Harmondsworth, Penguin.
LINDSEY, R. (1962), 'Socialised Medicine in England and Wales, the National Health Service, 1948-1961', North Carolina.
LONDON, P. (1964), 'The Modes and Morals of Psychotherapy', New York, Holt.
MITCHELL, J. (1973), 'Psychoanalysis and Feminism', Harmondsworth, Penguin.
NAVARRO, V. (1975), The Industrialisation of Fetishism or the Fetishism of Industrialisation: A Critique of Ivan Illich, 'Soc. Sci. and Med.', 9, 351-63.
NODDER, T.E. (1980), 'Organisational and Management Problems of Mental Illness Hospitals', DHSS.
PALLIS, D.J. and STOFFELMAYR, B.E. (1973), Social Attitudes and Treatment Orientation Among Psychiatrists, 'Br. J. Med. Psychol.', 46, 75-81.
ROAZEN, P. (1979), 'Freud and His Followers', Harmondsworth, Penguin.
ROSENHAM, D.L. (1973), On Being Sane in Insane Places, 'Science', 179, 250-7.
RUSSELL DAVIES, D. (1970), Depression as Adaptation to Crisis, 'B. J. Med. Psychol.', 43, 109-16.
SCHEFF, T.J. (1966), 'Being Mentally Ill: A Sociological Theory', Chicago, Aldine.
SCOTT, R.D. (1973), The Treatment Barrier: Part 1, 'B. J. Med. Psychol.', 46, 45.
SCOTT, D. and STARR, I. (1981), A 24-hour family oriented psychiatric and crisis service, 'J. Fam. Th.', vol. 3, 177-87.
SEDGWICK, P. (1972), 'Mental Illness is Illness', National Symposium on Deviance, York.
SIEGLER, M., OSMOND, H. and MANN, H. (1969), Laing's Models of Madness, 'B. J. Psychiat.', 115, 525.
SZASZ, T.S. (1970), 'The Manufacture of Madness', New York, Harper Row.
SZASZ, T.S. (1972), 'The Myth of Mental Illness', London, Paladin.
TURKLE, S. (1978), 'Psychoanalytic Politics: Freud's French Revolution', New York, Basic Books.
USDIN, E. and FORREST, I.S. (1976), 'Psychotherapeutic Drugs', New York, Decker.

Chapter 9

THE INTERNAL POLITICS OF PSYCHOTHERAPY
Don Bannister

Psychotherapy happens within the context of an institution (with or without walls) and the institution happens within the context of a society. It follows that, in psychotherapy, the political themes of institution and society, their power structures, are immanent. Therapists and clients swim in political waters.

In exploring this situation my examples are drawn from the classic therapeutic situation, the encounter between one therapist and one client. Work in other modes, such as group or family therapy, alters some detail of the political infrastructure but it does not gainsay it - therapists carry their institutions in their heads and to move into the family is to move into yet another institution.

Clearly, the relationship between therapist and client is initially neither reciprocal nor equal. If you are the therapist then you and the client sit on either side of your desk, in your office, on your patch. Your presence signifies qualifications, expertise and prestige; the client's presence signifies that he or she has 'given in', 'confessed failure'. You, as therapist, represent (socially, if not in fact) the healthy ordered life while the client represents 'sickness' and confusion. You prescribe the pattern of the relationship - you decide time and frequency of meeting, termination of meetings, form and duration of converse. You may decide to be non-directive but, even so, it will be you that decided to be non-directive. You may negotiate all things but you negotiate from a position of power. Clients may strive for equality but they strive from a disadvantaged position. One of my clients used to bring two cans of beer to every session and firmly refuse my coffee but both she and I recognised a symbol for what it was - a symbol. At its starting point, the psychotherapeutic relationship is cousin to lifeboatman-distressed sailor, warder-prisoner, teacher-student and all those relationships where the meek do not necessarily inherit the earth.

METAPHORS FOR THERAPIST AND CLIENT

We can begin a more detailed examination of the social role relation-ship between client and therapist by considering the social metaphors

for relationships that seem to be implied in different forms of psychotherapy. We can apply, by analogy, traditional social relationship
titles to various approaches to psychotherapy and consider, in each case,
the implications of the relationship for (i) the implied imbalance of
expertise between therapist and client, (ii) the formulation of the
problem, (iii) the style of interaction, (iv) the interplay of talk and
behaviour and (v) the intended outcome.

Doctor-patient

This is the most traditional style of relationship and it accords best
with the medical model implicit in psychiatry. It is a style of
relationship familiar to most clients, who have been meeting doctors
since they were children and it fits most easily into the organisational
systems adopted in psychiatric institutions. Conventionally, it is seen
as a relationship of honour and authority with a historical halo
compounded of science and saintliness.

Balance of expertise: The doctor-patient relationship explicitly argues
that the doctor is the expert who knows generally how people function
and who can specifically diagnose and treat what is wrong with a
particular client. The client is seen as an ignoramus who can only
confuse matters if he or she attempts any kind of self-diagnosis. The
client may be a clear or confused reporter of 'symptoms' but it is the
doctor's province to determine and treat the underlying 'illness'.

Formulation of problem: In its classic form the doctor-patient relationship implies that the problem is essentially an 'illness'. The doctor
will consult his diagnostic classificatory system and label (and may
later re-label and re-label) the 'illness'. Any insistence by the
client (who is now known to be suffering from 'depression',
'obsessionality', 'schizophrenia' and whose thoughts are therefore
suspect) that his or her problem is to do with spouse, job, religious
conflict or whatever, can only be seen as symptomatic evidence for the
diagnosis itself. In practice, psychiatrists seem to find it easier to
use diagnostic labels in the context of physical treatments in
psychiatry: when involved in psychotherapy they often begin to listen
credulously to the client's personal story. However, if the story
becomes hard to understand the conviction that they are dealing with an
'illness' (he or she was walking along one day and caught 'depression')
tends to come to the fore again. Clients often collude with the notion
that they have been stricken by an illness, partly out of deference to
the doctor's expertise (which seems very expert to someone in a confused
and unhappy frame of mind) and partly because it relieves them of guilt
(you can be 'guilty of making a mess of your life' but not 'guilty of
falling ill'). It is easier to face friends, relatives and society as
a sick person, rather than as someone whose interpersonal mistakes have
caught up with them.

Style of interaction: The doctor-patient relationship inevitably
encourages the patient to be passive, waiting for cure and the doctor
is saddled with total responsibility for cure - both roles which carry
threat with them.

Talk and behaviour: Within the doctor-patient relationship the client's
talk is seen as useful only because it reveals symptoms and is evidence
for a diagnostic formulation. The talk of the doctor is seen as
primarily instructional (and incidentally comforting) with the
behaviour of the client, within and between sessions, being valued
insofar as it follows the guidelines indicated in the doctor's talk.

Outcome: The doctor's formulation of 'what is wrong' necessarily
defines successful outcome, e.g. the 'depression' has been got rid of.
This is problematic in the sense that it may ignore what the depression
was about and prevent it being taken as a reasonable signal to the
client that the basis of his or her life needs re-examining.
Interestingly, it is the client's own declaration that his or her
symptomatic experiences no longer occur that is taken as primary
evidence of 'cure'.

Trainer-trainee

The behavioural psychotherapies appear to have adopted what might
broadly be called a trainer-trainee model of relationship between
therapist and client. The concept of a maladaptive learned habit
translates easily into loss of, or non-acquisition of, skill (note -
the term skill and the term training are explicitly combined in 'social
skills training'). The emphasis on detailed programs of behaviour
modification following behavioural analysis suggests a technical-
instructional and impersonal (if courteous) relationship between
therapist and client. Additionally, the simple logic of behaviourist
psychology and its mechanistic picture of human functioning argues for
'training' as a central mode of psychological change. This is historically related to the origins of behaviourism in animal psychology.

Balance of expertise: The assumption seems to be that the therapist is
initally expert both in the skill to be conveyed (the paradox of the
socially inept social skills trainer is ignored) and in general
techniques of training. The client is seen as initially ignorant but
able to acquire a basic degree of competence given therapy. Indeed,
the degree of ignorance assumed on the part of the client, in classic
forms of conditioning therapy, is remarkable. Clients are assumed to
be without any teleological capacities whatever. The transvestite
receiving electric shocks while wearing women's underwear is apparently
expected to ignore the fact that, in the outside world, women's underwear is rarely electrified. Patients responding to a token economy
programme are assumed not to ponder the fact that once in the outside
world, tokens for good ward behaviours will not be forthcoming.

Formulation of problem: Skill learning is, by definition, specific.
What is lacking and what is to be mastered are assumed to be highly
definable so that methods of teaching and acquiring skills can be
equally precise. We can be trained to read, to play chess, to juggle,
to operated a capstan lathe. It may be this lust for specificity that
has caused behavioural psychotherapists to over-define the content of
human problems and to become involved in an endless search for the
mythical mono-symptomatic complaint. The client may be tempted to

collude in an over-specified contract as to 'what is wrong', partly
because it engenders hope if a problem is given very definite boundaries
and partly because others (doctors, friends, relatives) grow impatient
and unhelpful when faced by relatively formless complaints. Thus the
'agoraphobic' client contracts with the therapist to tackle the problem
of 'going out' whilst largely disregarding the issue of going out for
what purpose. The social isolate contracts to learn how to talk with
others, largely without reference to the question of what he or she
wants to talk about. The vaguely depressed person, for whom life is
a mess, must either be ignored or agree to complain about a specific
this or that. Having one's life in a mess is difficult to define as a
'maladaptive learner habit' and training courses for learning not to
make a mess of life, are difficult to design.

Style of interaction: It may be that the interchanges between
behavioural therapist and client are more intimate, more of an inter-
personal duet than the clinical reports of behavioural programs would
lead one to suspect. Nevertheless, it seems likely that therapist and
client are distanced from each other and the range of their engagement
inhibited by the requirements of a trained-trainee model of interaction.

Talk and behaviour: Classic behavioural theory demoted talk (subjective
report) as a resource and as a process and although the trend to
'cognitive' behavioural therapy has modified the picture, the pivot of
change is still seen to lie in modification of the client's behaviour.
In practice, conversation between therapist and client is implicitly
recognised as important both in 'gaining rapport' (a process which is
considered essential but which is curiously unanalysed by behaviour
therapists) and in formulating a behavioural analysis of the client's
problems. What does not seem to be acknowledged is that the repetition
of approved behaviour may have no long term effects if the client fails
to see any significance in it, makes no sense out of it. It is the
conclusions we draw from our behaviours (about ourselves and others)
that we carry into the future, not the mechanically performed
behaviours themselves.

Outcome: By defining, in very specific and behavioural terms, 'what is
wrong' with the client, behavioural psychotherapists optimise the
chances of 'success', e.g. if the complaint is agreed to be a wasp
phobia then a client who learns to remain calm in the presence of wasps
is recorded a 'successful case', however miserable the rest of his or
her life may be. Extreme specificity in complaint masks the confusions
of both client and therapist about the nature of psychological distress
but if the contract de-limiting complaint can be adhered to, ground
will be thought to have been gained.

Friend and friend

Some of the humanistic approaches to psychotherapy (e.g. client-centred
psychotherapy) seem to have a friendship metaphor underlying their
conception of the therapist-client relationship. Their emphasis on
warmth, regard and mutual honesty seem to derive, to a fair extent,
from our traditional understanding of what is involved in friendship.

The call for a degree of self-disclosure on the part of the therapist
as well as the client, also hints at this kind of interplay.

Balance of expertise: Initially the client is seen as spiritually
ignorant but as having within him or her a potential for personal
enlightenment, (e.g. the concept of self actualisation) which they can
realise, largely through their own efforts. The therapist is expert in
the sense of being facilitative.

Formulation of problem: The underlying conviction that the client is
engaged in the pursuit of 'personal growth' suggests a non-specific
formulation of the problem. Life is the problem and (though
difficulties may be seen as embodied in this or that context) a narrow,
contractual formulation of 'what is wrong' is clearly discouraged.

Style of interaction: Humanistic psychotherapies, in so far as they
follow a friendship model, allow informal and diverse styles of interaction but they can suggest a particular stance for the therapist. The
non-directive mode, in which the therapist reflects the client's
assertions, can become stylised. Equally the stance of 'unconditional
regard' takes the customary natural approval of friends to an extreme
point, perhaps to an unnatural point. The therapist may consider his
or her regard 'unconditional' but the client may perceive it as
implicitly demanding the attainment of very high, almost impossible,
emotional standards. It can be read as saying 'I do not explicitly
state the conditions needed to win my approval because I know you will
surpass the implicit conditions which you know apply.' Additionally,
the 'friendship' made of interaction between therapist and client may
create confusion since so many aspects of the relationship are, in
practice, not reciprocal and not 'friendly', e.g. people are not paid
to be your friend, times, places and purposes of meetings between
friends are mutually negotiated and not prescribed by the one 'friend'
and so forth.

Talk and behaviour: Between 'friends' talk and behaviour are only very
vaguely distinguished. Intimate conversation can be the quintessential
'behaviour'. In much of humanistic psychotherapy the quality of
intimacy and mutual insight between therapist and client and the
fantasies and enactments explored can represent both the conversational
and behavioural heart of therapy.

Outcome: Since, in humanistic psychotherapy, purposes are broadly
defined under headings such as 'growth', outcome is seen not as the
getting rid of specific complaints but as involving reaching new levels
of awareness and interpersonal relationship. Humanistic therapists
seem to accept that this greater ambition, on the part of both
therapist and client, will inevitably make criteria of 'cure' more
difficult to define and their measure may be, in part, the process and
state of the client-therapist relationship itself.

Priest-penitant

Psychoanalytic psychotherapy, while having strong echoes of doctor-patient, can be characterised as establishing a form of priest-penitent relationship between therapist and client. Freudian theory and its variants propose that, as part of our infantile development, we inherit psychodynamic conflicts and a consequent intrinsic human inadequacy. The severity of the internalised conflicts may vary as between those choosing to enter therapy and those not so choosing but the argument is still that psychodynamic conflict is, like original sin, a natural state. By bringing unconscious conflicts into consciousness and resolving them, psychoanalytic therapy enables the person to evolve to a singular level. Since all analysts have been analysed they undertake work from this singular, evolved level and it is in this sense that the metaphor of priest-penitent is appropriate - by virtue of being absolved the analyst can give absolution, by virtue of access to the truth of human nature the analyst can offer the possibility of transcendence.

Balance of expertise: The psychoanalytic therapist is an appointed expert in two senses; in that he or she has personally resolved (relative to unanalysed humankind) the psychic confusion which plagues us and in that he or she is intimate with the base theory which explains our nature - just as the priest has access to and intimacy with, theological doctrine. The client is, initally, not only ignorant but the victim of false knowledge. He or she can attain understanding - a kind of lay expertise - essentially through therapy.

Formulation of problem: Psychoanalytic theory defines the nature of 'what is wrong' in subordinately broad and superordinately specific terms. A vast range of particular behaviours and interactions can be seen as symptomatic of 'the problem' but 'the problem' will always be specifically narrowed down to historic, infantile conflict and its later forms of working out. Thus the content of problems can be seen as varied but their form is always specific and relates to a special story about the human journey from birth.

Style of interaction: The priest-penitent mode seems to be reflected in the confessional attitude of the client and the authority, dignity and impersonal stance of the therapist. In accepting transference (the client's shifting of emotion applicable to other persons onto the psychoanalyst) the therapist manifests both the priest's capacity to forgive and his generally Christlike stance.

Talk and behaviour: The primary tools of psychoanalytic therapy (e.g. transference, free association, dream work, the gaining of insight by the client through the theoretical interpretations of the therapist and so forth) place an emphasis on talk. The behaviour and experience of the client between sessions is only partially relevant as material for the sessions themselves. Significantly, central aspects of emotional processing, such as catharsis and abreaction, are expected to take place during the therapeutic sessions. This, along with the high frequency of sessions and the prolonged duration of treatment, places a primary value on the therapeutic engagement itself, as contrasted with the client's life between sessions.

Outcome: The state of grace aimed at through psychoanalytic psycho-therapy is conceived of as broad in its effects but theoretically highly definable in that it must comprise the bringing into consciousness of previously unconscious psychodynamic conflict and thereby resolving it. The therapist is theoretically the best judge of whether outcome has been 'successful' being professionally undeceived by 'flight into health' or other defence mechanisms (False knowledge).

Supervisor-researcher

Kelly explicitly offers the metaphor of academic supervisor-researcher as a model for the therapist client relationship in personal construct theory psychotherapy. The model is problematic in that it is unfamiliar: only a few people in our society experience this mode of relationship, as contrasted with the many who have come to understand the parameters of doctor-patient, trainer-trainee, friend-friend and even priest-penitent.

Balance of expertise: As between supervisor and researcher, there is a differential and complementary expertise. Any research student inevitably knows a great deal more about the specific focus of his or her research, than the supervisor, since they live with it day by day. The supervisor's expertise is of a different kind. It is to do with experience in experimental design, the formulation of problems, the working out of research strategies. This is his or her specific contribution. Thus the metaphor links back to Kelly's argument that 'the client is the only informed expert on himself or herself' while allowing that the therapist has a particular expertise on issues such as how questions can be formulated and issues explored.

Formulation of problem: Construct theory is presented at a very abstract level and therefore offers no particular cultural content as inevitably underlying human problems, e.g. it has no equivalent of oedipal conflict. Yet, since it argues that a person's construct system, their way of understanding this world, is integrated in some way, there can be no truly isolated problems. There can be no single thing that is really 'what is wrong'. Thus in construct theory psychotherapy the formulation of 'the problem' is part of the psychotherapeutic process itself and the issue of what is really wrong may be negotiated and re-negotiated many times in the course of therapy.

Style of interaction: The emphasis of the approach (on personal experiment as the key mode for exploring problems) calls for very varied style of interaction, though, if the model of relationship (supervisor-researcher) is read literally, the style of interplay may become stilted.

Talk and behaviour: The metaphor of supervisor-researcher offers a fairly explicit forecast of the interplay between talk and behaviour. Just as the researcher moves from conducting experiments (behaviour) to reflecting on their meaning and generating further hypotheses (talk) with the supervisor, so the client moves from ventures between sessions to reflection within sessions. True, within sessions (in the form of role playing and through interplay with the therapist) real life behaviour is manifest but the underlying argument is that construing cannot change without validating or invalidating evidence, nor can effective experiments be undertaken without reconstruing. Thus the review-action process is seen as cyclical.

Outcome: As in the humanistic psychotherapies, personal construct theory takes a broad (and phenomenological) view of both 'what is wrong' and what might become 'right'. Broadly, it sees 'what is wrong' as some form of psychological imprisonment and entrapment. The client is unable to elaborate his or her life but is either forced into over defined circular patterns of living and relationship or equally imprisoned within that kind of vagueness and confusion which cannot generate testable purposes and engagements. Successful outcome is signified by psychological movement (liberation as experienced by the client) though the therapy does not specify movement in any particular direction.

THE FORMAL QUALITY OF PSYCHOTHERAPY

The models of relationship between therapist and client sketched out in this essay are, at one level, metaphors or cartoons, At another level, they point to ways in which interaction may be limited and shaped by the broad approach taken to the whole process of psycho-therapy. Psychotherapy is a way of formalising human interaction for particular purposes. For example, the primary issue in psychotherapy is the human situation of the client, not the human situation of the therapist - it is formalised thus, regardless of what dire straits the therapist may be in. This does not mean that the problems of the therapist cannot be raised or explored if they have relevance for the client or that they do not exist. It does mean that the relationship is not reciprocal, The client is at the centre of the interaction. The way in which the interaction is seen and formalised can be facilit-ating or hindering. A potentially useful aspect of all forms of psychotherapy is that they place the client (who by definition has difficulties in relating to people) within a relatively intimate and confronting relationship. This experience, of itself, provides him or her with the opportunity to experiment, to negotiate understanding, to explore their own nature, the nature of another and what lies between the two. Thus, the ways of formalising the psychotherapeutic inter-action which deny its human base, which make what happens invalid as evidence for the client, threaten the whole purpose of the venture. Some years ago, I was asked to see (as a prospective client for psychotherapy) an eighteen-year-old girl who had been brought into the hospital because of severe drug addiction. I disguised my instant dislike of her (as self-indulgent and careless of others) by pretending to empathy and warmth. After twenty minutes of this she suggested that if I disliked her that much I might just as well piss off. The client thus rescued the engagement from a possible fate as a kind of psycho-logical nonsense.

SOCIAL ROLE VERSUS ROLE RELATIONSHIP

A psychotherapeutic approach becomes invalid if there is too great a distance between the social role adopted by the therapist (and thereby forced upon the client) and their role relationship. I am using the term social role to point to a presentation which prescribes, in some detail, the content and limitations of the interaction and which requires those engaged, to play out some kind of traditional and socially determined script. Kelly defined role relationship, in his sociality corollary, in the following terms: to the extent that one person construes the construction processes of another he or she may play a role in a social process involving the other person. This makes our role relationships spontaneous and exploratory, in that they evolve to the degree that we can understand how the other person is making sense of us and how they are making sense of our way of making sense of them. In psychotherapy, while the very postures of 'therapist' and 'client' guide the forms of interplay, they must not prevent therapist and client from making discoveries about each other. Structure and method are of the essence of psychotherapy but they must not be allowed to deny the humanity of those engaged or smother it under social roles.

THE PRIMACY OF PERSONAL MEANING

The social role of therapist and client and its attendant prescriptions may obscure the issue of personal meaning. The client is (like the therapist) contending with the world in terms of the personal meanings he or she attaches to it, bearing in mind that 'the world' includes self and the meanings attached to self. They will escape from their personal imprisonment in so far as they can reinterpret who they are, what has happened to them and how they may engage with it. There are many prescribed constructs which can be applied by therapists in their social role, in such a way as to hinder both therapist and client in their attempt to uncover past and discover future meanings for events. For example, 'frigidity' is often treated as if its nature were defined and understood (i.e. its public meaning is accepted), and its elimination is thereby seen as a technical (if complicatedly technical) task. But 'frigidity' can mean many different things to the person alleged to be 'suffering' from it. This becomes obvious if we consider what, for different persons, the contrast pole of frigidity might be. The issue might be one of frigidity versus promiscuity, or frigidity versus male domination, or frigidity versus loss of control, or frigidity versus the ability to undertake the dull, domestic chore of sex, or frigidity versus social conformity, or frigidity versus loss of valued sexual fantasies. Any of theses (or many others) may be the actual contrast pole for a person, as opposed to the traditional frigidity versus sexual enthusiasm. Modes of psychotherapy which impose traditional, pseudo-medical definitions, as opposed to exploring personal meanings, espouse the socio-political ideology underlying the public definition and force this on the client.

THE POLITICAL CONTEXT OF PSYCHOTHERAPY

It was argued, initially, that psychotherapy takes place within an institutional and social surround and whether this dominates the process or not, depends , to a large extent, on the degree of

awareness of that institutional and social surround which therapist and
client can develop. What we are not aware of we cannot effectively
contend with. Frequently, the content of psychotherapy is discussed as
if it were independent of institutional structures. Texts of psychotherapy often ignore the fact that what goes on within therapy is in
play with both an administrative framework and the dominant ideological
themes of the time.

Let me offer, as a moral tale for this issue, the story of a therapy
group which I once conducted with a colleague. We had been pondering
the issue of 'who is suitable for group psychotherapy'. There are
vaguely formulated but very influential criteria for the selection of
clients for group psychotherapy. These include proposed
characteristics such as being young, intelligent, articulate,
emotionally responsive, not very disturbed and well mannered. Such
criteria clearly have their origins is what is currently socially
valued, what would be acceptable company for a middle class
professional. Paradoxically, they seem to suggest that the only
people suitable for group psychotherapy are those who patently do not
need it. In order to question the kind of social norms underlying
this kind of selection procedure, we asked the charge nurses and
sisters on eight different wards to select for us the patient on their
ward who they saw as the least suitable for group psychotherapy.
Inevitably, the group assembled consisted of eight long stay patients
from what are ominously termed 'back' wards and were classified in
psychiatric terms as 'chronic psychotics". Once in being, it became
clear that the psychotherapy group would accept none of the
conventional rules of procedure (sitting still in a circle, talking
one at a time, working for a fixed period, politely heeding what went
on, treating the professionals as group 'leaders' and so forth).
However, there seemed to be some enthusiasm for the group and in time
one of the conventional rules rejected by the group was the rule by
which psychotherapists control membership. Conventionally, the
members of a psychotherapy group are those people invited to join by
the therapists but our group members frequently brought friends or
acquaintances and thus the total group membership was erratic and
unpredictable. Rapidly, this brought us into collision with the
consultants responsible for (i.e. having power over) those patients
who were invited by their fellows. It was officially pointed out that
permission had never been sought for their participation in psychotherapy. Our 'excuse', that we had never known that they were going
to attend, was not accepted and indeed, in terms of the mores of
political control by professionals, it must have seemed foolish.
Eventually, the group had to be discontinued because there was no way
in which (under administrative pressures) we could continue it, without
enforcing a structure upon it (specified membership) that was not
acceptable to its members. Thus the hierarchical structure of the
institution and the nature of its regime affected (as it always must)
what was possible and not possible in terms of the content of psychotherapy.

DEMOCRATIC PSYCHOTHERAPY

As was stressed at the beginning of this essay, the psychotherapeutic situation involves an initially non-reciprocal relationship in which the balance of power lies with the therapist and which, thereby, is not a democratic situation. Additionally, the concept of psychotherapy itself is part of that ideology which is built around the managerial notion of an expert – an ideology which argues that a small number of middle class professionals – politicians, managers, doctors, engineers, psychologists and so forth – will be primarily responsible for the solution of society's problems. Nevertheless, the theme of democracy can be introduced into psychotherapy at two levels.

Firstly, the explicit purpose of psychotherapy can become the destruction of the non-reciprocal power relationship which is its starting point. 'Cure' can be defined as reaching a level at which the client can effectively contest the psychotherapist's view of life, i.e. the level at which the client does not need psychotherapy or the psychotherapist. When a person enters psychotherapy he or she is admitting that their personal resources, their relationships, their engagement with their own community, has failed them. They can no longer elaborate their life, resolve their problems and engage with their conflicts in direct personal terms. They are calling for what is essentially an artificial aid. Conversely, successful psychotherapy is characterised by a return to personally chosen life strategies. It is not marked by the disappearance of problems or conflicts – it is doubtful if these ever disappear in anyone's life. It is marked by the pain and the problems becoming the possession of the client and psychotherapy becoming unnecessary. Its continuance, beyond that point, turns it into a social luxury.

Secondly, as part of the increasing level of awareness which is aimed at in psychotherapy, there should evolve, for both therapist and client, an increasing awareness of what is not democratic and reciprocal between them and what is not democratic within their context. Both should become increasingly aware that, if they are not simply to reflect the ideology and the pressures of their surrounding institutions and society, they must come to understand how those pressures obtain: the potential tyranny of the family and the immanent dictatorship of the administrative hierarchy must be equally under- stood, if they are to be gainsaid.

PSYCHOTHERAPY AS A POLITICAL PIVOT

Most people who come within the ambit of psychiatry will receive no psychotherapy. So long as the medical model and its attendant economics and power structure remains in force, most patients (and they will be conceptualised as 'patients') will be treated by in-line production methods, i.e. drugs and electro-convulsive therapy. The operating model is that of mass repair, modified by the incidental humanity or occasional clinical insights of hospital staffs.

In this situation the value of psychotherapy is ideological not

economic. All forms of psychotherapy involve, to a greater or lesser
degree, seriously listening to the client, paying some heed to the
personal nature of their complaint. The experience of psychotherapy
contradicts the notion that psychological distress can be categorised
into broad classes and relieved by essentially impersonal techniques –
it leads toward the conviction that psychological distress is part of
living, relates to the particular content of a person's life and cannot
be functionally separated from the particular nature of the person. In
so far as this is true, then whatever the problematics of psychotherapy,
it proposes a philosophy of caring, alternative to that which has
dominated the field since it was taken over by medicine in the
nineteenth century.

True, psychotherapists have struggled to avoid this ideological
responsibility, e.g. be largely ignoring those termed psychotic and
by otherwise trivialising their undertaking. But the implications of
seeking to understand a person's confusion and assist his or her own
efforts to resolve it, remains powerfully in contradiction to the
strategy of classifying it and responding to it with pseudo-technical,
mass repair methods. It is this divergence, this refusal ultimately to
distance the so-called disturbed from the so-called normal, that
gives psychotherapy its pivotal, political role.

THE FUTURE OF PSYCHOTHERAPY

Psychotherapy has developed, in part, out of our acceptance of the
social ideology which dictates that the authorised professional rather
than the community shall be the agent for bestowing competence and
resolving conflict. We are only slowly coming to recognise that the
therapeutic milieu is preferable to the therapist and a social
collective within which people can freely elaborate their lives is
preferable to either. A parallel kind of recognition is slowly
taking place in the field of education. Even within conservative
educational institutions there is some awareness that the scholarly
community should become something which is, by its nature, educational
rather than that it should be nothing but a matter of teachers teaching
pupils. We should work towards a time when communities have
therapeutic qualities which render unnecessary the specific roles of
therapist and client.

Chapter 10

CAREER STRESSES ON PSYCHOLOGICAL THERAPISTS
Glenys Parry and Dan Gowler

INTRODUCTION

In recent years, professionals (and professionalism) have attracted a considerable amount of adverse criticism. Furthermore, this chorus of complaint has been directed mainly at the so-called 'caring' or 'liberal' professions, for example, doctors, lawyers and teachers. These have been charged with serious shortcomings, ranging from arrogant elitism to monopolistic exploitation. For example, Robinson (1978) writes of the professional and the client inhabiting 'worlds apart', where professionals seriously fail their clients by giving unworkable or inconsistent advice, not explaining adequately what their decisions or prescriptions involve, lacking in genuine sympathy or concern, judging clients' needs inappropriately, and using their status to render the client powerless and at their mercy. Such charges as these have culminated in the general allegation that these professions actually 'disable' their clients through the creation of spurious 'imputed needs' and 'expert solutions' (Illich et al., 1977).

These charges have been accompanied by the 'revolt of the client' (Haug and Sussman, 1969) on the one hand and the emergence of 'radical professionals' (Perucci, 1976) on the other. To the relatively detached eye of the historian or sociologist, however, these trends are clear manifestations of the processes of professionalization, de-professionalization and re-professionalization (Gerstel and Jacobs, 1976) generated by long-term changes in markets, technology, social organization, values and so on. But, as far as individual professional practitioners are concerned, they may experience these trends as a set of personal and interpersonal difficulties, which are unlikely to be dispelled by the knowledge that they are the inevitable result of remote, impersonal forces beyond their or anyone else's control.

The job-related stress of the 'caring' professions has been acknowledged and described in studies of 'emotional burnout'. This alarming syndrome is, it is claimed, unique to those doing 'people work' (Maslach, 1976; Maslach and Jackson, 1981). Consider the following passage:
Early studies of the burnout phenomenon identified several useful

dimensions for describing how providers of human service react to
their jobs ... Regardless of whether they feel effective ... the
close contact these workers have with other people's problems often
leads to a feeling of emotional exhaustion ... care-givers feel
strained after working closely with people day-in and day-out.
Feelings of frustration, tension, and psychological fatigue become
constant reminders of the burden of responsibility these workers
feel they must carry. Perhaps as a defensive strategy ... many
care-givers begin to depersonalize their recipients, treating them
as if they were objects rather than people; the once caring
professional helper now feels emotionally calloused and uncaring
(Jackson and Maslach, 1982, p. 64).
Here an account of the personal stress experienced by some caring
professionals is interwoven with an account of why the stress exists.
We question, however, whether the burnout phenomenon is a result of
working closely with the emotional problems of others, rather than
intrinsic to the professional role itself in contemporary circumstances.
We describe a model which has been derived from the study of a range of
professional occupations (Gowler and Legge, 1980), but is here applied
to psychological therapists, and in particular the profession of
clinical psychology. By doing this, we attempt to reduce the variety,
complexity and scale of impersonal forces by describing a 'mechanism'
that not only transforms these remote pressures into personal problems
but at the same time presents a range of possible coping behaviours.

THE CRUCIFORM EFFECT

A number of commentators have not only drawn attention to the shortcomings of professional practice but have also emphasized that professional roles should be reconsidered in the light of current organisational structures. For example, Daniels (1975) makes some interesting
comments about professionals in organisations, and writes that:
    The traditional model of the professional has always been one of
    the free agent contracting to perform a service for a client. It
    is thought that the client can choose his own professional and the
    first loyalty of the professional is always to his/her client.
    This conception has recently been challenged, however, on the
    grounds that it gives little attention to the numbers of
    professionals who have always been employed in organisations and
    the changes which such employment brings about in the professional
    relationship over time. Unfortunately, the notion of the 'free
    professional' ignores the ways in which conflicting values exert
    pressures upon the professional particularly where third parties
    intervene in a relationship with a client. Professionals with a
    basic mandate to provide a personal service to some individual
    may find this mandate directly and indirectly challenged by
    organisational priorities which require either the practitioner
    or the client to give primacy to other considerations (pp. 345-6;
    emphasis added).
It might at first appear that psychological therapists have an
exceptionally clear and unambiguous mandate to act in the interests of
their clients. (This is not to imply that an unambiguous commitment
to clients' needs does not bring its own problems.) The professional/

client relationship is, in this case, explicitly concerned with acceptance, empathy, good communication. It could even be argued that successful therapy depends on the professional and client not inhabiting two 'separate worlds'; treating the client as an impersonal object seem guaranteed to make therapy fail. Psychological therapy is almost always practised within a profession structure, and additionally within an organisation. (Although we concentrate on the clinical psychologist, much of this analysis could be applied to psychiatrists and social workers.) The psychological therapist attempting to fulfil this basic mandate soon becomes aware of other powerful, competing pressures. There is a need to plan one's therapeutic work within the constraints of, for example, scarce resources, bureaucratic controls, jostlings for power of other professional groups, or challenges to the legitimate limits of therapeutic intervention. Many people find that it is not easy to discover a niche within an organisation or career structure which allows an unambiguous commitment to the therapeutic relationship. We suggest that in entering the career structure of a given profession, the individual becomes subject to the stresses resulting from the ambiguity that is built into professional roles. At this point it is interesting to note that, like those of political parties, professional mandates appear to require frequent discussion and reformulation. However, we believe that these basic mandates are stated in such a way as to reflect and, to some extent, resolve the problems commented on above.

To establish claims to professional status in the face of role ambiguity, occupational rhetorics or justification have emerged. In other words, professional groups attempt to persuade others (and themselves) that their claims to authority and scarce resources are fully justified. These rhetorics also serve to reconcile claims to elite status and dominance with adaptations to technical, economic and bureaucratic constraints. Moreover, as illustrated in Figure 1, the structure and content of this rhetoric simultaneously expresses and attempts to resolve that characteristic pattern of stresses and strains we term 'the cruciform effect'. The term expresses metaphorically a set of demands which pull in opposing directions, such that whichever way one twists or turns, it is not possible to find a comfortable position.

While we treat the cruciform effect as prior to the development of the rhetoric of justification, Kat (1979) suggests that for clinical psychologists, we might reverse the logic. For example, he comments:
    It seems to me that as a professional group we are in the middle
    of a protracted process of deciding the grounds on which we wish
    to persuade other people that clinical psychology is a good thing.
    It is precisely because clinical psychology does not have an
    established rhetoric of justification, that individuals are
    particularly likely to experience the cruciform effect.(p. 38;
    emphasis added)

We return to this point later, but suffice to say that, for both Kat and ourselves, the rhetoric of justification functions as a device for coping with certain aspects of occupational stress, especially those manifested in the competition for professional status, rewards, resources and control.

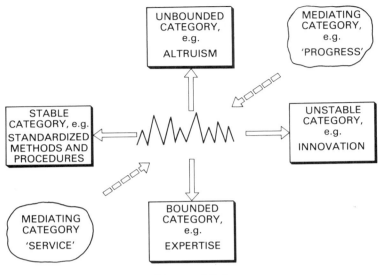

Figure 10.1
THE CRUCIFORM EFFECT

When viewed functionally, the rhetoric of justification may help professionals cope with the more immediate aspects of the problems and pressures commented upon above by simplifying and transforming complex issues into acceptable images and propositions. Thus, in Figure 10.1, the vertical axis illustrates how professional status may be established by claiming moral superiority (for example, by asserting altruism) and technical competence (for example by asserting expertise). The horizontal axis illustrates how professional status may also be established by claiming to achieve the control of care (for example, by asserting the existence of standardized methods and procedures) whilst at the same time claiming to improve the quality of care (for example, by asserting a relatively high level of innovation).

To summarize these comments, to the observer, the rhetoric of justification may be treated as a mask that conceals the details but reveals the contours of a variety of occupational stressors, that is, the cruciform effect (Gowler and Legge, 1980). Thus, claims about altruism and expertise are shaped by direct challenges to professional competence, whilst claims about standards and innovations are shaped by the constraints of bureaucratic control (Elliott and Kuhn, 1978). However, whilst may clinical psychologists might deny that they actually possess an 'established rhetoric of justification', most would find it relatively easy to give examples of direct challenges to their professional competence and/or the frustrations of bureaucratic control.

RHETORIC IS NOT ENOUGH

A closer look at the rhetoric of justification is instructive, because not only does it reflect the stresses and strains of professional life, but also it is itself unstable, and its various elements may be seen to 'pull' in opposite directions. For example, altruism is, by definition, unbounded, valid in its own terms, self-denying, concerned with the whole person, and stands in opposition to expertise (forms of specialisation) which is bounded, validated by external criteria (for example utility), self-affirming, and concerned only with particular aspects of a person.

The tension between expertise and altruism is inherent in the role of the clinical psychologist when he or she is working as a psychological therapist. A lengthy university training as a scientist is combined with a caring, helping stance towards the patient. Hildebrand, speaking from a psychoanalyst's perspective remarks that:

I do not feel ... that the university stimulates the possibility of the development of a capacity for warmth, empathy, understanding and the ability to recognise the work with the meanings of another person and their inner and outer worlds ... the average British department of academic psychology with its laudable emphasis on perceptual process, operant paradigms and cognitive modelling is not the best background for the psychotherapist who needs to have absorbed something of the study of the humanities allied to a good chunk of life experience, knowledge which it is far too easy to avoid amid the attractions of models of cognition and the computer programmes.

Yet it is precisely on its expertise in 'perceptual process, operant paradigms and cognitive modelling' that clinical psychologists have, as a profession, staked their claim to professional status.

A further example of the use of these aspects of the rhetoric is contained in the arguments put forward for the registration of psychologists as a profession. These arguments evoke both the claim to specialised knowledge, which should be protected, as it were, by the registered trade mark 'psychologist', and the claim that registration will protect the public from incompetent practitioners. Bannister (1981) has pointed out some of the flaws in these arguments, exposing the myth that specialised (and protected) expertise is unproblematically compatible with altruistic concerns about the public's best interests.

The tension between altruism and expertise is also apparent in the discrepancy between the techniques described in psychotherapy research and the everyday practice of psychotherapy by psychologists committed to helping their clients. Whilst not denying the utility of a coherent theoretical framework within which to work, it is the case that clinical practice is more eclectic than implied by most textbooks or clinical outcome studies. Expertise, in the sense of a blind adherence to the textbook version of a theoretical perspective, precludes the full flowering of an altruistic stance towards the client. Indeed, although many graduates entering clinical psychology courses may be motivated to do so by altruistic concerns, reference to this is remarkably rare once training has begun.

In the same way as the tension between altruism and expertise, the

routines of standardised profesional practice, with their emphasis
on stability, precedents and the minimisation of risks, stand in direct
opposition to the demands of necessary but unstable forms of innovation.
This oppostion is clearly felt in the profession. A typical training
in clinical psychology equips the tyro with psychometric and behavioural
treatment skills. The emphasis is on standard treatment 'packages' for
particular constellations of symptoms, which in turn produces a need to
match these procedures to the needs of the client. The justification
is that there are excessive numbers of clients and limited time
available. Yet the practising clinician cannot ignore for long the
preponderance of non-standard clients who do not 'fit' routinised
procedures. Innovatory treatments, therefore, demand the attention of
the clinician, or at least the need to take forms of therapy not
traditionally part of the psychologist's role into everyday practice.

Figure 1 also illustrates the point that other categories are created
to mediate between the contradictions commented on above. For example,
the inconsistency between professional expertise and routinised
procedures can be reduced by recourse to the concept ot 'service':
similarly, between altruism and innovation by the concept of 'progress'.
We argue, however, that because of the inherent instability of the
rhetoric of justification, such inconsistency-reducing categories are
likely to disintegrate when those involved reflect upon or attempt to
act out this rather unsatisfactory myth.

One consequence of all .this is that those concerned find it increasingly difficult to perform the requisite mental gymnastics in the face
of criticism from clients, administrators, politicians and competing
professional groups. Indeed, it could be predicted that if
professionals attempt to withstand these pressures by espousing and
conforming to all the conflicting demands,they will probably experience
a stressful combination of role overload and anomie. It is in such
circumstances that 'burnout' can occur, and the therapists themselves
are likely to become suitable cases for treatment.

THE CRUCIFORM EFFECT IN PRACTICE

It is worth outlining some common circumstances where the cruciform
effect may be clearly apparent for clinical psychologists functioning
as psychological therapists. Psychotherapy with hospitalised patients
is a good example. Psychiatric hospitals are, more often than not,
large, bureaucratic institutions with their own long-established
routines and procedures. Psychological therapists working in this
environment find themselves attempting to weld together contradictory
ideologies. There are three obvious ways in which this happens.
First, a common task for the therapist is to help the client experience
and honestly face painful, primitive or destructive emotions. In
opposition to this the organisational structures of the hospital can be
seen as adapted to defend against the anxiety of facing the realities
of mental pain and suffering (Menzies, 1970). The fundamental principle
of confidentiality in the therapeutic relationship is also challenged
by routine case conferences where it sometimes seems that everybody's
and anybody's observations or opinions about the patient are openly

discussed. A further problem concerns the principle that the patient's involvement in therapy should be entirely voluntary. This term can have an unusual meaning in the hospital setting: for example, when a 'voluntary' patient has to await the consultant's authority before being allowed home for weekend leave. It may be that the 'ideal' free contractual arrangement between client and therapist is rarely a reality in the NHS in any case, but in hospitals the contradictions are more clearly seen. For those working in secure hospitals the prisons the problem is even more acute. Bergman and Segel (1982) have addressed these issues and suggest that the problems would be alleviated in a well-run therapeutic community. Our analysis would suggest that the problems are more deeply entrenched than this implies, and the history of the therapeutic community movement could be taken as confirmation of this.

A second example of the cruciform effect is where a recently trained clinical psychologist, aspiring to be psychological therapist, takes on a 'difficult' client. The 'standard package' of techniques will fail to help such a client, who may even get worse rather than better. It is, of course, possible for the psychologist to terminate therapy and to tighten his or her selection process when deciding whom to accept into therapy in the future. We shall discuss this strategy later. It is, however, not uncommon for the young professional to struggle on aimlessly from session to session, attempting to use whatever their hurried reading or their commonsense may provide. It is often very difficult indeed to receive the support, supervision or continued advice of a more experienced therapist as a legitimate activity within one's professional structure. (There may be specialist settings where this is not so, but we speak of a general case.) We would argue that this at first surprisingly lack of support is predictable, since the rhetoric states that, as a fully-fledged member of the profession, one must by definition have the 'requisite expertise to help the client, using standard routines and applying the most up-to-date knowledge'. We suggest that the problem lies not so much in having inadequate knowledge, but in having adopted a professional role which does not allow the worker to admit their inadequate knowledge. To admit this would not only threaten one's own professional identity, but would challenge the rhetoric 'my professional training means that I am particularly well-equipped to help the people referred to me'.

In a similar vein, and in order to demonstrate that clinical psychologists are not uniquely subject to these pressures, it is worth noting the recent report on an enquiry into 18 serious cases of child abuse, where all but two resulted in the death of the child (DHSS, 1982). The enquiry found that in many cases either newly qualified or untrained social workers and health visitors were left in unsupportive circumstances to cope with these most difficult situations. It is reasonable to ask what the senior and experienced members of these professions were doing during these grisly events. A partial answer to this may be found by examining how professionals learn to cope with the cruciform effect.

COPING WITHOUT CLIENTS

Our observations of professional behaviour reveal that there are
several ways of coping with the dislocation of action and meaning that
stem from the pressures of the cruciform effect and the inadequacies of
rhetoric. As illustrated in Figure 10.2, these may be characterised in
terms of four main types of role expectations and performances.

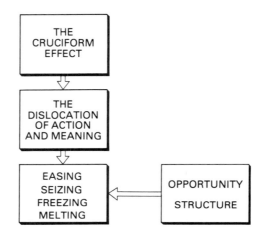

Figure 10.2
COPING WITH THE CRUCIFORM EFFECT

We have termed the four commonest types of coping behaviour 'easing',
'seizing', 'freezing' and 'melting', and they all have one important
characteristic in common: they each help relieve the stresses of the
cruciform effect by avoiding their major structural determinant, that
is, the problematic client-professional relationship. In other words,
it is easier to cope without clients. Moreoever, these patterns of
avoidance are made possible and, indeed, are legitimised by the
structure of roles and social supports created by membership of
professional associations. Thus, the very machinery that ensures that
an individual is capable enough to evaluate and treat other individuals'
mental states and behaviours, also provides a number of ways of
avoiding some of the most difficult aspects of these 'privileges'.

    Professionals who practise 'easing' (Cain, 1973) reduce their contact
with clients by spending considerable proportions of their time
'servicing' their colleagues. For example, they may undertake
administrative duties, attend or chair committees, organise
professional conferences, edit books or journals, and/or manage the
selection, instruction and examination of potential practitioners.
Alternatively, they may continue with a substantial case load, but ease
the strain by allowing crucial decisions to be 'unduly' influenced by
the latters' own lay definitions of problems. More senior clinical
psychologists may serve on BPS working parties, or on District and
Regional advisory sub-committees. Alternatively for professionals
lower in the hierarchy, a legitimate easing may be to work as an

advisor to groups of other professionals (for example, GPs, nurses or social workers) in what could be labelled 'skills diffusion' activities. Whilst these forms of coping appear to involve very different behaviours, they serve a smiliar function, since they all reduce potential conflicts and tensions be avoiding face-to-face confrontations with clients.

Similarly, those who practise 'freezing' close their eyes to the strains inherent in the traditional model of professional-client relationships and profess 'the only way to conduct professional practice'. They are able to maintain these protocols by the careful 'creaming' of clients (McKinley, 1975). Put another way, they select only those clients (and colleagues) who are prepared to accept this limited definition of their needs and of appropriate professional-client relationships. Moreover, such practitioners are likely to become experts on 'professionalism', for example, on occupational ethics and etiquette. Then, as guardians of tradition they occupy a prominent role in the internal regulation of the profession and the control of colleagues. Consequently, they are likely to become somewhat 'spiky' allies of colleagues who practise 'easing', whom at times they closely resemble.

'Freezing' psychologists are those who define the correct role for clinical psychologists rigidly and unequivocally. For example, there are those clinical psychologists who have firmly embraced the behaviourist tradition and are dogmatic in their adherence to standard techniques. Verbal psychotherapy may be seen as dubious and almost mystical, a pastime beyond the pale of correct professional practice. Another example is provided by the recent debate, full of feeling, between a group of psychologists defending the use of psychometric tests as evidence in court and another psychologist who appeared as an 'expert witness' and challenged the supremacy of such tests (Tunstall et al., 1982; Heim, 1982). Without wishing to comment on the rights and wrongs of the particular case, the arguments advanced in the papers do illustrate the characteristics of 'freezing'.

The above axample shows that 'freezers' may also be identified by the fact that, when expressing their preference for 'doing things by the book' they recount cautionary tales of unfortunates who did not. Additionally, this rather conservative stance is often justified by senior professionals as a corrective to 'abuses of professional freedom' and a necessary control upon the wayward behaviour of some of 'the more recently qualified members'.

By adopting such opinions and modes of behaviour, 'freezers' avoid many of the complex difficulties associated with innovation. Further-more, they may even go so far as to accuse those colleagues who do seek to implement (say) changes in therapy as guilty of 'charlatanism', 'an unprofessional lack of proper caution' and so on. Consequently, they are very likely to be especially critical of those we have labelled 'seizers'.

The professional who 'seizes' avoids clients by embracing those technologies and categorisations that enable him or her to reformulate the holistic complexity of a human being into a series of technical

problems. In doing so, 'seizers' may cultivate a 'backroom boy' image
and role, leaving colleagues to manage the potentially stressful
interactions with 'whole' or 'real' clients. The ultimate expression of
such a 'seizing' coping style is the retreat into research. Some forms
of research have the advantage for the 'seizer' that they avoid human
beings altogether. Other research can transform people into 'subjects';
that is, recast the problematic client in a form more amenable to the
researcher - as a dependent variable, for example. In extreme
circumstances, the canons of experimental science actually insist upon
the use of methods that ensure the segregation of those conducting
experiments from those being experimented upon.

'Seizing' may also involve an intense interest in a new technology
or specialist technique, so that the professional becomes an expert in
this limited sphere. There are a number of such techniques available
to the professional psychologist at any time. Current examples might
include Beck's cognitive therapy for depression, repertory grid testing
using microcomputers, magical therapy, biofeedback or attribution theory.
In these examples, the cruciform effect is diminished by defining the
problematic therapist/client relationship as primarily concerned to
handle the technical issues involved in the procedure. Thus many
potential stresses of taking on the client as a whole person are avoided
by defining the problem is advance; for example, as reducing emg
activity in the frontalis muscles, analysing the grid, formulating the
client's attributional style. Beck's therapy has the advantage of
subsuming even more complex concepts such as 'transference' in its
treatment approach by re-naming it 'static' (because it interferes with
the therapist's message being received loud and clear by the client).
Thus potentially complex issues of human relating can be reduced to a
technical hitch in the procedure.

The fourth escape route from the cruciform effect is taken by some
professionals by 'melting'. Briefly, this complex and ambivalent form
of coping involves those concerned in 'dissolving' their relationships
with their more conventional colleagues, whilst embracing a radically
new (or resurrected) ideology. Melters are radical psychologists who
are only too aware of the discomfort of the cruciform effect. They
may be vociferous in their criticism of 'easers', 'seizers' and
particularly 'freezers'. Such coping is in direct contrast to freezing,
and is one source of intraprofessional tension. 'Melters' can be seen
to be attempting to resolve the same set of stresses, however, by
turning away from conventional ideologies and the one-to-one therapist/
client relationship. They attempt to dissolve the 'ideal' relationship
with the individual client, by emphasising the needs of indirect,
impersonal clients, that is the community. When adopting this mode,
the professional justifies his or her form of service in terms of
social criteria, especially the needs of certain disadvantaged groups
and categories of people. Thus 'melting' may involve a commitment to
the idea of community psychology, or preventative work in large
populations rather than in individuals. At the same time, the melter
is committed to demystify the skills of the psychotherapist, and tries
to disown professional status. In doing so, but remaining on the
payroll of a conservative organisation, we would predict that the
dilemma of the melter is rarely resolved.

OPPORTUNITY TO COPE

As indicated in Figure 10.2, however, the individual does not always have the opportunity to adopt these coping styles. Consequently, the existing opportunity structure becomes a crucial factor in whether or not those concerned can alleviate the stresses of the cruciform effect. Furthermore, these issues become complex because certain forms of coping, especially 'easing' and 'seizing' have to be acted out for the maintenance and development of the professional institutions concerned. Consequently, some people are attracted to these roles and activities and do not necessarily enter them in order to cope with stress. Indeed Kat (1979) contends that: 'such opportunities are not an escape from work, but part of the work itself. What might be an escape strategy for one person could be a job description for another' (p. 38).

Whilst we accept that this may be true, we find that these coping behaviours, with the possible exception of melting, become even more widely practised with increasing seniority. We might even construe them as some of the perks or rewards of long service. It is certainly commonplace for psychologists in the basic grade, far from finding themselves in 'a period of advanced, specialist training' (Mair, 1980), to be left with the bulk of the face-to-face contact with clients to quite an overwhelming degree. Rather than basic grade workers having the opportunity to select clients carefully for training purposes, they may be left with complex and difficult cases to deal with.

We would argue that an awareness of the cruciform effect, and a curiosity to note its manifestations in our professional life, is a necessary first step to changing this state of affairs.

REFERENCES

BANNISTER, D. (1981), Registration - Yes or No?, 'New Forum', 7, 51-3.
BERGMAN, E. and SEGEL, R. (1982), The captive client: dilemmas of psychotherapy in the psychiatric hospital, 'Psychotherapy: Theory and Research Practice', 19, 31.
CAIN, M.E. (1973), 'Society and the Policeman's Role', London, Routledge & Kegan Paul.
DANIELS, A.K. (1975), 'Professionalism in Formal Organizations Behaviour', London, Holt, Rinehart & Winston.
DHSS (1982), 'Child Abuse: A Study of Inquiry Reports, 1973-81', London, HMSO.
ELLIOTT, C. and KUHN, D (1978), Professionals in Bureaucracies: some emerging areas of conflict, University of Michigan Business Review', vol. XXX, no. 1. January.
GERSTL, J. and JACOBS, G. (1976), 'Professions for the People: The Politics of Skill', New York, Schenkman.
GOWLER, D. and LEGGE, D. (1980), Evaluative practices as stressors in occupational settings, in C.L. Cooper and R. Payne (eds), 'Current Concerns in Occupational Stress', Chichester, John Wiley.
HAUG, M.R. and SUSSMAN, M.B. (1969), Professional autonomy and the revolt of the client, 'Social Problems', vol. 17, no. 3.
HEIM, A. (1982), Professional issues arising from psychological

evidence presented in court: A reply, 'Bulletin of the British Psychological Society', 35, 332.

HILDEBRAND, P. (1980), Therapeutic paradigms - psychodynamic therapy, 'New Forum', 7, 30-3.

ILLICH, I., ZOLA, I.K., McKNIGHT, J., CAPLAN, J. and SHAICKEN, H. (1977), 'Disabling Professions', London, Marion Boyars.

JACKSON, S.E. and MASLACH, C. (1982), After-effects of job-related stress: families as victims, 'Journal of Occupational Behaviour', 3, 63-77.

KAT, B. (1979), Rhetoric for survival, 'New Forum' 6, 38-9.

McKINLEY, J.B. (1975), Clients and organization, in J.B. McKinley (ed.), 'Processing People: Class in Organizational Behaviour', London, Holt, Rinehart & Winston.

MAIR, M. (1980), BPS report on the psychological therapies - a personal view, 'New Forum', 7, 39-41.

MASLACH, C. (1976), Burned-out, 'Human Behaviour', 5, 16-22.

MASLACH, C. and JACKSON, S.E. (1981), Measurement of experienced burnout, 'Journal of Occupational Behaviour', 2, 99-113.

MENZIES, I. (1970), The functioning of social systems as a defence against anxiety, 'Tavistock Pamphlet No. 3',London, Tavistock Institute of Human Relations.

PERRUCCI, C. (1976), In the service of man: radical movements in the professions, in G. Gerstl and G. Jacobs (eds), 'Professions for the People: The Politics of Skill', New York, Schenkman.

ROBINSON, T. (1978), In Worlds Apart, 'Professionals and their Clients in the Welfare State', London, Bedford Square Press.

SCOTT, R.L. (1976), Dialogue and Rhetoric, in J. Blankenship and H.G. Stelzner (eds). 'Rhetoric and Communications', Urbana: University of Illinois Press.

TUNSTALL, O., GUDJONSSON, G., EYSENCK, H. and HOWARD, L. (1982), Professional issues arising from psychological evidence presented in court, 'Bulletin of the British Psychological Society', 35, 329-31.

Chapter 11

WOMEN AS CLIENTS AND THERAPISTS
Sue Llewelyn and Kate Osborn

1   INTRODUCTION

Even the most cursory glance at the take-up of psychiatric services
suggests that there is a difference between the sexes in the
distribution of pathology (Klerman and Weissman, 1980; Goldman and
Ravid, 1980) diagnosis (Warner, 1979; Whitley, 1979), and treatment
offered (Chesler, 1973; Cooperstock, 1979; Tudor et al., 1977).   Why
is this so, and what are the consequences for clients and therapists?
The chapter attempts to offer some answers to these questions, by
examining the meaning of each of the differences.   Because of the
large number of observations that can be made regarding both sexual
differences and feminism on the one hand, and mental health and
pathology on the other, some theoretical or organisational framework is
needed.   The most helpful framework that we have found which organises
our observations into an explanatory and practical format, is
feminist psychotherapy.   The first part of this chapter will therefore
consist of an outline of feminist psychotherapy, and the insights it
offers to an understanding of female psychology and therapy.   This will
be followed by an overview of the particular issues which characterize
the difference between women's and men's experience of mental health.

The aim of this chapter is, however, not just to consider women 'out
there'.   Standing back from the content of our clinical work for a
while, we, as female workers in the field of mental health, notice some
important features of our lives, which may contribute towards the
project of understanding women's psychology.   The first feature is that
there are close similarities in the skills that we use in what is
classified as 'work' (that is, caring for clients), and in 'private
life' (that is, caring for our families and each other).   The second
noticeable feature is that there are close similarities in the
difficulties being faced by the consumers of our skills, that is, our
clients, and those being faced at one time or another, by ourselves.
Much conventional psychology is based on an explicit rejection of
reflexivity, hence a perception of this similarity is not normally
encouraged.   The second part of this chapter therefore explores the
nature of these similarities, and the consequences of them for the
therapist.

2   ORIGINS OF FEMINIST PSYCHOTHERAPY

Much research, in the last two decades, concerning women and mental
health has been based within the confines of a number of different and
exclusive disciplines. Hence sociologists have drawn attention to the
impact of social structures on women (e.g. Brown and Harris, 1978);
psychologists have looked at the effects of sex role stereotyping
(e.g. O'Neill, 1981; Bem, 1974); social anthropologists have drawn
attention to the significance of cultural symbols for marking various
aspects of gender (e.g. Ardener, 1981); biologists have looked at the
interaction between psychological and cultural influences on gender
(e.g. Money and Erhardt, 1972). Within feminism, women writers have
detailed the distorting process of discrimination and prejudice against
women in present day society and throughout history (e.g. de Beauvoire,
1949; Rowbotham, 1964). Most of these studies have, however, been
carried out in ignorance of the implication of the other studies; there
has been some work which examines the process by which the social
structures, stereotyping and discrimination are handed on from parents
to children, but little on the process by which the individual woman
actually feels and experiences the legitimacy of those structures or
limitations. A theory is needed which accepts the insights of a
politically aware or 'feminist' sociology, and at the same time works
with the individual woman as the unit of consciousness which is aware
of and is actively participating in creating her own life. Such a
theory has to reject the notion that people are simply 'determined' by
their society, but equally, cannot accept the idea that a person
becomes a person in a social and interpersonal vacuum.

Feminist psychotherapy has its roots in three specific spheres of
study. Firstly, it is based in the women's liberation movement, which
has always insisted that the 'personal is political'; secondly, it
draws on gender identity research suggesting that biology and culture
must be considered as separate (although interacting) determinants of
gender; and thirdly, in Britain at least, in the object relations
school of psychoanalysis as developed by Fairbairn (1952) and Guntrip
(1961, 1968), building on the work of Melanie Klein (1937). In this
sense, feminist psychotherapy is a developmentally based politically
aware theory (see Eichenbaum and Orbach, 1982). Feminist psychotherapists insist that the theory in materialist, in that it sees the
relationships in which the child is involved as being 'real' rather
than fantasy-based; and feminist, in that it sees the mother's own
psychology within patriarchal society as being crucial in any understanding of the mother/child relationship, and hence of the psychology
of the developing individual.

It should perhaps be noted at this point that in recent years, a
number of women therapists or psychologists have developed methods of
helping women or thinking about womens' psychology which do not draw
so heavily on object relations theory; these include the feminist
therapy groups which have developed throughout the UK and the USA, as
detailed by Ernst and Goodison (1981) and Gilbert (1980). Also, some
have pursued the insights of psychoanalysis in understanding the
longevity and prevalence of patriarchy, for example, Coward (1979),
who has used the work of Lacan to examine the significance of the

phallus in culture, and Mitchell (1974) who attempted to redefine
Freudian theories within a feminist perspective. We do not discuss
these approaches in such depth in this chapter because we have not
found them as rich in explanatory value as feminist psychotherapy,
although they undoubtedly contributed much to the development of the
theory.

Nor do we think that feminist psychotherapy is likely either to
degenerate into a mimicry of the so called 'growth' movement (see
Llewelyn, 1982), or to develop the exclusivity of psychoanalysis, cut
off from social awareness.

3   ASSUMPTIONS OF FEMINIST PSYCHOTHERAPY

In attempting to understand the psychology of women, three basic
assumptions about the social world can be made, which have enormous
influence on woman's experience. The first is that women are, by and
large, in a position of deference with regard to men, occupying
positions of lower status and with less overt access to power than do
men. In the USA, for example, 'although women comprise 39 per cent of
the labour force, less than 5 per cent of those earning more than
$10,000 per year are women' (Turkel, 1980). That ultimate authority
is presumed to rest with the male is recognised in law as well as
custom. Desire for overt power is presumed to be primarily masculine,
and the right of access to power by the male has been enshrined in the
laws of thousands of cultures for thousands of years. Female power
has been seen to lie primarily within the emotional sphere, which has
been separated off as somehow unpredictable, unstable, dangerous, and
from a 'male' point of view, unimportant. We would suggest that women
have never considered the emotional to be unimportant, and have, of
necessity, developed skills in this area as an alternative form of
power, which may them come to be seen as manipulative or covert.
Jean Baker Miller (1978) points out that a group with low status can
only maintain some degree of control over what happens to it by
learning how to interpret, manipulate and persuade the powerful, or to
corner off some area as it's own speciality. In this connection, it is
interesting to note that women do have superior skills in decoding non-
verbal signals (Hall, 1978), suggesting a greater degree of sensitivity
to emotionally laden communication. Thus women, as a subordinate group,
have had to learn the skills of manipulation and emotional responsiveness to the needs of others in order to maintain some form of self
determination (Chodrow, 1978). A consequence of this is passivity, an
increased ability on the part of the woman to be aware of the feelings
and needs of others, and yet a feeling that her own needs are somehow
wrong, and not to be considered (Dinnerstein, 1978). For a woman to
take overt power in any situation risks loss of femininity (Turkel,
1980); she is seen as castrating, demanding or aggressive where a man
is seen as assertive and admirable. A woman is, on the whole, most
valued as a woman when she is caring, loving, and self sacrificing.
Consequently, many women come to experience their needs as overwhelming,
bad and manipulative, and their own power as frightening (Moulton,
1977).

The second assumption of feminist psychotherapy is that women are, by and large, required by society to be 'connected' to men, so that the achievement of psychological and social autonomy is very problematic. Despite evidence to the contrary (Gigy, 1980) it is often assumed that the single woman is only single because she could not 'catch a man' and must therefore be pitied. This lack of self confidence in the woman is paralleled by a lack of confidence by the rest of society in her. Consequently, many women report that they do not 'feel' right if the single status is forced upon them, for example by divorce or widowhood; in addition they may lack the social and psychological resilience to cope with the feelings of abandonment or loss. In many societies women are severely restricted in their movements when unaccompanied by men (Ardener, 1981), and in most societies, woman's marital status defines her title, name and sexual availability. Undoubtedly there are problems for single men in a largely monogamous culture; however the economic and personal penalties are not likely to be as strictly enforced. Hence the psychological sense of 'oddity' is likely to be less for men.

The third assumption is that the issue of sexuality is immensely difficult for women. The achievement of a healthy enjoyment of the body is not easy for either sex, but in a society which values virginity in women, while characterising many sexual women as prostitutes, whores, easy lays and the like, it is understandable if women have mixed feelings about becoming sexually active. The use of the female body to sell goods in advertising, and the growth of pornography may further alienate the woman from her sexuality as she compares her own body (fat, spotty, wrinkled and human) to the perfect image on the screen or advertisement. However, it is noticeable that the increasing demand by woman for control over their bodies (through abortion and contraception for example) and for participation in sexual activities, is associated with an increased degree of impotence in the male (Moulton, 1977); it is almost as if in some cases, male sexual potency is dependent on female 'impotence'.

These three assumptions (of overt powerlessness coupled with the need for emotional sensitivity, of the need for connectedness, and of the problematic nature of sexuality) are basic to an understanding of the content of women's psychology in this particular historical epoch; it is not assumed that these tendencies in men and women are inevitable, fixed or genetically 'wired in'. They occur because of the nature of the society in which each child is brought up, and their apparent inevitability occurs because of their centrality to the developing child's personality. In a different social context with different mother/child interactions, the psychic structure might well be different.

It is, however, in the mother/child relationship that all the above assumptions are initially made, and hence, structured into the developing personality. Differential handling of the sexes reinforced throughout life by social structures, gives substance to an individual's identity as male or female. It goes without saying that boys, too, are subject to systematic restrictions in their development; in this sense feminist psychotherapy could have an enormous impact on

our view of male psychology. O'Neill (1981) for example, has detailed
the considerable implications of sexism for men, with regard to the
pressures, conflicts and limitations which the sex role entails.

4   THEORETICAL BACKGROUND OF FEMINIST PSYCHOTHERAPY

Many women therapists, who were bringing to their work situation their
feminism, were searching in the early days of feminist therapy for a
theoretical and practical orientation that reflected the depth and
extent of the emotional experiences women were talking about in their
consciousness-raising and self-help groups, and in their counselling
sessions. Again, and again, women described the conflictual nature of
their personal relationships, with partners, children and parents. It
became apparent that the psychodynamic aspects of women's emotional
lives required a careful and detailed analysis, in the context of the
reality of women's political and economic position in society.

Although critical of many lingering sexist assumptions, feminist
therapists in the UK have developed and extended the object relations
approach to therapy, as being the most fruitful in developing an understanding of women's emotional distress within patriarchal society.

Object relations theory gave the first truly psychological account of
human development,focussing on the salience of personal relationships.
All other work, before that of Fairbairn (1952), retained the biological
determinism which was central to the instinct theory of Freudian
psychology. For Freud and his followers (e.g. Jones, 1954), emotional
development depended upon the unfolding of innate psychological
processes in the context of life events. In a revolutionary way,
Fairbairn stressed the urgency of personal relationships to physical
and emotional development, thus stating the primacy of psychological
factors, in human beings, who according to Fairbairn are born with the
potential ability to form relationships with others.

Early in development, the infant's relationship with others is
governed by their responsiveness to her needs to be physically and
emotionally nourished. One of the main foci of the quality of such
centres around feeding, which explains why Klein(1937) in her
observations of infants found that many of their fantasies and conflicts
were concerned with 'taking in' the nourishment that was offered by
others. Significantly in our culture this involves what is offered by
the mother, since women are still primarily expected to fulfill this
role. The mother's anxiety or conflict concerning mothering, which
can occur for a variety of reasons, are then experienced by the child,
and according to Klein, may give rise to strong emotions which are both
loving and hating. The baby, Klein said, reacts to unpleasant stimuli
and to the frustration of pleasurable events with angry feelings which
are projected onto the mother herself, and are thus experienced by the
child as coming from the mother. This arouses anxiety in the child,
who finds it difficult to have such angry feelings coming from the
mother, since, as we will show later, motherhood tends to produce a
conflict of emotions for women.

Fairbairn (1952) saw that we are all liable to this cycle of reactions to emotional frustration which originated in the child coming to feel both that she is not really loved for herself, and that her own love is not valued and accepted. The child in this position may therefore come to feel that loving relationships with others are precarious, defensively split off and hide much of her own love and keep it inside rather than showing it. The extent to which an individual develops an integrated self, or ego, which is relatively intact rather than split, depends on the adequacy of interpersonal experiences from these early interactions onwards. To the degree that these relationships were, as Winnicott (1965) described, 'good-enough', the child can mature through stages of transitional dependence into an adult capable of leading an autonomous life where she is separate from yet able to have loving relationships with others. The goal of development as described by Fairbairn, is mature dependence, where the fully adult person can live without being dependent on others, and yet can enjoy intimacy with others without the fear of being suffocated or abandoned by them. A therapy based on such object-relations theory, as we will describe it later, reproduces the behaviour of the good-enough parent for the infant, and this gradual passage towards mature dependence is the goal of the therapy relationship (Guntrip, 1968).

5   THE MOTHER-DAUGHTER RELATIONSHIP

Inevitably, the demands of parenting, even if only to be minimally good-enough, stretch the resources of many of us. Children are conceived from a range of motives and for many women the perpetuation of male power over the availability of contraception and abortion facilities limits the extent of their control over their own reproduction. For many women, the desire to produce a tiny baby of their own may stem from the belief that at last they will have one human being who will thoroughly love them. For others, a pregnancy means enduring an invasion from a foreign body, or simply an extra mouth to feed, signifying economic hardship. Although conventionally, object-relations theories have argued that conflicts for mothers abound irrespective of the sex of their baby, Chodrow (1978) has shown how different the relationship can be for mothers between sons and daughters. There is already well documented evidence showing behaviourally how differently boy babies are treated from their sisters (Katz, 1979); what feminist therapists have found in listening to women are the powerful identifications complicating the relationship between mothers and their daughters. Whilst recognising that they have a little girl-child who they want to protect from the pains of the outside world, just as they themselves would have liked to have been protected, women also experience their daughters' needs as being overwhelming, wishing instead that in some sense their little girls could look after them. Daughters are therefore often both over-protected, for example, their sexuality denied, or their exploration of the world hampered, and at the same time at another level their emotional needs to be loved and cared for in themselves are not fulfilled. Hence the beginnings of women's psychology that we have already described: from an early age women learn their role as nurturers in taking care of their mothers, while at the same time their conflicts over dependence and independence begin.

   Chodrow (1978) argues that as long as women are primarily responsible
for child-care this dynamic will continue. She looks optimistically
towards a time when men will become more involved in the day-to-day
parenting, thus diffusing this powerful dynamic and allowing both boy
and girl children more realistic relationships with their mothers and
their currently absent fathers. So long as children have to rely
solely on their mothers for emotional and physical nourishment, boys
will always harbour deep resentments about women not being good-enough,
blaming and yet idolising their mothers for their bad and good
experiences (Dinnerstein, 1978). Similarly, girls, who are expected in
a heterosexual world finally to give up their mothers and transfer
their love and affection to men, will continue to resent and mistrust
women, competing with others for male attention and always feeling a
lingering responsibility for their mothers.

6   PRESENTING SYMPTOMS

The theoretical formulation of feminist psychotherapy suggest that
certain issues are likely to be problematic for women in patriarchal
society. These include firstly, assertion and the expression of needs;
secondly, autonomy and dependence; and thirdly, sexuality and body
image. This indeed is what is commonly found in clinical practice.
A number of issues will now be discussed in the light of the feminist
psychotherapeutic analysis as described above. This will, of course,
not be a comprehensive discussion of all presenting symptoms commonly
seen.

(a)   Hysteria

One particularly 'feminine' diagnosis is that of hysteria (Warner, 1979).
This is generally understood to result from an inability to express
real feelings or desires, such that a manipulative or dramatic
deception is presented to the world and to the self. Chodoff (1978)
notes the characteristics of hysteria to include emotional storms,
attention seeking and sexually seductive behaviour which tends to be
superficial rather than erotic, and a 'performing' presentation which,
he suggests, betrays a lack of self: 'a self image of inauthenticity
rather than one of integrity ... submissiveness and eagerness to please
in reciprocal relationship with a kind of ruthless wilfulness' (p. 499).
This description in many ways represents what Chodoff calls 'a
caricature of femininity' in which the expression of needs in a
straightforward way is not possible. It seems that the woman, feeling
ill at ease with her ability to 'own' her own needs and feelings,
tries to use a number of self-deceptive and manipulatory ways of
making sense out of her experiences, and of getting what she wants.
Tragically, she is often then misunderstood, and misunderstands herself.
Khan (1975) argues that women with hysterical symptoms typically
attempt to deal with emotional needs through sexual involvement, which
is bound to fail since sexual gratification was not actually the aim.
Inviting a sexual response, the woman then feels grossly misunderstood

when her seduction is taken at face value; yet if she does not receive
a response her sense of self is threatened. Within patriarchal society
the 'hysterical' path is only too available to young women who do
receive some gratification from their attractiveness. The hollowness
of some of this gratification can, however, subsequently prove very
distressing, and this distress is often manifested by a number of
puzzling symptoms and a sense of 'grudge' which may confuse both the
woman and her therapist.

(b)   Agoraphobia

While there may be a number of factors involved in the genesis of agoraphobia, one factor to which feminist psychotherapy calls attention is
that is a conflict over autonomy. Just as hysteria allows avoidance of
open expression of wishes and needs, so agoraphobic symptoms temporarily
'solve' a conflict over independence and dependence by the 'substitution'
of a phobic problem. Symonds (1971) notes the frequency of onset of
agoraphobia after marriage, especially but not only when there are
marital difficulties. She suggests that phobias after marriage are a
'declaration of dependence'. A need to restrict activity away from the
home may mean that the woman does not have to struggle between her
desire for independence and her newly married responsibilities. A
client seen by one of us, who got married for the first time at the age
of 48, to an older man, began shortly after her marriage to experience
panic attacks when visiting the local town, and progressively became
unable to leave her new home. She had previously been used to
considerable independence and had enjoyed many driving holidays abroad.

    Although therapy was initially successful, it was terminated at her
husband's request, since he disapproved of her need to attend therapy
sessions at the local hospital, claiming that it caused her unacceptable
distress. It seems that she was willing to accept his ruling on this,
rather than challenge the basis of the marriage. This seems to be a
relatively common finding. Milton and Hafner (1979) note the
frequency of relapse after initial improvements, which seems to relate
to marital conflict.

(c)   Identity problems and depression

A number of different symptoms, such as depression and poor self-esteem,
seem to relate to a conflict over autonomy, dependence and identity.
Because of the problems involved in adequate separation from the mother,
and autonomy, as noted above, a woman may have difficulty knowing
exactly where the boundaries are between herself and the other. Such
difficulties occur especially at points of transition, when a woman is
having to adapt to new social demands, and are exacerbated if her
resources are too firmly rooted in a limited 'feminine' sex-role (see
Block et al., 1973; Spence, 1979 and others, for evidence concerning
the paucity of adaptive resources available in the feminine response to
stress). Hence, if changes in life situation result in too great a
demand being placed on an ego which is not sufficiently resilient or
individuated, the response by the woman is, obviously, psychological

distress. We shall now examine some of these transition points in more detail.

Having failed to achieve adequate separation many new mothers themselves experience difficulty in distinguishing between their own needs and those of their children. Hence crises often occur after the birth of children (Wilson, 1979), or, alternatively, departure from home (Bart, 1971). On both these occasions, the woman may experience anxiety about her adequacy as a person presented either directly, or more typically through depression and poor self-esteem. On occasion the self-doubt may be shown through obsessions, which can be seen as an attempt to retain some form of control on boundaries. In all these cases, the woman's underlying sense of self is deficient, and inter-personal relationships consequently deteriorate.

The suggestion that the woman attempt to regain some more adequate sense of self by returning to work and developing a career has been welcomed by the feminist movement, and may on many occasions indeed be of considerable help (Weissman and Paykel, 1974; Cochrane and Stoeps-Roe, 1981). However, additional problems do sometimes result. Moulton (1979) describes the ambivalence that career women may feel over motherhood, and the high degree of conflict that some women experience in having to make choices between home and family. Mogul (1979) notes that women in mid-life who are returning to work frequently experience difficulties in facing issues such as dealing with authority and ambition, which have previously been avoided by concentrating on motherhood. In all these cases a woman may find herself struggling with her own fears about her duties, role, dependency needs and autonomy, as well as the social sanctions that may overtly or covertly be placed on her as a working mother. This in combination with the exhaustion resulting from her 'dual' career, can sometimes provide too much of a strain on her resources, with a resulting sense of failure, poor self-esteem and depression.

A last area where identity problems may arise through a transitional stage is on widowhood or divorce. If the woman's sense of value as a person has been dependent on her social and economic position as determined by a partner, she will on widowhood or divorce, need to re-establish herself in her own right. Possibly she no longer possesses the skills necessary for independent living, or cannot consider herself worth the effort. If the marital relationship has been primarily one of dependence, the difficulties associated with inadequate individuation will be raised again. The problems are worsened if the woman has few friends, which is likely if her view of woman is that they are, like mother, not to be trusted or relied on. Again, low self-esteem leading to depression is a likely outcome.

(d)   Body-related symptoms

The alienation which may women experience from their bodies is reflected in the number of symptoms which concern ambivalence about the body. Many of these symptoms centre on physical appearance, sexual or food-related issues; indeed it is sometimes difficult to separate them in the genesis of any one particular symptom.

Only a few such symptoms can be mentioned which illustrate the ambivalence over sexuality and ingestion. Although there are some men with similar symptoms, anorexia is primarily a female disorder and is normally seen as relating to a profound dread of female adulthood (Bruch, 1973). Macleod, in an account of her anorexia, described how anorexia symptoms simultaneously allowed her a systematic denial of what she construed as womanhood, creativity and productivity and at the same time, satisfied her desperate need to be in control of something (Macleod, 1981). Most women do not, of course, develop anorexic symptoms; nevertheless a preoocupation with the adequacy of and need to control the body size of shape is so widespread amongst women as to be almost universal. Orbach suggests that weight disorders are an expression of a woman's discomfort with the patriarchal world in which she lives, especially with regard to sexual issues (Orbach, 1978). Certainly, in a therapy group which one of us has been running for women with compulsive eating problems, the prospect of losing weight was contemplated with some dread because of the opportunities the group members then perceived for promiscuity.

We would like to suggest that, in many instances, these symptoms seem to represent the woman's ambivalence about control over boundaries, in that they involve conflict over 'taking in', i.e. either ingestion of food or sexual penetration. Needs are not experienced as 'normal', but rather as excessive; or else, are denied completely. The emotional conflict over boundaries and needs may well become conflated with social pressures, so that the woman's body becomes a battleground for competing physiological, social and emotional influences from intra-psychic forces, as well as from social forces. The need to be the 'right' shape, or to respond in the 'right' way to the 'right' sort of male (given heterosexual society) means that having control over these needs may become more important than the needs themselves. This can apply to both sexuality and eating. Control of sexuality may, for example, become more important than its enjoyment. It is then hardly surprising that the difficulties than women present with concerning sexual behaviour tend to centre on an 'inability to let go', or an inability to enjoy sex, experiencing themselves as really being there in an active way, rather than as an outsider observing what someone is doing to them. It is also noticeable that for many women who eat or diet compulsively, or become anorexic, the enjoyment of the taste of food becomes secondary to the number of calories consumed and the sense of gaining or losing control.

Looking very briefly specifically at sexual problems, a considerable amount of work has been done by feminist psychotherapists (for example, Ernst and Goodison, 1981) in rediscovering for women their own sexuality, by shifting the focus of inquiry away from the penile penetration as the ultimate aim and expression of sexual love. Anorgasmia, and disappointing sexual feelings, are in our experience widespread and chronic problems, which often remain undisclosed. Clearly such difficulties have enormous implications for a woman's self-image, and her relationship with her spouse or lover. An adequate understanding of such difficulties can only be reached if the social context in which they occur is also understood.

7   ADDITIONAL ISSUES EFFECTING WOMEN: POWERLESS NESS AND VIOLENCE

The nature of relationships between men and women in patriarchy can be
seen to affect women's psychological health particularly in the
expression of anger, violence and sexuality, and in the way that men
can use their power to enforce their assumed control. It has been
shown above how men's fear and resentment of women can be understood
within the context of mother-rearing. Chesler (1980) has re-examined
the important implication of men's envy of women's child-rearing, life-
giving functions as fuelling the frequency of male violence against
women, although this, she claims, has its source in men's anger against
other men. Women, being easier targets, act as absorbers of male
violence.

Therapists working with women clients need to be aware of the
frequency of the threat and actual occurence of violent experience in
women's contact with men. For example, 25 per cent of all reported
violent crime is wife assault, which is undoubtedly a low estimate if
the amount of unreported crime is considered (Bristol Women's Studies
Group, 1979). For many years now women have worked together on a
self-help basis to provide refuge and support for those women and their
children who need to escape from violent men they have been living with.
Similarly, rape crisis centres have been set up to counsel those women
who experience sexual abuse and harassment. Research on sexual
violence challenges existing myths about rape (Osborne, in press). For
example, rapes are seldom explosive events as might be expected from
the prevailing ethos of uncontrollable male sexual urges, in that
generally three-quarters of all rapes are planned, especially group
rapes. Similarly, rape is not a crime conducted in a dark alley by a
complete stranger; in almost half of the cases studied, the victim and
offender were acquaintances, neighbours or members of the same family,
and the rape was often in the home of the raped woman or her attacker.
In many rape attacks, far more force is used than is necessary for the
act of penetration. A feminist analysis argues that rape is
essentially an extreme form of violence towards women, rather than an
act of sexuality (Brownmiller, 1975). Yet still the prevailing
attitude among professionals and lay people involved is that the woman
must have 'asked for it'. Rapists are more likely to avoid conviction
if the woman was found to be dressed in a manner considered to be
provocative or to have behaved in ways not suitable to feminine
stereotypes. The expression of such opinion by both family and public
can enhance the woman's feelings of guilt and self-punishment, making
both short-term crisis counselling and longer-term therapy more
difficult. The psychological results tend to leave the woman
temporarily, if not permanently, more dependent on others and may
augment her feelings of being cut off from having a trusting, loving
relationship. Typically she may show the symptoms of such increased
dependency, such as feeling agoraphobic, unsure of her sexuality and
out of touch with her own body.

One final example of the expression of the power balance between men

and women in families is in the frequency of incest. Once again it is
usually young women and girl children who are the targets of
incestuous relationships with their father, brother and uncles (Summit
and Kryso, 1978). Incest, more than many other such situations, can
involve immature and dependent young women in relationships which
exploit their vulnerability and powerlessness at a time when their
images of their sexuality are still developing. As with the married
woman who is being battered, escaping from a person on whom one is
financially, socially and emotionally dependent is a difficult task.

Yet rarely in the therapeutic literature is there a clear critique
of the effects of the violence of men's relationships with women and
the frequency of these experiences for women seeking therapy. Few
therapists are specifically trained to deal either with crisis-
counselling in such situations, or the extent to which women's self-
blame leads them to hide such experiences even from their own therapist.
More strikingly, when women turn to professional therapists for help
they may find that their domination is perpetuated. As we have found
in our support work with self-help groups formed to assist women who
are the victims of male violence, previous experiences of medical and
psychiatric care make many women suspicious even of feminist therapists.

8   THE THERAPEUTIC RELATIONSHIP

A woman may present for therapy with any of the issues or symptoms
noted above, but she will also present her resolution of the inter-
personal and intrapersonal questions faced by all women. The therapy
relationship ideally provides an arena in which her symptoms and the
adequacy of her resolution can be examined, with a therapist who is
either aware of such issues, or is prepared to learn about them.
Unfortunately not all therapists are able to examine issues in a way
which respects the social situation of women, or allows a woman to
think critically about dependence, independence, assertion, autonomy
and other tricky areas.

There is evidence for example, that sexism is prevalent in psychotherapy, so that sex-stereotyped patterns of interaction between
therapist and client are encourage (Chesler, 1974), or that sex-typed
standards of mental health are advocated (Broverman et al., 1970;
Whitley, 1979). The American Psychological Association's Task Force
on sex bias and sex-role stereotyping in psychotherapeutic practice
(Brodsky and Holyroyd, 1975) documented sex bias in the encouragement
of traditional sex-roles, sexist use of psychoanalytic concepts, and
the treatment of women as sex-objects. The sexual mis-use of women by
their doctors is appallingly widespread (Holyroyd and Brodsky, 1977);
Burgess, 1981), and places women in a particularly difficult position,
not dissimilar to that of the incest victim. In this situation, it is
not very easy for a woman critically to examine her sexuality or
feelings about her sex-role.

Turning now to the details of the therapeutic relationship itself,
we consider that there are two important aspects of the therapist's
work; firstly to get behind the presenting symptoms and to help the

the woman to examine her current attempts to resolve conflicts; secondly and at the same time to offer the building blocks of a caring relationship. Inevitably, in the light of previous failures, this offer can be perceived as being very threatening for a woman in distress, and the therapist has to be sensitive to the defensive boundaries used by the woman to shield her from what might be too frightening. Intermingled with feelings of distrust and unworthiness are frequent expressions of relief that there is someone who apparently does care. In the early stages of feminist psychotherapy women clients often express relief that they are talking to another woman and may find it easier to trust the therapist because of this especially since some similar values are assumed about women's position in society and the nature of women's roles. Yet later this may be more problematic as the woman may fear overburdening the therapist due to her desire to take care of the therapist just as she takes care of everyone else; conversely she may feel competitive with the therapist and resent the difference in their two positions.

If a successful therapeutic alliance is formed and the woman is able to let herself feel emotionally cared for by her therapist, much of the nurturing 'repair work' can be done, both within the exploration and reviewing of previous relationship experiences, and in the giving and receiving within the new relationship with the therapist. Here the therapist as a woman herself can acknowledge the same process of socialisation and the nature of women's oppression. There are therefore both transference and real aspects of the therapist-client interaction, both of which need to be acknowledged and allowed for. At this stage the woman may experience strong dependency upon her therapist, which may be extremely exhausting for the therapist herself to bear. One of the most painful aspects for the client at this stage, however, is the nature of the power relationship in that the woman needs the therapist, but the therapist does not have the same need for the client. This is not, therefore, an egalitarian relationship as the therapist is required to bring her integrated adult self into the room, not her vulnerability.

The aim of the therapy relationship is that the woman is able to internalise the nurturance, give up some of her dependency on the therapist and be capable of making other new relationships which are maturely based and not formed from old patterns of clinging and rejecting. This inevitably takes a varying length of time, depending on the client. Such an approach can be profitably made use of by some clients within a relatively short space of time; for others a lengthy period of contact is needed. The timing of the termination of the therapy is perhaps the most difficult aspect of the whole process. Many women may feel that they ought to go prematurely, due to their concern not to wear the therapist out; such women may need to be encouraged to stay and to examine their fantasies about how much they can lean on other women. Other women may fear leaving their therapist and either produce new symptoms or start to rework old material.

As in any form of therapeutic contact, the transference aspects of the relationship interact with the real relationship being offered. Both of these elements pose particular problems for .a feminist

therapist. The parenting dimensions of what she offers will often
elicit powerful feelings in the client, so that at times she will feel
unable to cope in her world without the therapist being 'on tap', or
alternatively she may feel that however much the therapist gives her,
it cannot possibly be enough, perceiving rejection in every nuance of
the therapy contact. It is at these times in particular that the
therapist has to be very clear about setting boundaries. In our
experience these issues are particularly heightened with lesbian clients
who may eroticise their transference feelings and have difficulty in
accepting the limitations of the therapeutic contact. Feminist psychotherapy would argue against the classical interpretations of this being
merely a transference neurosis, instead acknowledging the reality of
women's love for each other, but working hard to clarify the difference
between what a therapist has to offer compared with what a lover
relationship brings. Eroticised feelings have been particularly
difficult to manage in very regressed women, who may well benefit from,
and indeed only be able to feel safe with, a therapy who can physically
hold them in a secure way (Balint, 1965). For most clients, however,
the containment of what the therapist is emotionally offering (Guntrip,
1971) produces sufficient security for the relationship to develop and
the psychological work to be done.

9   WOMEN AS THERAPISTS

In this last section we intend to turn the analysis developed throughout
this chapter upon ourselves as therapists, to see whether such an
analysis can assist us in understanding our own difficulties and
dilemmas as therapists. It is perhaps a commonplace that therapists
become therapists because of particular constellations of personal
characteristics and unresolved questions; Guntrip (1975) reports
Fairbairn as remarking 'I can't think what could motivate any of us to
become psychotherapists if we hadn't got problems of our own'. As
feminist psychotherapists we are trying to understand those 'problems',
not merely because we do not wish to impose them on our clients
(although this is important), but also because we recognise that we,
like our clients, are women with unfulfilled needs, and in understanding their genesis we may become wiser therapists and happier
women.

    A person who devotes a considerable amount of time to listening to
and trying to understand another is likely to be one who has recognised
the importance of feelings, both unexpressed and expressed, in
personal relationships. As has been suggested earlier, this
sensitivity to and caring for others is likely to be a particularly
'feminine' characteristic, although it is by no means peculiar to
women. Such caring is also demanded in relationships within the family,
and between friends. Thus a woman therapist may find that she is
doing a very similar job at work and at home. Being an emotional
resource for others in too many spheres can lead the women to a neglect
of her own needs for care and space. This is confounded by the woman
therapist's own psychology as a woman. As has been suggested above,
it is not easy for women to accept and state their own desire for
dependency; equally, it may be difficult for the woman therapist to

assert herself in other ways, and to feel happy about exerting her
autonomy and authority, for example in setting limits to the amount she
is able or prepared to give. Both these aspects of women's psychology
may cause problems for the woman as a person and as a therapist, and
are additionally complicated by the issue of identification with the
client. On the one hand, the woman therapist has feelings and needs,
which must be faced and accepted so that they are not imposed on the
client, but on the other hand, being a woman in patriarchal society,
the chances are that the therapist has herself experienced many of the
issues also being faced by the client. Because feminist psychotherapy
is based on a materialistic analysis of psychological distress, the
therapist cannot construe the client's problems as projections or mere
distortions, but rather tries to accept the problems as reality based,
and as such accepts that such problems are as potentially distressing
to the therapist. But she must avoid the risks of imposing her
solutions onto the client; as Kenworth (1979) and Lerner (1978) point
out, the androgynous ideal is not workable for all women in all
situations no matter how useful it may seem to the therapist herself.
The therapist has therefore to avoid seeking 'validation' for her own
attempts to deal with emotionally difficult situations either
vicariously through her clients' lives, or through destructive,
exploitative relationships with her clients.

    The stereotypically feminine ability to sense others' unexpressed
desires and confusions is of course a vital part of therapy. It does,
however, 'cost' the therapist in emotional terms. Closeness to
emotional trauma is distressing, and the therapist who identified too
clearly with the client will become overwhelmed by distress. But, to
be an effective therapist it is also necessary to use skills beyond
the traditional 'feminine' skills of empathy, that is, the skill of
setting limits, clarifying objectives, and the acceptance of a degree
of authority. Kaplan, in her exploration of sex-role related issues
in the therapeutic relationship comments (1979, p. 114):
    Consider the task facing the female therapist. Her challenge is
    to accept the legitimate authority of her role as therapist in
    the face of cultural pressures to be deferential, and to integrate
    that stance with expressions of warmth and empathy without letting
    the latter feeling predominate as she has generally been encouraged
    to do.
Failure to develop both aspects of the therapeutic task limits the
effectiveness of the therapist, as of any woman. Kaplan points out
that uneasiness with authority may lead the therapist either to
develop a nurturant or protectively maternal role with her clients,
or to tolerate abuse of the therapeutic relationship herself can
become exhausted, invaded and undermined. In addition, there may be
pressures on the therapist to change what she knows to be important
guidelines for therapeutic practice. This is a crucial area, since
an incompetent therapist, even if she shares the same values, is no
more desirable than an incompetent doctor or lawyer who happened to be
a feminist. However, as we know from American research, women who
seek out feminist therapy are more likely to be feminists themselves
or to hold radical opinions (Maracek et al., 1979). Thus, if the
feminist therapist is active more generally in the women's movement,
as we would argue she should be if her therapy is to be a part of more

general societal change, she may risk contact with her clients in social
situations which allow her no privacy and inevitably cause conflict for
the client. This may cause the therapist to feel she has to restrict
her other activities and lead to her increased isolation.

Because of the probable identification with the client, the emotional
demandingness of close therapeutic contact, hesitancy in assertion, and
the need to avoid dependency on the client, support for the woman
therapist herself is vital. She needs this support to deal with the
paradox that being a therapist means acting out in force a feminine
role, caring for others, and denying her own needs at least during
working hours (and frequently when the phone rings at night). Her task
is to help other people to get what is best for them, which is women's
role once again. However, such support is not always available, for
two main reasons. Firstly, the woman, in respecting the limits of
others, may not feel too happy about asking for support, and secondly,
she may not know where or from whom to obtain it. Moulton (1977)
comments 'many women who can earn their own living, have a professional
identity of their own and could be 'free agents' have great difficulty
in doing so. They have too much anxiety about being 'feminine' due to
cultural and psychological pressures, and need much reassurance from
men' (p. 83). She suggests that successful professional women often
have unexpressed dependency needs, which their partners may discourage
them from expressing because of their own need for care. In addition,
a woman therapist may have a partner who finds her emotional commitment
to others too demanding on her attention; he or she may become, in a
sense, jealous of her clients.

None the less, emotional support from a partner, friend or lover can
of course be of tremendous value. But recognising the impossibility of
any one relationship being sufficient to meet all of anyone's needs,
some women have developed ways of obtaining support from other women
therapists. In this way, therapists can build into their lives some
taking as well as giving. Dunbar et al. (1979) describe the women's
group that they have established, which they suggest helps women
members deal with particular areas of stress, which include (a) dealing
with competition, (b) acceptance of personal dependency needs, and
(c) integration of identities as women and as professionals. In the
UK, too, many therapists are getting together to form feminist
psychotherapy support groups (Osborne, 1982). Most women professionals
know the pressure they feel under to succeed at everything they do,
which includes the 'traditional role' of women; as Dunbar expressed
it 'all had tried at various times to be superwives, supermothers,
superlovers, gourmet cooks and knockouts' (p. 44). There is
considerable evidence in the psychiatric field (e.g. Soloman, 1979),
that it is harder for a woman professional to be taken seriously than
for a man, hence she must strive even harder to succeed, and is even
more likely to experience these pressures. Thus she is in even greater
need for support, at the same time as being seen as the emotional
resource for others.

However, the achievement of personal support networks cannot be the
only way forward for dealing constructively with women therapists'
difficulties. Women therapists do not exist in a political or social

vacuum, anymore than their clients do. Contact with groups that are
actively seeking to promote social change can, in itself, be a
liberating experience. The lessons learned from the women's liberation
movement, that sharing the experience of oppression is the first step
towards resisting it, has been a useful one for many feminist psychotherapists who have maintained their links with various women's groups
and political groups. As noted above, however, this can itself pose
problems to the feminist psychotherapist who may have to attempt to
draw support from a group which also contains her clients. None the
less, whatever form it takes, feminist therapists would argue that
through their own personal development they have learnt a great deal
about relationship needs, and whether or not they are in couple
relationships, they place high value on their contact with other women.

10   SUMMARY

Feminist psychotherapy has provided the beginnings of an analysis of
psychological development in the context of a patriarchal culture.
It acknowledged the importance of that culture in shaping the conscious
and unconscious needs of men and women, and the way in which society
prescribed roles and behaviour which are gender-differentiated. In
stressing the importance of early relationship experiences in the
formation of adult people, feminist psychotherapists have observed the
centrality of the mother-daughter relationship in a society where
children are predominantly mother-reared. Young women internalise the
social requirements of femininity and are particularly vulnerable to
various forms of male oppression; at its extreme form expressed through
rape and incest. Because it is expected that they should be attractive
to please their menfolk, women frequently express their emotional
distress through symptoms concerning their appearance and the
repercussions of their dependence.

Therapists, whether male or female, need to examine the nature of
their own analysis of women's psychology and women's social role. In
particular, in a mother-rearing society, they need to be clear about
the residual power of the nature of their own primary relationships
with their mothers, and the effects this has on their relationships
with women. Most particularly for women therapists, as we have learnt
ourselves, the model we use to understand our clients' distress is
also applicable to our own development. In utilising the nurturant
aspects of women's psychology in a professional role, we as therapists
also need to be 'good-enough' to ourselves.

REFERENCES

ARDENER, S. (ed.) (1981), 'Women and Space', Croom Helm, London.
BAKER MILLER, J. (1978), 'Towards a New Psychology of Women', Penguin,
Harmondsworth.
BALINT, M. (1965), 'Primary Love and Psychoanalytic Technique', London,
Tavistock.
BART, P.B. (1971), Depression in middle aged women, in V. Gornick and
B.K. Moran, (eds), 'Women in Sexist Society', New York, Basic Books.

BEM, S. (1974), The measurement of psychological androgeny, 'Journal of Consulting and Clinical Psychology', 42, 155-62.
BLOCK, J. et al. (1973), Sex role and socialisation patterns, 'Journal of Consulting and Clinical Psychology, 41, 321-41.
BRISTOL WOMEN'S STUDIES GROUP (1979), 'Half the Sky: an Introduction to Women's Studies', London, Virago.
BRODSKY, A. and HOLYROYD, J. (19750, Report of the Task Force on sex bias and sex-role stereotyping in therapeutic practice, 'Newsletter, Division 35', APA, 2,7.
BROVERMAN, I.K. et al. (1970), Sex-role stereotypes and clinical judgements of mental health, 'Journal of Consulting and Clinical Psychology', 34, 1-7.
BROWN, G. and HARRIS, T. (1978), 'The Social Origins of Depression', London, Tavistock.
BROWNMILLER, S. (1975),'Against Our Will: Men, Women and Rape', New York, Bantam Books.
BRUCH, H. (1973), 'Eating Disorders', London, Routledge & Kegan Paul.
BURGESS, A.W. (1981), Physician sexual misconduct and patients' responses, 'American Journal of Psychiatry', 138, 1335-42.
CHESLER, P. (1973), 'Women and Madness', Avon, New York.
CHESLER, P. (1980). 'About Men', New York, Bantam Books.
CHODOFF, P. (1978), Psychotherapy of the hysterical personality disorder, 'Journal of the American Academy of Psychoanalysis', 6, 497-510.
CHODROW, N. (1978), 'The Reproduction of Mothering', University of California Press, London.
COCHRANE, R. and STOPES-ROE, M. (1981), Women, marriage, employment and mental health, 'British Journal of Psychiatry', 139, 373-81.
COOPERSTOCK, R. (1979), A review of women's psychotropic drug use, 'Canadian Journal of Psychiatry', 24, 29-34.
COWARD, R. (1979), Significant thinker, 'New Forum', 5, 51-3.
DE BEAUVOIR, S. (1949), 'The Second Sex', Paris.
DINNERSTEIN, D. (1978), 'The Rocking of the Cradle', Souvenir Press, London.
DUNBAR, C. et al. (1979), Successful coping styles in professional women, 'Canadian Journal of Psychiatry', 24, 43-6.
EICHENBAUM, L. and ORBACH, S. (1982), 'Outside In...Inside Out', Harmondsworth, Penguin.
ERNST, S. and GOODISON, L. (1981), 'In Our Own Hands', The Women's Press, London.
FAIRBAIRN, W.R.D. (1952), 'Psychoanalytic Studies of the Personality', London, Routledge & Kegan Paul.
GIGY, L.L. (1980), Self concept of single women, 'Psychology of Women Quarterly', 5, 321-40.
GILBERT, L.A. (1980), Feminist Therapy, in A.M. Brodsky and R. Hare-Mustin (eds), 'Women and Psychotherapy', New York, Guildford Press.
GOLDMAN, N. and RAVID, R. (1980), Community surveys: sex differences in mental illness, in Guttentag, M. et al. (1980).
GUNTRIP, H. (1968), 'Schizoid Phenomena and Object Relations', London, Hogarth.
GUNTRIP, H. (1971), 'Psychoanalytic Theory, Therapy and the Self', New York and London, Basic Books.
GUNTRIP, H. (1975), My experience of analysis with Fairbairn and Winnicott, 'International Review of Psycho-analysis', 2, 145-56.

GUTTENTAG, M. et al. (eds) (1980), 'The Mental Health of Women', Academic Press

HALL, J.A. (1978), Gender effects in decoding nonverbal cues, 'Psychological Bulletin', 85, 845-7.

HOLYROYD, J. and BRODSKY, A. (1977), Psychologists' attitudes and practices regarding erotic and non erotic physical contact with patients, 'American Psychologist', 32, 843-9.

JONES, E. (1954), 'Sigmund Freud: Life and Work', vol. 1, London, Hogarth.

KAPLAN, A.G. (1979), Toward an analysis of sex-role related issues in the therapeutic relationship, 'Psychiatry', 42, no. 2, 112-20.

KATZ, P.A. (1979), The development of female identity, 'Sex Roles', 5, 155-78.

KENWORTHY, J.A. (1979), Androgyny in psychotherapy: but will it sell in Peoria, 'Psychology of Women Quarterly', 3, 231-40.

KHAN, M. (1975), Grudge and the hysteric, 'International Journal of Psychoanalytic Psychotherapy', 4, 349-57.

KLEIN, M. (1937), Love, Guilt and Reparation, in M. Klein, 'Love, Guilt and Reparation and Other Works, 1921-1945', 1975, London, Hogarth.

KLERMAN, G. and WEISSMAN, M. (1980), Depression among women: their nature and causes, in Guttentag, M. et al. (1980).

LERNER, H.E. (1978), Adaptive and pathogenic aspects of sex-role stereotypes: implications for parenting and psychotherapy, 'American Journal of Psychiatry', 135, 48-52.

LLEWELYN, S.P. (1982), The challenge of feminist psychotherapy, 'New Forum', 8, 51-4.

MACLEOD, S. (1981), 'The Art of Starvation', Virago, London.

MARACEK, J., KRAVETZ, D. and FINN, S. (1979), A comparison of women who enter feminist therapy and women who enter traditional therapy, 'Journal of Consulting and Clinical Psychology', 47, 734-42.

MILTON, F. and HEFNER, J. (1979), The outcome of behaviour therapy for agoraphobia in relation to marital adjustment, 'Archives of General Psychiatry', 36, 807-11.

MITCHELL, J. (1974), "Psychoanalysis and Feminism', Harmondsworth, Penguin.

MOGUL, K.M. (1979), Women in midlife: decision, rewards and conflicts related to work and careers, 'American Journal of Psychiatry', 136, 1139-43.

MONEY, J. and ERHARDT, A. (1972), 'Man and Woman, Boy and Girl', Baltimore, Johns Hopkins Press.

MOULTON, R. (1977), Women with double lives, 'Contemporary Psychoanalysis', 13, 64-83.

MOULTON, R. (1979), Ambivalence about motherhood in career women, 'Journal of the American Academy of Psychoanalysis', 7, 241-57.

O'NEIL, J.M. (1981), Male sex role conflicts, sexism and masculinity: psychological implications for men, women and the counselling psychologist, 'Counselling Psychologist', 9, 2, 61-80.

ORBACH, S. (1978), 'Fat is a Feminist Issues', London, Paddington Press.

OSBORNE, K. (1982), Women as Therapists, 'Bulletin of the British Psychological Society', 34, 380-2.

OSBORNE, K. (in press), Sexual Violence, in P. Feldman (ed.), 'Developments in the Study of Original Behaviour', vol. 2, Chichester, Wiley, 67-88.

ROWBOTHAM, S. (1972), 'Women, Resistance and Revolution', Penguin, Harmondsworth.
SOLOMAN, K. (1979), Sexism and professional chauvinism in psychology, 'Psychiatry', 42, 374.
SPENCE, J.T. (1979), Traits, roles and the concept of androgyny, in J.E. Gullahorn (ed.), 'Psychology and Women: in Transition'.
SUMMIT, R. and KRYSO, J. (1978), Sexual abuse of children: a clinical spectrum, 'American Journal of Orthopsychiatry', 48, 237-51.
SYMONDS, A. (1971), Phobias after marriage: women's declaration of dependence, 'American Journal of Psycho-analysis', 31, 144-52.
TUDOR, W. et al. (1977), The effect of sex role differences on the social control of mental illness, 'Journal of Health and Social Behaviour', 18, 98-112.
TURKEL, A.R. (1980), The power dilemma of women, 'American Journal of Psychoanalysis', 40, 301-11.
WARNER, R. (1979), Radical and sexual bias in psychiatric diagnosis, 'Journal of Nervous and Mental Diseases', 167, 303-10.
WEISSMAN, M.M. and PAYKEL, E.S. (1974), 'The Depressed Woman: a Study in Social Relationships', University of Chicago Press.
WHITELY, B. (1979), Sex-roles and psychotherapy: a current appraisal, 'Psychological Bulletin', 86, 1309-20.
WILSON, M. (1979), Guilt-edged security, 'New Forum', 5, 57-8.
WINNICOTT, D. (1965), 'The Maturational Process and the Facilitating Environment', London, Hogarth.

Chapter 12

PSYCHOLOGICAL THERAPY AND PERSONAL CRISIS - THE CARE OF PHYSICALLY ILL PEOPLE
Keith Nichols

For some time, psychologists with an inclination towards the business of psychological therapy have debated out <u>what</u> exactly they should do. Now a new debate is surfacing, centred on the related problem of <u>where</u> exactly they should do it. Hawks (1981) catches the dilemma. There are hopelessly too few psychological therapists in the UK to deal directly with the known incidence of psychological problems or to make more than a token contribution to the existing service of psychiatry. Attempting moves into new areas such as primary health care or the general hospitals can, Hawks argues, at best only be 'an extravagant experiment' that is clearly unrealistic or, at worst, a form of escape.

This chapter is concerned with promoting the work of psychological care in certain sectors of the general hospitals. Clearly, therefore, I must account for myself in relation to this position, otherwise we need go no further.

In order to expand into general medicine without abandoning present commitments, there will have to be a steady expansion in the numbers of psychological therapists. However, the principle of expanding the number of therapists appears to bother Hawks since he feels it implies a passive acceptance of the current levels of psychopathology. Better, he insists, to redeploy the current workforce in the task of primary prevention in order to reduce the incidence of psychological problems and thus begin an era which requires fewer therapists. One to one therapy has little relevance to prevention and so it would rapidly diminish in the role specification of the clinical psychologist.

In general terms this vision has some appeal but I am not sure that it deals with the real world. The business of health education, educating health educators, changing nursing and medical attitudes, engineering educational and institutional change and so on which will be the basis of a major scheme of primary prevention is highly labour intensive. We would almost certainly need more psychologists than we have at present to do it effectively. It is also questionable that the body of psychological therapists would find widespread support from allied professions (who would be left to deal with the individual psychological problems in this major shift of role) and consent could

be important. Discarding completely the one to one therapeutic role
in the manner that Hawks suggests runs the risk of being badly
misunderstood and consequenly sacrificing support. Rather than a rapid
transition it will probably prove better to aim for an extension of the
clinical psychologist's role to include and progressively emphasise
preventative work. This will, though, necessitate a continued pressure
to build up the number of psychologists to cater for the additional
activity.

A last point in my response to Hawks is that it is unreasonable to
link,as he does, an increase in numbers of therapists with a static
adherence to established practice. There is no good reason to believe
that an enlarged workforce will not shift into an increasingly
preventative emphasis as quickly as the present workforce. In fact,
the increased numbers ought to allow accelerated progress. My view
then is contrary to that of Hawks. We need to press steadily to expand
the body of psychological therapists, and, as part of a rational
strategy, some of these must be occupied establishing a presence in
the general hospitals.

Why specifically the general hospitals? The case for this move has
been argued in greater length elsewhere (Nichols, 1979 and 1981) and
below, but it is useful at this point to clarify the main points
particularly in relation to this discussion on the value of increasing
emphasis on preventative work and the current limitations in the
numbers of psychologists available:
1   Psychologists would do better in the present circumstances to focus
efforts at development on areas of high need where intervention can, in
part, take the form of preventative work and where an effective
demonstration of the relevance and positive effect of psychological
care are likely.
2   The general hospitals fit this requirement because they act as a
contact point for large numbers of physically ill or injured people who
are known to manifest a very high incidence of psychological distress
and who must make very considerable psychological adjustments (Lancet,
1979). There is no formal provision for the psychological care of
these people at present. Basically it is an area of high need and
near total neglect.
3   The nature of psychological distress encountered in general
hospitals is very varied. A proportion of people inevitably require
the individual attention of a skilled psychological therapist.
However, as described later, it is clear that much of the work that is
required (both preventative and supportive) can be dealt with by people
trained in basic counselling techniques, nurses for example. Thus the
ingredients of a situation in which the psychologist can use another
profession to extend his contribution are present. His function will
be that of continued modelling through some one to one therapy,
together with training, advising and supporting those involved in
psychological care. Recent developments in the nursing profession
indicate a growing readiness for this kind of work and a receptivity to
this kind of alliance (see below).
4   Without doubt some psychological distress common in general
hospital populations derives from the traditional attitudes and
practices of the medical and nursing sub-cultures (again, this is

expanded below). In working towards good psychological care for the
physically ill, psychological therapists will find themselves forced to
give a high priority to the work of changing these sub-cultures as one
of the key components to effective prevention. While this will be no
mean task it is sufficiently circumscribed to be within our range as a
profession and, therefore, a hopeful investment of effort. This
contrasts perhaps with some of the preventative ambitions involving
widespread social and political change.

Thus, far from being an 'extravagant experiment', the expansion of
psychological therapy into the general hosptials is long overdue since
it is an ideal setting to implement the type of development that Hawks
and many others envisage. In the spirit of this argument, the
following material has been prepared as an encouragement and primer for
clinical psychologists to pursue the opportunities for psychological
care and therapy in general hospitals.

ORIENTATION (1) A BRIEF HISTORY

The psychology of physical illness has taken significant strides in
recent years. The development springs from the late 1940s. Scattered
articles began to appear with a focus of concern largely directed
towards the contributing effects of personality and stress on the
incidence, character and outcome of illness. Alexander (1950) is a
typical example of this psychosomatic interest.

Psychotherapeutic intervention as we know it today was not a focal
issue in the literature at that time. Throughout the following years,
the concern to establish whether or not psychological factors have a
causal relationship with illness has remained very much alive with
behaviouristic psychosomatic interpretations enjoying a period of being
fashionable (e.g. Lachman, 1972). Other interests expanded though. In
particular, various writers turned to the issue of psychological
process in relation to the experiences of illness and injury. Janis
and Leventhal (1965) wrote, for example, on the nature and function of
reflective grief and reflective anxiety. Without the work of worry,
they argued, emotional innoculation is minimal and without the work of
grief, adaption to life after illness or injury may never be completed.
In a similar vein, some considered the psycho-social determinants of
recovery from illness, e.g. Querido (1959) and Imboden (1972). Here
the significance of the psychological context in which the illness
occurred was emphasised as governing the reaction pattern which then
influenced the rate and extent of recovery. A closely related
literature to this trend has been the discussion concerning coping
styles and the importance of support, Adams and Lindemamm (1974) and
Funch and Mettlin (1982).

By the mid-1970s the literature had become substantial. Moos (1975)
and Howells (1976) were typical in collecting together sets of articles
dealing with the psychological consequences of many forms of disfiguring
or disabling illness. The theme of intervention by psychological
therapists was developed in noticeable strength in many of these later
publications. For example, Kaplan de-Nour (1970) wrote on psychotherapy

with dialysis patients and Roskies (1980) discussed therapy programmes
for Type A personalities at risk for coronary heart disease.

Lastly, a further theme has been the concern to provide psychological
services for physically ill people. An early plea for the presence of
psychologists in British general hospitals to add to the overall care
offered was advanced by Hetherington (1967).   Recently this plea has
been converted to a demand, Nichols (1981).

ORIENTATION (2) UNDERSTANDING THE UNFAVOURABLE INTERPERSONAL SETTING
IN BRITISH GENERAL HOSPITALS

The organisation of general hospital services gives little sign of
recognition of the psychological distress known to be associated with
serious illness and injury. As a rule hospitals do not operate, nor
request, psychological services of their own. It is true that medical
social workers are employed to maintain a caring contact with the users
of general hospitals but neither their training nor their role is that
of specialists in psychological care. The psychiatric service is
available, of course, but it functions as a separate institution and is
normally only involved on a casuality basis, that is, where psychological complications are overtly displayed or are a nuisance.

Latterly there has been an increased awareness of the need for psych-
logical care on the part of the nursing profession. With the development of hospice care for the dying the nurse has a greater
responsibility for basic psycholgocial care. The role has clearly
shifted into that of nurse and support figure (Webster, 1981).
Encouragingly there are signs that this trend is influencing nursing
practices in other areas of medicine. Recent arguments for the
introduction of the so-called nursing process (Dickenson, 1982) with
an apparent person-centred emphasis are evidence of this. However, the
trend is in its early phase and can only be seen as a move towards very
basic psychological care as opposed to the provision of an adequate
service which includes psychological therapy.

It is more difficult to find evidence of general trends towards
psychological mindedness in the medical profession. There are some
indications of growing awareness ('The Lancet' (1979), for example, ran
a short but powerful plea for action on the alarmingly high incidence
of psychological distress in general hospital populations) but I have
little evidence of a general shift in practice. There may be an
increased effort in teaching psychology to medical students (Weinman,
1978) but on the whole the atmosphere in British hospitals is, at
first sight, unfavourable and discouraging for the psycholgoists. The
issue of importance here is to understand why, after centuries of
development, the medical profession has failed to see the need and make
provision for psychological care, and why it may even have actively
suppressed this development. Similarly, until very recently at least,
why it is that the nursing profession has opted to collude with this
position despite the greater level of contact with the psychological
distress of physically ill people. <u>Whatever influences are responsible
for this situation they probably still operate and will, therefore,</u>

affect a psychological therapist attempting to function in this work environment.

    In searching for an explanation to these questions, I want firstly to discuss the 'medical style of relating'. The medical profession is, of course, composed of individuals of differing specialities, training and philosophy. In reality, there is a wide range of interpersonal styles manifest by doctors from the very sensitive and caring to the grotesquely insensitive and inhumane. This presents a problem in attempting to assess the profession as a whole. Clearly there is a danger of injustice that results from construing the profession as an entity embued with a single set of characteristics. Nevertheless, an overview is of relevance here and I ask that the following comments be taken as alerting readers to likely circumstances rather than absolute facts.

    Hauser (1981) gives an impressive review of the state of knowledge regarding doctor/patient relationships. The overall findings are not good. A high proportion, at times reported to be as high as 70 per cent, of people using medical services find doctors unhelpful in a personal sense. Much of the trouble is with unsatisfactory communication, in particular the so-called doctor-centred style of communicating. This takes the form of an efficient but mechanistic encounter which allows little recognition of the needs or experience of the client. The focus of the doctor's attention is on physical aspects and obtaining key bits of medical information whilst 'managing the patient'. The doctor thus relates to only part of his client's needs, the predominant pattern in the communication being that of partial or nondisclosure of information to the client.

    This style of communicating signals a particular type of inter-personal stance which Hauser talks of as over-detachment. It is the most common interpersonal style in experienced doctors, although trainee doctors tend to be less socially distant. This distancing and focus of attention on physical function is damaging since it removes the opportunity of making hospital care a composite of medical, psychological and social concerns.

    The origins of over-detachment are of importance because the psychological therapist needs to understand the feelings and motives of the medical profession if he is to function effectively in a medical setting. I want to put stress on this point. In general hospital work, the therapist may well experience many instances in which the client's distress is directly provoked by the manner of communicating and inter-personal style of the doctors and nurses. Consequently anger and feelings of protectiveness on the part of the therapist is a real possibility. The risk is obvious. An angry therapist may lose clinical judgment and sacrifice rapport with the colleagues he is trying to influence and educate. The better the understanding of the dynamics that sustain people in the medical style of relating, the better the insulation from unproductive anger (a statement which, I may add, carries with it the history of some salutory personal learning experiences).

The literature dealing with medical communication in extensive and
it best suits the purpose of this section to make a brief synthesis of
the various factors claimed to be responsible for the medical style of
relating.
1   The social distance and selective perception characteristic of
over-detachment are maintained by the doctor as an active and necessary
psychological defence. Exposure to the acute distress, fright and anger
of another person, coupled with responsibility for that person, makes
doctors and nurses very vulnerable people. Without the defence of
over-detachment many doctors would find the role highly destructive,
particularly in cases involving severe pain and loss of physical
function or disfigurement. Identification with the client's distress
can not only be a profoundly disturbing event but it can distract from
effective decision-making. As an evolved psychological strategy to
deal with this, Lief and Fox (1963) argue that distancing is instilled
as a coping device in medical trainees. Menzies (1970) wrote of the
defence against this type of psychological trauma that nurses employ.
The nurse cannot avoid contact with her client's distress with the
strategies that doctors use and, therefore, it is claimed she partici-
pates in a collective defence which involves an anxious subservience to
the doctor as the sole custodian of clinical responsibility. The
point being made is that responsibility can be tolerated with the
defence of distance but where that distance is not possible then the
responsibility becomes intolerable and is avoided.
2   The over-detached style of the doctor and the seeming passive
acceptance of their clients are best seen as aspects of culturally
prescribed roles. Medical students undergo a lengthy period of
socialisation to this role (Hauser, 1981) which is an extension of
prior informal socialisation to the roles of doctor and patient that
children normally receive in Western culture. This is, of course,
Parsons's (1975) position and he further argues that the over-detached
style of relating which I refer to here as unfavourable is, in fact,
functional and inevitable. He perceives the doctor as an accepted
agent of social control who must adopt and preserve an asymmetric power
position. I would add to this the comment that part of the socialisation to the roles of doctor and patient involves the separation of
the concept of patient from that of person. Doctors relate to
patients in a manner that they do not usually use in other situation;
patient is not synonymous with person. There is, in my observations,
a cultural permission for the discourteous, authoritarian handling of
patients which fosters a lack of contact with their needs as people.
This is antagonistic to genuine care.
3   The medical and nursing professions have become enmeshed in the
'myth of medicine'. The threats and potential psychological trauma of
serious illness, injury and death loom over us all. In Western society
these threats are counterbalanced by a denial and general tendency to
project power and invincibility onto the medical services. There is a
myth of medical power and medical excellence. This anxiety-reducing
attribution of healing power is accompanied in many by a disowning of
personal responsibility for health and a denial of the realities of
illness and limitations of medicine. In its development the medical
profession has colluded with this myth and is now its captive victim.
The problem of medical mistakes illustrates this well. It is clear
that large organisations like hospitals have a 'mistake rate'. By this

is meant the approximate frequency of errors in communication, losses in the transfer of information (e.g. from one shift of nurses to the next), erroneous diagnoses, procedural errors and instances of inability on the part of doctors to understand or correct certain medical problems. Most staff in a hospital clearly recognise this and wards, surgical teams or units may be known as above or below the average mistake rate. In reality the mistake rate can be surprisingly high in medical settings, although this does not usually seem to produce irreversible harm on too many occasions. The important thing to note is that the tension and anxious pressure by the users of medical services for those services to be ideal, and the collusion with this myth by medical staff, produces a permanent and difficult problem. Hospitals have a mistake rate and probably can never improve beyond certain levels because of the nature of bureaucratic institutions. Yet they are not allowed either by their own posture or by the pressure from the users to admit that mistakes are commonplace. Communications and relationships are inevitably influenced by this. Millmann (1962) describes three lines of defence that physicians use against mistakes being identified: (a) witholding information from clients and so limiting their understanding and power – the primary defence, (b) refusing to evaluate the competence or performance of others involved in the care of the client, and (c) discrediting the client in a way which deflects blame away from the doctors or nurses.

It is relevant to note that the type of relationship which doctors and nurses maintain in hospice care is entirely different. Here there is a positive effort to attend to the needs of the person rather than just the body of the patient. Rapport is usually good and staff are instructed in the need to give time to dying people and to explore with them their questions and fears (Webster, 1981). The essential difference is that the myth of medicine has been dropped by both staff and the users of the service. It is accepted that medicine does not have the power to avert death and the defensive strategies are abandoned. This is the opposite effect to the crisis in a general hospital when a serious mistake comes to light. The extreme anger and need for retribution through law and the tenacious defence by medical personnel underlines the lack of reality in the position of the profession and their clients. Mistakes are not allowed and they cannot be admitted, yet they occur all the time.

4   The medical style of relating as a means of maintaining power. It is noted above that a stable characteristic of the medical style of relating is the strategy of non-disclosure of information. This may take the form of very guarded and incomplete information, unusable information (e.g. inappropriate language) or simply the absence of any information, sometimes because the doctor himself is absent or because confusion is maintained by a succession of different doctors in the so-called committee style of case management (Duff and Hollingshead, 1968). The effect of this on the client is, of course, uncertainty. If this is an evolved social strategy it will have a purpose, so how should the habit of withholding information be construed? We have the concepts listed above but to this must now be added the less benign idea that it is to do with personal and professional power. In the eyes of Waitzkin and Stoeckle (1972), 'a physician's ability to

preserve his power over the patient in the doctor-patient relationship depends largely on his ability to control the patient's uncertainty.' The possibility arises that the power needs of individual doctors are met in this way. On a broader plane, medicine may be seen as a power-holding bureaucracy which will attempt to enhance and defend its power. Either way, the observed behaviour is concerned with the retention of power and has little to do with medicine and care.

Can the issue of the comparative importance of these explanations be resolved? Possibly, but I do not wish to take it further here. My objective has been to sensitise readers to the possibilities.

In conclusion I will note that psychological therapists working with physically ill people are likely to become enmeshed in triangular relationships with doctors and nurses on the one hand and the client on the other. The therapist will encounter differing experiences which will suggest various of the influences described above. Sometimes, for example, the therapist may experience a doctor as a person who has daily to defend against very disturbing experiences and deserves care himself. There will inevitably be the opposite experience, with the therapist stirred by the recognition that his client needs to be defended from the stress of damaging personal treatment by a doctor. As in all therapy, the better the therapist understands his own motives and those of the other people involved in a case, the better his chances of being effective.

THE EXTENDED ROLE OF THE PSYCHOLOGICAL THERAPIST.

Throughout this article the term psychological therapist has been used as opposed to psychotherapist. This is, perhaps, a somewhat laboured way of signalling that work with physically ill people demands an extension of the usual role of the psychotherapist. In the psycho-dynamic style of therapy, as set out by Malan (1979), for example, the therapist and client are encapsulated in a world and task of their own. The therapist's intervention is limited to using the content of sessions as material to facilitate personal education and insight. However, when a psychological therapist has a concern for the overall psycho-logical care of physically ill clients, he cannot limit his role in this way. Psychological care will include psychotherapy but there is much active intervention necessary as well, including various educational and information-based interventions together with inter-ventions involving medical staff, nursing staff and relatives. This statement is not, it should be emphasised, an idealistic or theoretical stand but describes the working role into which I have been 'shaped' by the realities of providing a psychological service in a kidney unit and occasionally to orthopaedic and other sections of a general hospital.

The various aspects of this extended role are very well illustrated by reference to the experience of people suffering unexpected kidney failure and then surviving by means of haemodialysis. The following sections are given over to a detailed account of work as a psychological therapist with these people although the principles involved apply to most other sectors of general medicine.

The clinical material is derived from contact with approximately
fifty dialysands or their partners. Material is also presented here
which is drawn from a survey of the psycho-social difficulties of users
of the kidney unit. The survey, conducted in 1980, was based on an
interview combined with a questionnaire termed the Dialysis Problem
Check List. Tables I and II give, respectively, the percentage of
dialysands and their partners who identify particular difficulties as
applicable to themselves (this data is a limited selection, the
complete report will be presented elsewhere).

KIDNEY FAILURE AND THE PSYCHOLOGICAL THERAPIST

Kidney failure may be progressive or quite unexpected, the latter often
being a complication of other problems such as high blood pressure or
viral infections. While those with progressive kidney failure can make
some adjustments for the life to come, those suffering a sudden failure
undergo the transition from unsuspecting normal health to the life of
chronic illness in two or three days, with no opportunity for
adjustment whatsoever. Their lives are radically changed as they enter
a phase of what some workers in the field regard as a terminal illness,
involving eventual multisystem failure (Woodhams, 1981). Dialysis
averts death and restores a viable physiology but nevertheless there is
a slow deterioration in various systems (e.g. vascular, neuromuscular)
which results in a considerably reduced life span. The transplantation
of a functioning kidney may be successful in giving a limited period
of relatively normal physiology. Life after kidney failure can prove
an exceptionally difficult experience. As Kaplan de-Nour (1981)
discovered from her sample of one hundred cases, 37 per cent died
within five years, 30 per cent experienced moderate to severe anxiety,
53 per cent experienced moderate to severe depression and 77 per cent
failed to comply adequately with the dietary restrictions needed.

The nature of the psychological difficulties resulting from sudden
kidney failure and the necessary psychotherapeutic work can be linked
to several stages in the usual medical history.

STAGE 1: EMERGENCY DIALYSIS

The events

Following the complete failure of kidney function, uraemea and fluid
overloading rapidly develop. The victim will initially feel ill,
though not dramatically so. After two or three days the increasingly
alarming effects of severe nausea and neuromuscular weakness and pain
will become evident. It is a frightening transition from an apparently
everyday illness to something which is clearly of great gravity. The
general practitioner will be involved and once he has identified
possible kidney failure, blood samples will be sent for analysis. The
news that the blood condition confirms kidney failure marks the point
of entry into a new world, that of surviving by dialysis. The client,
now gravely ill, will be admitted to intensive care or a kidney unit

for the first emergency dialysis. This will either be the peritoneal
type (which involves pumping fluid in and out of the abdominal cavity)
or haemodialysis, using a temporary sub-clavian catheter for access to
the blood stream. Each of these techniques require minor surgery to
allow insertion of catheters. After adequate dialysis to reduce the
toxic state and fluid overloading, the crisis recedes a little and the
client and his family will begin to confront their situation. They will
probably know little of kidney function and the implications of kidney
failure. Their initial expectations may well be based on the hopes of
cure. The medical and nursing staff will begin explanations and the
key issue will emerge, namely that survival is the objective, not
cure. With dialysis three times a week involving a procedure that
takes about six and a half hours, death is inevitable. In the example
we are following, where long-term haemodialysis is intended, the
construction of a fistula (an anastamosis between a vein and artery in
the forearm which yields the blood-flow rate required for dialysis) is
required as soon as possible. The first few days then are spent with
emergency dialysis, another minor surgical event constructing the
fistula, and adjusting to life as an in-patient at the kidney unit.
A period of waiting ensues while the fistula heals and 'matures'. When,
several weeks later, it is ready for use, training in the technique
of haemodialysis can begin. In the meantime the staff cope with the
dialysis,the only change being that if the client's condition allows,
there is conversion to out-patient status.

The psychological therapist's task

For the purposes of clear illustration, I will assume that the role to
be described is in the context of a unit which is relatively naive to
the principles of psychological care. Thus the therapist will, in
the early days, have to cope with the work himself (kidney units do not
usually have a high rate of new cases and such a work level is quite
manageable).

   The manner is which the therapist begins working with the client
will depend on the nature of each client's initial reactions.
Predicting these is less than easy. The prior development of the
individual, the life context in which the kidney failure occurs and the
experiences with staff all exert varying influences, Levy (1974)
describes common stages. Initially, he claims, there is a 'honeymoon'
period characterised by gratitutde and hope. Later this gives way to
a lengthier period of disenchantment. British psychologists are, on
the whole, less inclined to see stages than our American counterparts
and although I know what he means, I cannot confirm that this
particular observation applies to the majority of cases seen. Dress
and Gallagher (1981) similarly describe some common patterns of
reacting, these being (a) depressed-helpless; (b) aggressive-protesting;
(c) denying-pseudo stable; and (d) adult-mature. They reflect, Dress
writes, the early developmental stages of ego growth. At a descriptive
level there is much that is familiar in this observation too, but
setting one package of observations against another I would argue that
stability within a pattern does not seem a characteristic in the early
weeks; many clients appear to slip from one pattern to another in an

unstable way. One fact is certain though. When making the initial
contact with these people a psychological therapist will be meeting
clients who are suffering a highly stressing psychological trauma.
Supplementing my own experience with a synthesis of reports from
Kaplan de-Nour (1976) and Levy (1981), it is clear that the following
pressures figure prominently:

1   Fright - Health has gone and life itself is threatened. There are
many unknown experiences ahead in terms of medical procedures and social
changes. The means of support for some (the job or business) are out of
reach and may stay so. The children or dependants of others are
having to cope alone, or with hastily improvised arrangements.

2   Helpless dependency - Continued survival depends entirely on a
complex technology and considerable medical and nursing skill. The
client can contribute nothing and, initially, probably understands
little. He has no control over events at all and is placed into a
position of regressed, passive dependency. This brings conflict. The
enforced regression may be welcome at one level as meeting a need to
seek nurturance in crisis but it involves the loss of adult status and
individual power, which can be threatening. The conflict invoked by
dependency is viewed by Kaplan de-Tour (1976) and Strain (1981) as a
source of much upheaval.

3   Factual confusion - Within the British system of medical care there
is rarely a consistent programme of education for people in hospital.
Information comes in fragments, from different sources. Facts, best
estimates, contradictions, differences of opinion and kindly cover-
ups are intermixed. To add to the problem, understanding kidney
failure and life on dialysis involves considerable learning and the
acquisition of a new vocabulary. This is at a time when one is
physically weakened and distracted by anxiety and learning powers are,
therefore, diminished. Lack of information, erroneous or conflicting
ideas and confusion are frequent findings in the early days.

4   Inter-personal confusion - The arrangement of working days, the
shift system and the avoidance of personal styles of nursing together
with the team arrangements for medical cover means that there will
usually be a good number of staff coming and going in a complex
pattern. Rapport may be established with a nurse one day who may then
be off duty the next. An important question arising from a
conversation with a consultant may be blocked because the next visit
(it is discovered) is three days hence and a senior house officer
arrives instead. In addition, the client has to accept the necessity
of a succession of strangers executing intimate tasks. At an emotional
level, there is often resentment resulting from this inter-personal
experience to which is added conflicting feelings aroused by the
enforced dependency.

5   Anger - Various of the experiences listed above may provoke anger.
So too can the illness itself, both from the imposed constraints and
discomfort of dialysis and the sense of being failed by medicine.
Expressing anger in the setting of a unit is difficult. One is both
grateful to and dependent on the staff and making anger explicit often
provokes guilt. Expressing anger against oneself is equally difficult.
Anger then tends to be held in, a psychodynamic event which presages
depression (Malan, 1979).

6   Reaction to losses - Depending on the accuracy of the person's
expectations and his operating level of denial, there may be some

awareness of the losses to come. Dialysis brings inevitable losses
in occupational, social and familial roles. The consequent sense of
being diminished as a person and of ambitions being relinquished can
trigger, of course, the powerful process of grief. This is perhaps
more likely in later months but the beginnings of awareness and reaction
are sometimes present after a few days.
7   Separation anxiety - Lastly, it is inevitably the case that the
setting in which these pressures have to be dealt with requires
separation from known and security-giving places, people and roles.
Strain (1981) records separation anxiety as a discernable consequence.

How should the therapist slant his work at this stage? My conviction
is that the care component of therapy is where the emphasis should be
placed. That is, attempting to make these distressed people more
psychologically comfortable by minimising psychological stressors and
facilitating normal psychological processes. Since some of the
stressors listed include separation, difficult relationships, powerful
triggers to the emotions of fear, anger, depression and grief which
may then be blocked from direct expression by the client, it is clear
that these have to be dealt with by the psychologist in a flexible
form of supportive counselling tailored to the individual's needs.

When working in this mode, the contrast with conventional therapy is
apparent at the outset since the therapist takes the initiative by
making contact with the client. In so doing, the preventative
emphasis is taken and immediate care is offered to all, rather than
waiting for casualties to develop. A time is chosen when the client's
strength and physical condition permit a meaningful encounter,
probably after the second dialysis. The therapist explains his
function in the unit and invites the client to use his support. He
aims to be construed by the client and staff as a person who is
concerned with the psychological well-being of those receiving treatment at the unit, who understands the experiences that the client is
going through, who specialises in dealing with psychological
difficulties, who recognises that these are virtually inevitable with
this type of illness and who will be reliably available on an agreed
basis. There is from the beginning a 'permission giving' communication
which validates the feelings and reactions within the client as a
natural consequence of severe personal stress. They are to be given
time and attention and valued as an important facet of the illness, not
discredited as a nuisance, nor to be pushed aside because they are
uncomfortable for the staff. As with all counselling, the therapist
aims to create a relationship wherein the client will feel safe to
express feelings and fantasy and will thus have the experience of being
received. It should be noted that not all clients are able to cope with
work of any emotional intensity since they are holding onto a powerful
defence of denial, a difficulty which Kaplan de-Nour (1970) records in
her description of psychotherapeutic work with dialysands. Here the
therapist may have to limit his work to the second, more practical
aspects of psychological care, the information-based interventions
aimed at minimising uncertainty and the damage of false hopes and fears.
When circumstances permit,the therapist repeats his invitation to the
immediate relatives. The parents of a child on dialysis or a marital
partner clearly have equally demanding difficulties to deal with.

Other than noting that work with relatives is an important aspect of care, I will not be able to deal with this topic in any further detail here.

Much earlier in this paper the communication difficulties within medicine were discussed in some length. Once engaged with a client, the therapist may encounter evidence of distress from communication styles and over-detachment on the part of medical staff. The therapist will probably have to deal with the problems directly, although with patient neutrality. He will do well to bear in mind two 'laws'. People in hospital who are anxious are not good listeners; they tend to listen selectively and remember inaccurately. Staff in hospitals who are defensive or not able to cope with emotion in clients and relatives are not good communicators. They tend to opt for placatory, anxiety-reducing statements or avoid giving difficult information in an attempt to deal with their own difficulties. Examples are legion. An anxious man training in peritoneal dialysis sought information on how long he was to stay in the unit. His business was suffering in his absence and he was wanting to get back to it urgently. He was given various opinions by staff which basically suggested several weeks. An insecure trainee nurse was pressed to be more specific and gave an unrealistically hopeful estimate of two weeks. Days later he was greatly angered and distressed when a date four weeks away was suggested since he 'knew' he had been told two weeks. The staff were similarly aggrieved because they 'knew' they had not given him such an unrealistic estimate.

From this and many other similar instances I have realised that one of the most helpful routine tasks in psychological care is constantly to monitor what exactly a client does know and how this shapes his expectations in relation to those of the staff. The therapist may then work to obtain relevant missing information for the client and maintain understanding and accurate recall. Always it must be borne in mind that something told does not equal something heard. Repeated checks and rehearsal of information with, perhaps, written notes on individual case details are necessary.

In short, the therapist works to develop reality-based expectations and thus protects clients from the stresses of inadequate preparation through the ineffective transmission of information.

A last aspect of the work is the regular communication with staff. They need to be reassured that they are not failing if there is emotion evident in a client and given credible explanations to help them understand an individual's reaction. Otherwise staff may develop myths about individuals being difficult and become drawn into a collective rejection. Many also need assistance with the business of communicating. The lesson that the needs of the client have to be addressed rather than the anxieties of the doctor or nurse is an important one. So too the value of checking what a client knows and repeating information where necessary. Thus, if a nurse can look in to see a client an hour after a ward round she can go through again what was said and why, and may usefully repeat this exercise a day later.

STAGE 2: HAEMODIALYSIS TRAINING AND CONVERSION TO HOME DIALYSIS

The events

Training to full self-sufficiency in the technique of haemodialysis
takes a year or more. The basic skills that must be acquired include
taking physiological readings, preparation of the machine and dialyser,
care of the access sites, inserting needles into the access sites,
joining up blood lines, understanding and correctly responding to the
machine alarms, using a de-clotting agent, dealing with dialysis
problems (e.g. hypotension and pressure abnormalities, blood leaks,
etc.), coping with simple machine faults and coming off dialysis.

These are advanced skills and the consequences of error can be grave.
Naturally enough a substantial proportion of trainees find the whole
business quite daunting at first, particularly where there is no basis
of biological knowledge at all. Anxiety reactions develop in about
25 per cent of cases, though not all severe.

Normally training and dialysis take place three times a week on an
outpatient basis, with sessions taking place about six hours. The
partner or intended assistant will also be asked to attend sufficient
sessions to learn the basic skills. Life and work have to be fitted
around this commitment.

When skills are adequately developed to permit 'solo' dialysis,
conversion to home treatment is attempted. Typically this is some time
between the third and sixth month. It is usually a welcome event since
it relieves a family of the burden of travel and absences three times
a week. It does, however, bring the anxiety of independence, for
although the early home dialyses are supervised by a home sister, there
soon arrives the day when no support figures are physially present and
the only source of immediate help is the telephone link with the unit.
Experience accumulates and after a further six months or so most
common difficulties have been encountered and dealt with and while there
is no discharge as such, the dialysand will be regarded as self
sufficient.

Meantime the individual and the family will be encountering the
realities of survival by dialysis. Depending on the approach taken by
a unit on informing people in advance, this may mean a time of
disappointment, sometimes shock. The difficulties encountered are
governed by so many variables (age, health and associated complications,
prior personality, the social context of the illness, distance from the
unit, etc.) that generalisations are of little worth. Suffice to say
that dialysands in complete renal failure will be fortunate if they do
not encounter the typical effects of chronic uraemia, for example, loss
of energy, muscular weakness and cramps, proneness to breathlessness,
anaemia, prevailing tiredness, skin irritation, poor concentration,
impotence (and equivalent sexual difficulties for women) and emotional
instability. The way of life requires enormous adjustment. Many
dialysands need to limit fluid intake to 500 mls per day and to
monitor and regulate their diet in very exact terms. The ever present
necessity to dialyse three times a week is an onerous constraint for

most, it having many implications in terms of work, travel, social life
and rearing the family. In young people the possibility of having
children is extremely difficult. Where kidney failure occurs in the
context of a marriage which is failing, there are obvious problems.
The dialysand needs the partner as a dialysis assistant. The partner
would, under normal circumstances, want separation but is trapped by
moral obligation, guilt and, perhaps, pressure from unit staff.

Set against all this are the positive aspects. Death has been
averted and relationships can continue. There exists the hope of a
successful transplant attempt which could restore life to near normality
for a period of years. There may be a long wait for this, however, and
the chances of success are at best 70 per cent. The majority of
dialysis families do adjust and cope with the life, albeit with
sadness and the sense of a heavy burden.

The psychological therapist's tasks

Tables 12.1 and 12.2 give an indication of the type of difficulties
that dialysands and their partners are able to articulate and, therefore, some of the problems to which the therapist will have to address
himself. Together with these particular problems, the general pattern
of a person's reaction to the situation will emerge and it may be that
some dialysands and partners will self-refer, or nursing staff will
express concern on their behalf.

In maintaining a complete service of psychological care, the
therapist will find himself functioning in several modes:
(a)   The continuing work of basic psychological care outlined above.
That is, stressing the preventative aspects of supportive counselling
and information checking together with any liaison work required with
staff to facilitate good relationships between nurses, doctors and
clients. Ideally this will progress in the form of regular meetings as
the psychologist follows the client through his training.
(b)   Specific problem-oriented psychological therapy. As can be seen
from the tables, the incidence of psychological difficulties is high.
Many of these problems are best dealt with in a direct, practical way
using whatever means seem appropriate. Anxiety reactions to needling
and the responsibilities of running a dialysis, general physical
tension during dialysis, episodes of disturbing emotional upheaval,
inadequate social skills to engage staff in important conversations,
inappropriate styles in dealing with personal difficulties in the unit,
inappropriate and failing strategies of self-care (e.g. keeping to
fluid limits), relationship difficulties within a marriage arising from
dialysis and the problem of sexual relations are typical of the
problems which obstruct training and erode confidence. Both clients
and staff usually see a need for psychological aid, but in the training
phase at least, the pressure is to find a way to deal with specific
difficulties efficiently. It is a situation that requires a truly
eclectic psychological therapist, able to shift his style to meet the
client's needs rather than relabelling his clients needs to suit his
favoured approach.

TABLE 12.1   The percentage of a group of people in their first
                    year of dialysis treatment agreeing with items
                    from the Dialysis Problem Check List
                    (N=16)

TRAINING COMMUNICATIONS	Agreement
Finding that things are not explained well enough	56
Confused because different people tell you different things	50
The staff way I should feel well between dialyses, but I feel weak and ill	44
Feeling confused about dialysis techniques	44
Finding that I forget what I have been told	31
Wanting explanations repeated - too awkward to ask	25

GENERAL COMMUNICATIONS	
The staff do not realise how difficult life on dialysis is	44
Ashamed because I'm depressed	31
Ashamed because I'm anxious	25
Having difficulties, but not wanting to 'phone the unit because you feel such a nuisance'	25

DIALYSIS (AT HOME AND AT THE UNIT)	
Worried about having trouble with needles or the fistula	67
Feeling tense when putting the needles in	67
Feeling anxious before going on the machine	31
Feeling worried that I'll make a mistake	31
Feeling depressed while I'm on the machine	25
Feeling angry before going on the machine	25

RELATIONSHIPS	
Feeling no good as a parent (those with children)	60
Feeling that there is too much strain on my partner	57
I feel I'm spoiling my partner's life	50
Sexual relationships are difficult/have stopped	50
I'm difficult to live with	43
Feeling no good as a husband/wife	36
Feeling that I spoil my family's life	31

GENERAL PSYCHOLOGICAL DIFFICULTIES	
Angry that I can't do the things that I used to	50
Worrying a good deal about the future	50
I'm too moody	43
Craving for liquid	43
Feeling depressed much of the time	38
Feeling irritable much of the time	38
Feeling ruled by the dialysis machine	31
Feeling anxious much of the time	25
Sometimes wanting to take my life	19

TABLE 12.2   The percentage of a group of partners of people
                          in their first year of dialysis agreeing with
                          items from the Dialysis Problem Check List
                          (N=13)

TRAINING AND GENERAL COMMUNICATIONS	% Agreement
Reluctant to 'phone the unit when we have problems in case they think we are a nuisance'	54
Finding that things are not explained well enough	31
Confused because different staff tell you different things	31
The staff don't realise how difficult life is	31
Never being able to talk to the doctors because they are in such a rush	23
Needing to have explanations repeated but feeling too awkward to ask	23

DIALYSIS (IN THE UNIT AND AT HOME)	
Worried that I won't be able to deal with an emergency	46
Feeling anxious about being in charge of the machine	31
Frightened I'll cause harm or even death during dialysis	31
Feeling anxious about putting needles in	23
Helping with dialysis is a strain - my own health is deteriorating	23

GENERAL PSYCHO-SOCIAL DIFFICULTIES	
Feeling depressed at how he/she has changed	61
Feeling exhausted	54
Finding his/her depression hard to bear	31
Upset by the way our sexual life has suffered/stopped	31
I badly need a holiday	31
Feeling trapped because he/she depends on me so much now	31
Resenting the way he/she won't do things for him/herself	31
Worried about his/her attitude to other people now	23
Worried about the effects the situation is having on the children	23
Finding his/her tempers hard to bear	23
The future looks bleak	23
I badly need to get away for a day or two but never can	23

Stressing againt the extended role of the therapist, the tables demonstrate that some of the problems are with the staff, not the clients. Few nursing or medical staff are trained as teachers, which shows up on the check list items related to training communications. Few staff are trained to notice their own needs to deny distress and see the clients as doing well. Kaplan de-Nour (1981) reports that the physicians-in-charge who took part in her study badly overestimated the extent to which clients were progressing against objective indicators, a tendency which was linked to the level of denial in the doctors. This again shows up on the dialysis problem check list, 44 per cent of dialysands found staff reluctant to accept reports of not feeling well and unaware of how difficult their lives seemed. Similarly, staff are not usually trained into a positive attitude towards the predictable and normal psychological reaction to serious physical illness. As a consequence, 31 per cent felt ashamed of their depression and 25 per cent ashamed of their anxiety. Clearly the unit is the 'patient' with these issues and to be effective the therapist must aim to develop a strong influential presence, tackling these problems directly by tutoring, reminding and supporting staff.

(c) Long term psychotherapy. Some people lose their kidney function in circumstances that suggest psychosomatic overlay. Chronic hypertension may lead to kidney failure, for example, and this itself may be linked to certain personality disturbances. Abuse of certain drugs will damage kidney function and this again may be linked to long standing psychological difficulties. Amongst the population of dialysands, therefore, are a small number of people who were either already receiving or certainly needing psychotherapy. In assessing the demand for psychotherapy, one must also add the significant number of people who, while functioning normally prior to kidney failure, have clearly entered a state of psychological disturbance that resists the support work and limited approach to therapy spoken of so far.

In brief illustration, I may mention a forty-year-old Welshman who became agitated and very aggressive in his training months. He related very badly to the nurses and ran into severe problems with his needling skills because of an angry need to achieve success immediately. Similar difficulties arose in his negotiations with the administrator who he pressed angrily to have a machine installed at home in great haste. These were the early signs of several years of difficulty. He was, as it turned out, dreadfully ill-suited to the life of a dialysand. He had, through his life, striven constantly to achieve credit and recognition by driving himself excessively in work and recreation. Failure was an issue which had been attributed great significance by his father and he revealed himself in therapy to be a sad and damaged person in whom any personal behaviour which was seen as failing or just getting by was anxiously rejected. Feelings of security and worth seemed to come only through the medium of maximum effort. His agitation with us arose in construing his need for dialysis and the weakening effects of uraemia as permanently rendering him a failure. His angry struggle to achieve success in training and later in rehabilitation were frightened attempts to recover acceptability in his own eyes. There were many instances of transference problems with male authority figures at the unit and in his work and social life.

He felt rejected and humiliated in their eyes, responding with angry
defensiveness to a situation that mirrored his early experiences in
life.

Psychotherapy with such people is made more difficult in the sense
that work is often interrupted by illness and mediation is necessary
between the client and the staff who are often confused and respond
with a protective counter-rejection to such anger. Other than this, the
work of uncovering the dynamics and leading the client to alternative
ways of being is that of psychotherapy in any setting.

STAGE III: LONG-TERM DIALYSIS

This section will not be developed in detail because the work is
basically an extension of that discussed above.

People vary in the difficulties they encounter in the long term.
Some stumble from one physical crisis to another or survive a failed
transplant attempt which leaves them ill for months. Others dwell with
apparently adequate adjustment for years. The partners may 'burn out'
and enter a phase of great distress in emotional and physical
exhaustion. The therapist, hopefully by this time a known and trusted
figure, will attempt to care for them as their needs dictate.

OVERVIEW

I have now to link the themes of this chapter together. My concern has
been to show the need for psychological therapists to extend their work
to give care to the clients of general hospitals. This has been
illustrated with the example of people surviving by haemodialysis after
kidney failure. It would have been equally appropriate to use the
examples from many other specialities, such as orthopaedic hospitals,
coronary care units or surgical wards. The same arguments and
principles apply.

It has been emphasised that in the setting of the general hospital
the psychological therapist will need to adopt an adaptive attitude.
He will find himself in a caring relationship with people who are
themselves dealing with an institution which can unwittingly promote
psychological neglect, not care. Thus without prejudicing rapport
with nursing and medical colleagues, the therapist acts, in effect, as
an agent representing the psychological needs of his client. He will
have to influence the institution to encourage good care and to inter-
vene in the individual case to reverse the effects of damaging
experience as well as conduct conventional therapy according to the
needs of the person. The role is, therefore, demanding of a flexible
and wide ranging approach extending well beyond individual sessions in
a consulting room.

One obvious feature of the work of basic psychological care will
have probably struck most readers already. It can clearly be dealt
with just as well by other staff, assuming they have the basic

training. In the example given, I noted that the assumption was of work
in a unit naive to psychological care. This was, in fact, the situation
I encountered several years ago. Things have changed now. A period
ensued in which a close working relationship developed between myself as
psychologist and the nursing staff. The nurses were happy to attend
tutorials and sessions in counselling skills. They appreciated
individual case discussion and the senior nurses in particular sought to
develop themselves in the principles of psychological care. Now a
situation exists which I think may be labelled 'Hawk's fantasy'. The
senior nurses include basic psychological care as a routine part of
their duty. They are progressively taking on the business of
representing the basic psychological needs of clients with the medical
profession. They function in a basic supportive-counselling role
together with normal nursing duties and are collaborating in the
introduction of a scheme of preventative educational counselling for
new families as they become involved with the unit. The psychologist's
role has receded as the nurses have developed in strength and the
function is now to do with back up, teaching (a constant responsibility
which can never be relinquished with the constant flow of new staff) and
dealing with more difficult individual problems.

This outcome could so easily be repeated in selected hospital units
around the country. It waits only for the initiative to be taken by the
psychologists.

REFERENCES

ADAMS, E. and LINDEMANN, E. (1974), Coping with long-term disability,
in Adams, D. and Lindemann, E. (eds), 'Coping and Adaption', New York,
Wiley.
ALEXANDER, F. (1950), 'Psychosomatic Medicine', New York, Norton.
DICKINSON, S. (1982), The nursing process and the professional status
of nursing, 'Nursing Times', 22 June, pp. 61-4.
DRESS, A. and GALLAGHER, E.B. (1981), Haemodialysis, rehabilitation and
psychological support, in Levy, N.B. (ed.), 'Psychonephrology' I, New
York, Plenum.
DUFF, R. and HOLLINGSHEAD, A.B. (1968), 'Sickness and Society', New
York, Harper & Row.
FUNCH, D.P. and METTLIN, C. (1982), The role of support in relation to
recovery from breast surgery, 'Social Science and Medicine', vol. 16,
pp. 91-8.
HAUSER, S.T. (1981), Physician-patient relationship, in Mishler, E.G.
et al., 'Social Contexts of Health, Illness and Patient Care', London,
Cambridge University Press.
HAWKS, D. (1981), The dilemma of clinical practice: surviving as a
clinical psychologist, in Macpherson, I. and Sutton, A. (eds),
'Reconstructing Psychological Practice', London, Croom Helm.
HETHERINGTON, R. (1967), Psychology in the general hospital, 'Bulletin
of the British Psychological Society', vol. 20, pp. 7-10.
HOWELLS, J.G. (ed.) (1976), 'Modern Perspectives in the Psychiatric
Aspects of Surgery', London, Macmillan.
IMBODEN, J.B. (1972) Psycho-social determinants of recovery,
'Advancements in Psychosomatic Medicine', vol. 8, pp. 142-55.

JANIS, I.L. and LEVENTHAL, H. (1965), Psychological aspects of physical illness, in Wolman, B.B., (ed.), 'Handbook of Clinical Psychology', New York, McGraw Hill.

KAPLAN DE-NOUR, A. (1970), Psychotherapy with patients on chronic haemodialysis, 'British Journal of Psychiatry', vol. -16, pp. 207-15.

KAPLAN DE-NOUR, A. (1976), The psychiatric aspects of renal haemodialysis, in Howells, J.G. (ed.), 'Modern Perspectives in the Psychiatric Aspects of Surgery', London, Macmillan.

KAPLAN DE-NOUR, A. (1981), Prediction of adjustment to haemodialysis, in Levy, N.B. (ed.), 'Psychonephrology', I, New York, Plenum.

LACHMAN, S.J. (1972), 'Psychosomatic Disorders: A Behaviouristic Interpretation', New York, Wiley.

LEVY, N.B. (1974), 'Living or Dying - Adaption to Haemodialysis', Springfield, Illinois, Charles C. Thomas.

LEVY, N.B. (ed.) (1981) 'Psychonephrology', I, New York, Plenum.

LEIF, H.I. and FOX, R.C., 'Training for detached concern in medical students, in Lief, H.I. (ed.), 'The Psychological Basis of Medical Practice', New York, Harper & Row.

MALAN, D.H. (1979), 'Individual Psychotherapy and the Science of Psychodynamics', London, Butterworths.

MENZIES, I.E.P. (1970), 'The Functioning of Social Systems as a Defence Against Anxiety', Kent, Headley.

MILLMAN, M. (1977), 'The Unkindest Cut', New York, Morrow.

MOOS, R.H. (ed.) (1977), 'Coping with Physical Illness', New York, Plenum.

NICHOLS, K.A. (1979), Psychological care for the ill and injured, in Oborne, D.J., Gruneberg, M.M. and Eiser, J.R. (eds), 'Research in Psychology and Medicine', Vol. 2, London, Academic Press.

NICHOLS, K.A. (1981), Psychological care in general hospitals, 'Bulletin of the British Psychological Society', vol. 34, pp. 90-4.

PARSONS, T. (1975), The sick role and the role of the physician reconsidered, 'Millbank Memorial Fund Quarterly', vol. 53, pp. 257-78.

QUERIDO, A. (1954), Forecast and follow up - an investigation into the clinical, social and mental factors determining the results of hospital treatment, 'British Journal of Preventative and Social Medicine', vol. 13, pp. 33-49.

ROSKIES, E. (1980), Considerations in developing a treatment program for the coronary-prone (Type A) behaviour pattern, in Davidson, P.O. (ed.), 'Behavioural Medicine: Changing Health Lfestyles', New York, Brunner.

STRAIN, J.J. (1981), Impediments to psychological care of the chronic renal patient, in Levy, N.B. (ed.), 'Psychonephrology', I, New York, Plenum.

'The Lancet', (1979), 3 March, pp. 478-9.

WAITZKIN, H. and STOECKLE, D. (1972), The communication of information about illness, 'Advancement of Psychosomatic Medicine', Vol. 8, pp. 180-215.

WEBSTER, M.E. (1981), Communicating with dying patients, 'Nursing Times', 4 June, pp. 999-1002.

WEINMANN, J. (1978), Integrating psychology with general medicine, 'Bulletin of the British Psychological Society', vol. 32, pp. 352-5.

WOODHAMS, P. (1981), personal communication.

Chapter 13

SOCIAL CLASS ISSUES IN PSYCHOTHERAPY
Eric Bromley

One analyst, in fact, explicitly stated that he was trying to learn to speak with lower-class people again. He explained that he came from a working class family, but that he felt that as a result of middle-class encultivation - ... - he had lost his ability to speak with blue-collar people; he was trying to regain this ability and become bidialectic or diglossic.   (Meltzer, 1978)

PROLOGUE

As I start to try and write this chapter with one of its underlying themes being that of personalising what is written, several thoughts arise but the main ones are how personal, whether I will say anything new or useful or interesting and whether it's really going to be possible to 'synthesise' personal experience, ideas and emotions with discussion and review of 'learned' articles and books.

It seems hard to believe that social class can be anything other than a live and burning issue to any helping 'professional' from a working-class background. Specifically in the field of psychiatry, it is hard to perceive the scene as being anything other than largely middle-class professional elites (psychiatrists, psychologists, social workers) ministering to largely working-class populations in working-class ghettoes called psychiatric hospitals (often through a somewhat ignored and difficult to 'classify' corps of nurses). But surely that's an exaggeration, of course it is, or is it? But in any case what's all this got to do with psychotherapy? 'Certainly' (when that word is used to mean its approximate opposite) psychotherapy is used mainly with non-hospitalised non-working-class (or perhaps upper working-class) patients. Most psychotherapy takes place between mutually non-working-class people, most other psychiatric treatment takes place between non-mutual working-class patients and non-working-class professionals.

The play that follows is dedicated, I would like to say, to answering the question why but must honestly say the questions whether and how.

PSYCHOTHERAPY AND SOCIAL CLASS

A play in two acts

ACT 1

The scene is a lecture room. A learned conference is taking place. The stage is empty and in darkness apart from a lectern behind which stands a man, the lecturer, dressed in a white smock with violet coloured velvet edging and a conical white hat similarly embroidered. On top of the hat is a flashing green light. (McCue, 1977)

He is lit by a single white spotlight.

The man addresses his audience (which is the audience) in at first a nervous voice with much hesitation, coughing, etc. As he progresses, his voice and manner take on a firmness such that the final few paragraphs are presented with considerable flourish.

Lecturer:

Some issues in 'social class and psychotherapy'

In this paper, I would like to address myself to some of the problems in relation to, and issues raised by, psychotherapy with clients from different social classes. Immediately we are into several extremely interesting broad areas of discussion. To anybody who isn't completely unaware of social reality, class is important at both individual and political levels. To Marxists 'class' is almost equatable to 'politics' and other strands of political thought equally stress its importance if only by spending a fair amount of time in attempting to deny that class has any relevance whatsoever. But this paper cannot (and its author would not wish to) address itself to more traditional political dimensions of activity, but rather limits itself to a discussion of one particular form of activity at the level of the individual, namely psychotherapy.

For this is not a political conference, it is psychotherapeutic and my paper will limit itself to a survey of the issue and problems of psychotherapy with working class clients.

The literature on social class factors in psychotherapy is considerable.

Perhaps the earliest quotation of note is from Freud (1905) himself: 'those patients who do not possess a reasonable degree of education ... should be refused'. This class-laden sentiment fell apparently on receptive ears in the psychoanalytic/psychiatric field so that Davis (1938) for instance could angrily denounce the fact that few working class patients were accepted for psychotherapy as a manifestation of the 'invidious, discriminatory aspect of social life' in the mental health field. Very few empirical studies seem to have taken place till the pioneering work of Hollingshead and Redlich (1958) which showed very clearly the class discriminatory nature of psychiatric

services in general. More specifically, they showed that, at least as
far as their sample was concerned, lower class patients were much more
likely to receive therapy such as ECT, tranquilisers or confinement and
much less likely to receive psychotherapy than their higher status
countrymen. Hollingshead and Redlich's work was clearly of crucial,
seminal importance and led to a plethora of studies. These papers can
best be summarised under the headings of the questions which they
attempt to answer.

(1)   Are lower-class patients less likely to be chosen for psycho-
       therapy?

These studies fall into two groups, surveys of existing practices and
simulated studies in which social class in manipulated as a variable in
the selection procedure.

Simulated studies are few in numbers. Crocetti et al. (1976)
presented 30 psychiatrists in private practice and 38 experienced
clinicians in a community mental health clinic with 4 psychiatric case
descriptions of upper- and lower-class patients. They report that no
significant class differences were present in relation to recommended
treatment. Rowden et al. (1970) and Meltzer (1978) report contrary
findings. In the former study, 34 practising or trainee therapists
were shown 10 case records (based on case-notes but of hypothetical
patients) in which two variables, social class and 'insight-verbal
ability' were manipulated. They found that both variables significantly affected the likelihood of being chosen for psychotherapy -
the higher the social class (and the higher the 'insight-verbal
ability') the greater the chance of being chosen for psychotherapy.
Meltzer's paper contains a fairly sophisticated study in which 10
psychoanalysts, 10 trained non-analyst psychotherapists and 10
psychology undergraduate students were asked to assess suitability for
psychotherapy of 4 patients of different social classes on the basis of
transcripts of initial interviews. All three groups of therapists
were found more likely to assign the higher social class patients to
psychotherapy. (Correlations between 'social class' and 'assign to
psychotherapy' were .77, .65 and .62 respectively.)

Lee et al. (1970) presented an (acted) taped diagnostic interview to
four groups of 10 psychiatric residents. The first group were given no
prior information about social class and the fourth group were told
that the 'patient' was of lower class. The usual diagnosis in the
first group was 'normal with excellent prognosis' with respect of
psychotherapy and in the latter group, 'mentally ill with fair
prognosis'.

Studies based on actual practice are much more numerous. Overwhelmingly, they show that working-class patients are less likely to be
offered psychotherapy. Some of the very long list of studies showing
this bias are:
       (i)   Balch and Miller (1974) who studied 256 consecutive cases at a
              community based mental health centre. They found that advice
              and supportive psychotherapy was the modal treatment for all

socio-economic groups other than class V where the modal
treatment (45 per cent) was (of course?) medication.

(ii)   Marx and Spray (1972) in a survey covering 35,820 (!)
       patients seen privately for psychotherapy in three large US
       cities found that only 7.2 per cent were in their lowest
       class grouping (based on annual income).

(iii) Rosenthal and Frank (1958) showed that psychiatrists referred
       significantly more upper class patients for psychotherapy
       (and significantly more of their young, better educated and
       white patients).

(iv)   Schaffer and Myers (1954) found that only 3 per cent of Class
       V patients, compared to 64 per cent of Class II patients
       were accepted for psychotherapy in a low-cost clinic where
       fees were set according to income.

(v)   Schmidt and Hancey (1979) in a free, US Military Hospital
       found that although 'social class' (actually, in their study,
       army rank) did not affect the type of treatment offered, it
       did affect the length of psychotherapeutic treatment
       recommended.

Other studies showing a bias against offering psychotherapy to lower-
class patients include Bailey et al. (1959), Brill and Storrow (1960),
Cole (1962), Daly and Johnson (1970), Miller and Grigg (1966), Redlich
et al. (1955), Shader (1970), Thain (1968) and Yanamoto and Goin (1966)
in addition, of course, to Hollingshead and Redlich (1958) already
referred to.

There are relatively few instances reported of practices where lower-
class patients were accepted on an equal basis for psychotherapy.
Albronda et al. (1964) claims that psychotherapy was attempted with all
patients referred, irrespective of social class. Frank et al. (1978)
in a 'walk-in' clinic describes a negotiated approach based on initially
responding to the expressed 'wants' rather than professionally perceived
'needs' of the clients and claims no class bias in treatment choice.
Lowe and Ziglin (1973) studied 1061 white, male, voluntary first
admission alcoholic patients and found no significant differences in
treatment offered between different socio-economic classes. Wold and
Steger (1976) describe 'a clinic with therapists sympathetic to lower-
class values where no patients is judged unsuitable for psychotherapy'.
Finally Springer (1977) in a survey of forty mental health centres
suggests that assignment of particular forms of treatment had little
or nothing to do with social class.

The overwhelming evidence is then that, in practice, lower-class
patients are less likely to be offered psychotherapy and that this is
partially confirmed in more simulated, experimental, studies. One also
cannot help noticing the change over the time span of the studies
quoted in that, with the exception of Albronda, only studies in the
1970s show equality of treatment.

One qualification must be made immediately. All the studies quoted
so far in this section have been in a USA context. Indeed one theme we
will return to is the dearth of published research in countries other
than the USA. Only one directly relevant UK study could be found,

that of Freeman (1967) whose paper represents a retrospective analysis
of patients referred for free, NHS outpatient treatment to the
Lansdowne Clinic in Edinburgh. No patients referred from social
classes IV or V (Registrar General's classification) were offered
individual therapy, all thirty-eight such patients being offered group
therapy.

Studies of peripheral importance for our purposes but within a UK
context include those of Buglass (1976) who showed that depressive
parasuicides in social class V in Edinburgh were less likely to be
referred to psychiatrists (not necessarily for psychotherapy of course)
than similar patients from other social classes. (As a fascinating
but quite irrelevant aside, the same study showed that '20 of the patients
described as having no psychiatric or personality abnormality were
referred to a psychiatrist'!).

Studies in non-English speaking countries include those of Gisin et
al. (1978) in Switzerland, Shanan and Moses (1961) in Israel, both of
which confirm the expected connection between social class and the
likelihood of receiving psychotherapy. Wodak-Leodolter (1978) in
Vienna, though, reports a project on group psychotherapy with working-
class clients which, it is claimed, is proving successful – 'They are
well adapted to this speech situation and manage it well.'

(2) Do lower-class patients want psychotherapy?

Many suggestions have been made that one reason for the imbalance in
members of different social classes involvement in psychotherapy is
that psychotherapy is not what the working-class client wants. In
other words, the system is responding to the divergent demands of the
members of the different social classes (as consumers of what is on
offer) by providing divergent forms of treatment.

Thus in two studies Aronson and Overall (1968) and Overall and
Aronson (1963) administered a thirty-five-item questionnaire to two
groups of lower-class and middle-class clients to assess the expressed
wants of these groups. They claim that lower-class clients demand
more direction and support from the mental health sustem and adopt a
more passive role in their treatment. But they found no significant
differences in terms of demand for specifically medical help nor in
interest in dealing with psychological material. Balch and Miller
(1974) compared the clients' and clinic workers' perception of
presenting problem and treatment expectation of 256 consecutive
referrals to a mental health centre. They found a greater degree of
client/professional congruence among the higher social classes and
suggest lower social classes were more oriented to receiving specifically medical help (mainly medieation).

Somewhat similarly, Brill and Storrow (1960) claim to find that
lower-class patients have a tendency to see their problems in physical
rather than psychological terms, seek symptomatic relief rather than
overall help, lack an understanding of the psychotherapeutic process
and have little desire for psychotherapy.

Bookbinder and Gussman (1964) show a significant but small correlation (r=.34, n=63) between occupational/educational level and participation in treatment as judged by the therapist and Imber et al. (1955) claim lower class patients have little interest in, or ability to deal with interpersonal concepts.

Heitler (1974) suggests that working-class patients have very little idea what psychotherapy involves, so very little 'core of mutually understood role expectations' and that therefore there is no initial 'working alliance' with the therapist.

Fitzgibbons (1971 and 1972), though, suggests an 'impressive degree of similarity' exists between upper class and working-class clients on a number of factors relating to what patients wanted help with. Goin et al. (1975) showed that 52 per cent of lower social class patients expressed a desire to solve their problems by 'talking about their feelings and their past, i.e. through insight therapy'. (Of the remainder 34 per cent wanted advice and only 14 per cent sought medication.) Lorion (1974) in a commendably brief paper found no significant social class effect using mental attitude and treatment expectation surveys and concluded that 'low income patients do not necessarily have more negative pre-treatment attitudes and expectations than upper socio-economic status applicants'. Perhaps the most sophisticated attempt to assess what different clients, and different social classes want out of therapy is that provided by Frank et al. (1978). This study used a questionnaire (the patients request form) which measured what patients wanted out of fourteen categories of help. Class differences were limited to Class V compared to the rest on just six categories not including 'psychodynamic insight', 'clarification', 'confession' or 'reality contact' (all of which might be construed as being provided by psychotherapy). Class V patients did request more 'psychological expertise', succorance, community triage social intervention and administrative help.

The evidence (and again it is only evidence from the USA) is equivocal as to whether low social class patients have differing wants from, attempt to make differing demands on, the mental health system. Suffice it to say that there is insufficient evidence to suggest that the system in offering working class clients less chance of psychotherapy is doing so in response to working class demand.

(3) Do working-class patients do less well when 'given' psychotherapy?

In attempting to answer this questions one has, of course, to try and answer the question what 'doing well' in psychotherapy means. Most of the studies quoted here essentially duck the issue by using length of stay in psychotherapy as the criterion. Obviously, this raises quite serious conceptual problems, a discussion of which will be left till later.

An excellent survey of this question is that of Jones (1974). He quotes nine studies showing that lower class patients are more likely to be early drop-outs as against two, Overall and Aronson (1964) and

Lorr et al. (1958), who fail to find such a relationship. The latter
study involved two samples (of 115 each) taken from thirteen different
clinics. Each sample consisted of 57 'terminators', defined as those
terminating therapy within a shorter time than six weeks, and 58
'remainers' who had stayed in psychotherapy for longer than six months.
The hypothesis that terminators were more likely to be of low socio-
economic class was not supported as a statistically significant level
although the result was in the expected direction.

There are several papers not referred to by Jones (1974) which would
seem to support the view that working-class patients do benefit from
psychotherapy. Albronda et al. (1964) in a survey of five years work
in a clinic which offered psychotherapy to clients irrespective of
social class found no signficant social class differences with respect
to drop-out rate. Caligor (1969), referring to a Trades Union
organised therapy project among blue-collar workers, claimed that more
than a quarter of the clients benefitted from psychotherapy. Day and
Reznikoff (1980) found, in relation to psychotherapy with seven- to
eleven-year-old boys, that neither appointment keeping nor drop-out
rate was related to social class. Similarly, Love et al. (1972)
working with children aged eight to thirteen found no significant
social class differences in outcome. (Successful outcome in this study
was that of school grade improvement!) Pettit et al. (1974) in a study
involving 256 patient-therapist dyads and apparently sophisticated
statistical techniques, concluded that 'patients' index of social
position ... (did not account) for a significant portion of the
variance in duration of treatment.' Wold and Steger (1976) surveyed
279 consecutive cases in 'a clinic with therapists sympathetic to lower-
class values where 'no patient is judged unsuitable for psychotherapy'
and found that being unemployed was related negatively to staying in
therapy but that social class per se was not.

Gottschalk et al. (1967) claims low social class is predictive of
better prognosis in psychotherapy and appears to be the only study to
do so. Improvement was measured by the change in scores on a psychiatric morbidity scale (PMS) based on a structured interview. Therapy
consisted of a maximum of six weekly sessions of between twenty-five
and fifty minutes duration. The improvment in PMS scores was
significantly better for social classes IV and V as a group compared
to the others.

There are, though, a larger number of studies suggesting that low
social class is associated with poor outcome in psychotherapy. Cole
et al. (1962) found that 'survival rates' past thirty interviews were
13 per cent for class V and 11 per cent for class IV compared to 38
per cent for class III and 41 per cent for classes I and II combined.
Frank et al. (1957) found that, of 91 white outpatients, 41 per cent
of lower-class patients terminated before the fourth session compared
to 21 per cent of middle-class patients. Goldstein's general approach,
for example in Goldstein (1973A and 1973B) is based on the premise that
working-class patients in general do not benefit from traditional
psychotherapy. Terestman et al. (1974) using outcome ratings based
on case record data, and subjective ratings, found that blue collar
workers did do less well than other social classes. Yanamoto and Goin

(1966) show that lower-class patients are less likely to attend for first session when chosen for psychotherapy.

Again, all the papers cited under this heading so far have been based on patient samples in the USA. There are few studies elsewhere. Wodak-Leodolter (1978) in Austria has already been referred to and claims that working-class patients can benefit from (group) psycho-therapy. Arana Gallegos (1974) apparently takes for granted the difficulties in using psychotherapy with the poor, and questions whether basic attitudes within psychoanalysis perhaps engenders poverty. Freeman (1967) states 'There is little point, in the evidence drawn from the group results in offering psychoanalytic psychotherapy to ... patients ... belonging to social classes IV and V' which seeing that no patients in these two classes (and only one is social class III even) had been selected for individual therapy strikes at least this reader as somewhat perverse. Freeman's criterion for success appears to be a subjective rating of 'recovered' or 'improved' compared to 'no change'. (Freeman seems to have rejected any suggestions that any patients involved could have got any worse.) Reworking Freeman's figures of the 38 social class IV and V patients involved in the group therapy, 4 were rated as recovered or improved - in 34 there had been 'no change'. Sette (1972) in reporting on psychotherapy with low income patients in Brazil quoted a high drop-out rate of 75 per cent. Zuk (1973) reports a high drop-out rate among Spanish-speaking patients of low social class.

In summary then, the empirical evidence as to whether working-class patients can benefit from psychotherapy is, at worst, equivocal. The use of drop-out rate as a criterion, as is done in most of the studies, is extremely problematical. As Jones (1974) points out, although length in therapy has been shown in general to be predictive of successful outcome, it may be that a proportion of lower-class patients receive enough from a few sessions to either convince them psycho-therapy will not help them, or to help them in significant ways (perhaps in both cases because realisation dawns that their problems really are objective and situational rather than subjective and 'psychological'). Other criteria used seem, without exception, open to serious criticism as being highly subjective (rated improvement) or only marginally valid (e.g. school grade improvement).

(4)   Does the social class of the therapist have any effect?

One of the suggested explanations of the alleged difficulty of psycho-therapy with working-class patients is the 'social gap' theory - meaning, of course, that psychotherapy does not work, or is not offered, because of the social distance between therapist and patient. Most of the reported studies either assume that the therapist is middle or upper class, or that it matters not, anyway. Albee (1977) in a beautifully polemical paper argues that 'psychotherapy was created for the relief of the emotional problems of affluent clients' and points out, in relation to Clinical Psychologists, that 'As admission to clinical training programs becomes more and more selective and difficult, the lucky few who are admitted are obsessive

high-achievers with outstanding academic records and high test scores.'
In short, they 'are obsessives heavily indoctrinated about the
importance of time, inner control and research ... are selected from the
upper middle class and few of them speak the language, share the values,
or understand the problems of the poor.' He argues that the cultural
gap is so huge that there is no point providing (free at time of need)
psychotherapy because the poor cannot benefit from it and the non-poor
use it to deal with problems which are inherent in industrial civilisa-
tions rather than being ilnesses. A more empirical approach is that
represented by Carkhuff and Pierce (1967). They took two white and two
black counsellors (one each from middle- and lower-class backgrounds)
and assigned to them sixteen patients distributed equally among the
four combinations of class and ethnicity represented. Taped segments
of counselling sessions were rated in terms of clients' depth of
exploration (which previously had, it is claimed, been shown to be
associated with positive outcome in therapy). They concluded that 'The
patients most similar to the race and social class of the counsellor
involved tended to explore themselves most, whilst patients most
dissimilar tended to explore themselves least.' McNair et al. (1962)
and Carson (1967) both claim to show that therapists with mechanical-
technical interests are better in working with working-class patients
and whilst they do not related this finding to the social class of the
therapist, it could well be that this variable was so correlated
(i.e. that 'working-class' therapists are more likely to have such
interests). Of similiarly peripheral interest to the main question,
Harrison et al. (1970) showed in a child psychiatric setting that there
was considerable interplay between the social class of origin of the
psychiatrist, the social class of the patient and the diagnosis and
recommendation for treatment. For example working-class children were
eleven times (!) more likely to be given a 'chronic brain syndrome'
diagnosis and were less likely to be recommended for psychotherapy
by 'upper-class' as compared to 'lower-class' psychiatrists. Siassi et
al. (1976) suggest that middle-class therapists find it difficult to
identify with working-class patients and that this adversely affects
their therapeutic efficacy. Thain (1968) showed in a study which used
artificial behavioural descriptions of clients that the social class
of the rater 'therapist' and the rated 'patient' were both positively
correlated with a recommendation for psychotherapy.

    Butler (1978) investigated a sample of 202 working-class patients
in either family of individual therapy, found that the relationship
between the therapists' social class background and early termination
(one or two sessions) was nearly random and concluded that 'despite
previous research which has supported the similarity of therapists'
and clients' backgrounds to be important to continuance, this study
found no such relationship'.

    Burstein (1976) suggests that a 'social gap' between therapist
and patient may be irrelevant,or even facilitative, to the therapeutic
process. In arguing against the use of 'para-professionals' he cites
Keiser (1974) and Shapiro and Pinsker (1973) as showing that a cultural
gap can potentiate psychoanalytic therapy. In fact it is hard to see
that Keiser's paper does anything of the sort as it consists of
excellent 'clinical vignettes' of the type of problems engendered by

differing early family experiences among social extremes and has some very interesting comments to make about the role of language in therapy but nowhere suggests that a cultural gap is advantageous. Shapiro and Pinsker's paper is similarly anecdotal and relates essentially to ethnic rather than social class factors.

Other studies relevant to the question include those of Haase (1964) who used paired Rorschach protocols and accompanying social histories equated for all major factors other than social class. Haase gave these to seventy-five clinical psychologists from varying social class backgrounds. He found there was a significant and consistent bias against the lower-class 'patients' in terms of diagnosis and prognosis and that this bias was not significantly affected by the social class background of the psychologist. Marx and Spray (1972) in the survey previously referred to showed that the highly paid patient was more likely to be treated and that the 'social class origins of the psycho-therapist ... does not affect this pattern of preferential treatment'. It is of some importance to note that this study related only to patients seen privately.

So, once again, all the studies seem to be USA-based and to give conflicting answers about the effect of the social class of the therapist.

(5)   Why are there social class differences in psychotherapy variables?

One explanation, that of cultural (or social) gap has already been touched upon. There are two other broad categories of explanation.
(a)   The difficulties in psychotherapy are mediated by the language attributes of the working class client, or
(b)   by other 'psychological' mediators.

In some ways, the 'language' hypothesis is better worked out. The seminal paper is that of Bernstein (1964) in which he applies his concepts of restricted and elaborated code to the practice of psycho-therapy. Summarily, he claims that working-class culture consists of a restricted linguistic code which has the following features:
(i)   It is generated by relationships in which the intent of others is clear and can be taken for granted;
(ii)   it is relatively simple in structure and content and, therefore, more predictable;
(iii)   there is little, if any, verbal elaboration;
(iv)   the code signals social rather than personal identity;
(v)   it is therefore relatively impersonal;
(vi)   and becomes a vehicle for expressing group similarity and cohesion rather than for emphasising personal uniqueness;
(vii)   ofter personal identity is signalled through non-verbal channels;
(viii) emphasis is on the 'concrete here-and-now ... rather than reflective, abstract relationships';
(ix)   the restricted code does not facilitate an interest in (motivational) processes;
(x)   the self is rarely the subject of verbal investigation;

(xi) 'Speech is not used as a means for a voyage from one person
      to another', and

(xii) verbal control over behaviour is mediated by authority rather
      than logic.

In contradistinction the middle and upper clases are more able to
speak in elaborated code which has the opposite qualities.

Some of the empirical evidence for this analysis is to be found in
Bernstein (1971 and 1973)(1) and leads him to suggest that restricted
code leads to difficulties in a psychotherapeutic relationship because
the status relationship is ambiguous, there is a loss of social identity,
it does not facilitate personal insight and will tend to lead to
dependency as a defence against the lack of structure. Bernstein
himself does not postulate an impossibility in regard to psychotherapy
with working-class patients and, indeed, says 'I am not suggesting that
therapy with patients limited to a restricted code cannot be rewarding
and beneficial. The absence of so-called appropriate communications is
pregnant with meaning and significance for the therapist if he has a
more sensitive understanding of the predicament of the patient and a
willingness to adapt his technique.'

This approach to the problem is restated by Hallum (1978) in
claiming as a result of Bernstein's analysis that in the lower classes,
the purpose of communication is control rather than the exchange of
information, that lower-class speech does not promote the communication
of subjective experience and that 'Speakers of restricted codes do not
confront themselves, or the objective world in an analytic manner'.
As a result, Hallum argues that psychotherapy is no use to the working-
class and that behaviour therapy or Minuchin's 'structural family
therapy' ought to be applied.

Meltzer (1978) tried to test two hypotheses relating to Bernstein's
analysis: that patients are judged suitable for psychotherapy when they
speak an elaborated code and that this judgment will not consciously be
founded on language cues. He certainly found, as previously stated,
that higher-class patients were more likely to be judged suitable for
psychotherapy. Whether or not this was due to elaborated code speaking
was tested indirectly by generating, according to Meltzer, the hypothesis that if the significant factor is the elaborated code then there
should be no significant difference between the three groups of judges
(of differing degrees of psychiatric/psychological sophistication).
This was confirmed - there were differences but these were non-
significant. It is, though, by no means obvious, at least to this
reader, that the generated hypothesis 'proves' the original hypothesis
that the judgment is based on elaborated code judgments. Meltzer's
argument seems to be that the judgment cannot be a sophisticated
judgment of the psychological needs of the 'patients', can only be
based on their language because paralinguistic cues are removed by
using transcripts and therefore 'elaborated code'. But all three
groups of judges may be equally good at judging social class from
language cues which have nothing to do with elaborated code (for
instance 'picking up' upper-class restricted code markers). If this
were so, and if all three groups (unconsciously or otherwise) thought

upper-class patients more likely to benefit from psychotherapy, the result would be explained. Meltzer's third hypothesis that unconscious use is made of language cues seems to be supported in that only 15 per cent spontaneously remarked that language was a factor and even after direct enquiry 25 per cent failed to appreciate its importance. Meltzer's paper if not 'proving' at least gives weight to an 'elaborated code' hypothesis. It must remain an open question whether this is because (all the judges being middle-class anyway) 'status homophily' (Kandel 1971) was at work or as Meltzer claims because the chosen patients 'speak a semiotic code which facilitates the elaboration of individual experience and therefore allows a detailed exploration of their idiosyncratic world of intention and meaning'.

Other studies have attempted to find other psychological mediators between social class and psychotherapeutic variables. Potential mediators include level of (verbal) intelligence (which impinges on the above analysis of language behaviour) authoritarianism, psychological differentiation and locus of control. Dowds et al. (1977) found that verbal IQ locus of control and authoritarianism were all related to social class and to being rated as suitable for psychotherapy. They suggest, therefore, that all three are cognitive mediators in this respect. Rowden's (1970) finding that in a simulated study psycho-therapists were more likely to assign to therapy the patients with high 'insight-verbal ability' has already been referred to. One study of relevance to the question of authoritarianism as an intervening variable is that of Canter (1971) who used a sample of 220 inpatients, overwhelmingly of lower-middle or lower class and found that high authoritarian scoring patients preferred structured 'lectures' to less structured 'group therapy' sessions.

Two 'multivariate' approaches are those of Lorr et al. (1958) and Fontana et al. (1980). Lorr in the paper previously mentioned failed to find any single variable (including limited vocabulary, authori-tarianism and social class) which significantly differentiated the two groups. However, using item selection from the various question-naires used and multiple regression techniques he was able to differentiate the two groups (with cross-validation in that two sub-samples were used).

Fontana used the technique of causal modelling (or path analysis) in a relatively small sample of thirty male outpatients. He failed to find any mediating effect, between social class and suitability for psychotherapy, for five patient cognitive or communication variables (verbal productivity, degree of self-exploration, conceptual level, verbal intelligence and psychological differentiation). Psychological differentiation was found to act as a partial mediator when therapist communication variables are taken into account. The highest correlation with suitability still remained social class per se.

An interesting discussion concerning the role, or lack of it, for intervening variables is provided by Stern et al. (1975), Garfield's (1977) objection to Stern's conclusion and Stern's reply (1977).

In the 1975 paper Stern et al. criticise previous work relating the psychological characteristics of terminators by claiming that no adequate account was taken of social class as being a confounding variable. They successfully test two hypotheses, that social class differences will be found on 'terminator-remainer' questionnaire scales and that within each social class the scales will not differentiate between reaminers and leavers. (The terminator-remainer scales essentially purport to measure poor impulse control, authoritarian attitudes and low expressed anxiety.) They conclude that it is social class differences rather than personality variables which underly the 'problem' of early termination. Garfield questions this finding by denying there was a lack of control for social class in the earlier studies, remarking on the differing cut-off points for premature termination and refusing to accept the Stern finding till replicated. Stern et al. (1977) argue against Garfield's strictures. But a replication is, presumably, still awaited unless one accepts that Butler's (1978) finding implies that 'personality' intervening variables are unimportant. (She found that the only significant predictors of early termination in a sample of working class patients were: client/ therapist disagreement on problem area; inaccurate expectancy with respect to the therapy process; and shorter symptom duration.)

(6)   Can lower class patients be adequately prepared for psychotherapy?

If there are problems associated with psychotherapy and the working class client, is it possible to overcome these difficulties by some form of preparation? There have been several studies attempting to answer this question: Hoehn-Saric et al. (1964) used a role-induction interview involving a general exposition of psychotherapy, comments about the behaviour to be expected from the patient and therapist, a preparation for some possible phenomena such as resistance and stress was laid on improvement being unlikely before four weeks. They found that the experimental group given this induction interview were better than controls judged on various criteria of process and outcome. Strupp and Bloxom (1973) in addition to surveying several studies showing the use- fulness of some form of role-induction, present their own study using a role-induction film describing the experience of a truck driver with a volatile temper who joins a therapy group. They found that on most measures this film was superior to both a role-induction interview and a neutral film. Heitler (1973) showed that an 'anticipatory socialisation interview' was effective in potentiating therapeutic effects with a group of lower-class patients (compared to a control group of the same class).

Conclusions from research

Several general statements can be made about the various papers reviewed:
    (1)   Practically all the empirical research is from the USA.
    (2)   There is very little analysis of the concept of 'class' and
          how this might theoretically articulate with psychotherapy.
    (3)   Similarly, there is little theoretical discussion about the
          nature of psychotherapy in this context although it seems to
          be assumed that it is a process which is mainly about
          intellectual and verbal interaction, and not much else, between
          therapist and patients. (2)

(4)   Very little distinction is made between individual and group
       therapy and, for instance, where group therapy is under
       investigation we are rarely told whether the groups are mixed
       or not with respect to class.
(5)   Similarly little emphasis is placed on the sex of the client -
       some of the studies are men only, some are mixed but nowhere
       does it seem to be seen as a relevant variable.
(6)   There is overwhelming evidence that working-class patients are
       less likely to be offered psychotherapy than other social
       classes.
(7)   But very little evidence that this is because they do not 'want'
       it, and equivocal evidence as whether or not they benefit from
       it, compared to non-working-class patients.
(8)   The evidence relating to reasons for alleged problems in
       psychotherapy with working-class patients and how to prepare
       such patients for psychotherapy is therefore problematical in
       that the supposed difficulties and, therefore, the need for
       preparation is not proven.

Clearly, therefore, more research is needed particularly in view of
the virtually complete lack of any such research outside the USA.
Empirical research must though be accompanied by clearer theoretical
analysis of the issues involved.

ACT II

The scene is a bar in the University College which is staging the
conference. Four people are sat round dressed identically to the
lecturer of the first act except that they are (all) wearing different
hats. Hovering around this group is the barman dressed as, shall we
say, a normal barman. In his hovering he occasionally fills the glasses
of the people.

Person 1:
    I thought lecturer's paper was really quite interesting in pin-
    pointing some of the difficiencies in work that's been published so
    far. But the general drift backs up my view that psychotherapy with
    most working-class patients is just not on. They don't want to do
    anything themselves, can't talk meaningfully about themselves most
    of the time and really only want a magical cure from on high - whether
    it's drugs or some behaviourist to come along and teach them how to
    control anxiety or whatever.

Person 2:
    But that's just what you'd expect anyway. He didn't dare get into
    an analysis of class or of the interface between say psychotherapy
    and politics, the individual level and the social level, but your
    description is just what you'd expect if he did. You can't give
    the working class tools for analysis and you have to keep them passive
    otherwise they'd understand what was wrong in the world and do
    something about it.

Person 1:
God, he's on to politics again. What on earth has your Marxist stuff about class politics got to do with psychotherapy?

Person 2:
Well, what is psychotherapy?

Person 3:
The way lecturer described it you'd think it was nothing but somebody having a nice intellectual debate with their therapist about their feelings or whatever. No wonder if that's what they think in the States that they don't do very well with working-class patients - they probably think it's a complete irrelevant bore. No wonder they break off early while your intellectualising middle classes go on forever.

Person 2:
Well, psychotherapy as I see it is a combination of two processes - demystification and dealienation. You make sense of what's happening, of what you're about. And when you're doing that you can begin to bring into consciousness all the repressed, alienated parts of the self because you begin to understand what's led to the ego-splits in the first place. Now, that's very similar to Marxist politics. If the working class realise what's happening, what the system does to them, this will lead to them doing something about it and changing the system that keeps them alienated and oppressed. That's what politics has got to do with psychotherapy - they're the same revolutionary processes at different levels.

Person 1:
So what's stopping these revolutions taking place?

Person 2:
The ideological effect of the mass media. Take some of the descriptions the lecturer mentioned about the working-class restricted code and apply it to the language of say the 'Sun' as an example of the mass media. You'll find all the relevant ones can be applied there as well, it's simplified, lacking in any analysis, mediated by authority relationships, there is a core of mutual ideology which can be taken for granted, etc. So the working-class speak in a restricted code because that's the way they're taught to. And they're taught to so they can be more easily oppressed. The language mystifies and/or trivialises everything. That's why the revolution hasn't taken place, why psychotherapy doesn't work as well.

Person 1:
Rubbish, the restricted code is there just because they're not as bright and can't intellectually use words the same as we can. And there's strong evidence that intellectual level is genetic anyway. So psychotherapy is difficult with them because they're constitutionally unable to analyse well enough.

Person 2:
Not that chestnut again. You can't say it's genetic. All the work of

Kamin and people like that shows that. And anyway it's conceptually
all wrong. Have a look at the third note in Bromley (1983). (3)

Person 3:
   But you're both assuming an inability to speak in elaborated code is
   a disadvantage. It may not be an inability so much as an unwillingness. Several people have questioned the emprical and conceptual
   basis of Bernstein's ideas and ideas of cultural deprivation in
   general. Look at Labov (1969) for example who showed that given the
   right context really deprived working-class kids could speak in an
   elaborate, logically sophisticated, way.

   If it is an inability then it might be a useful one. It's all
   right Bernstein, Hallum, Meltzer and people like that saying the
   worker can't see things individualistically, can't analyse and
   emphasise individual, compared to group, motivations but perhaps,
   just perhaps his way of looking at life is nearer to reality.

Person 4:
   Now we're getting somewhere. What the real goal of psychotherapy
   should be is the realisation that individual identification is the
   supreme delusion. The whole emphasis of Watts and Zen therapists
   and so on is quite right. We have to break through this emphasis on
   individuality. That's why I agree about therapy not being about
   words being exchanged between therapist and client. We need to de-
   emphasise subjective language and motivation.

Barman: (Appearing with drinks but speaking directly to the audience so
   that the persons do not hear)
   I must have the ability and the patience to formulate what is not
   contained in the language of our time, for what is not intelligible
   is meaningless. Miller (1964).

Person 3:
   No, that mystical mumbo-jumbo isn't what I meant. Capitalist modes
   of production, capitalist ideologies alienate all social classes.
   But they are alienated in different ways. The working-class is
   alienated in that their creative power is expropriated. As
   individuals they have no power, their culture is destroyed by imposed
   mass culture. But as a class, collectively they are powerful and
   could be all powerful. Therefore their de-emphasis on individual
   motivational analysis is functionally useful. Collective, group,
   activity is all that is available for them to have an impact on the
   real world.

   . The alienation of the bourgeiosie is the split between their
   individual power, which to some extent because of their relationship
   to production they have, and their attitudes to this power. For
   some, this alienation leads to them fooling themselves about the
   individual selfishness of this power by offering help quote the
   less fortunate unquote and thereby helping to expropriate any ability
   the individual worker has to help themselves at the same time as
   ameliorating their own guilt feelings about their power. Hence the
   lady bountiful doer of good works, hence the helping professional

and hence the correctness of the working-class rejecting psychotherapy as presently practised. They dimly recognise it for what it
is - class cultural imperialism, an attempt to get them to think in
bourgeois, intellectualistic ways, rather than generate a collective
class-based ideology of solidarity, an attempt to expropriate, or
trivialise, their culture by emphasising individuality against that
collective. Mass media does it, helping professionals do it.

Person 1:
You'll have to put that more simply for me.

Person 3:
The worker is suffering from real, objective factors which can only
be solved collectively, politically if you like. The ruling class
and the bourgeoisie suffer from fantasy-based subjective factors
which can, arguably, be solved at an individual level - through
psychotherapy in the context we're talking about.

Person 2:
Plausible but dangerous I call your analysis. Psychotherapy if it
were available would help working class people. It would help them
to start using, if you like, an elaborate code, would help them to
gain, or regain, their analytical abilities. Potentially it could
be a demystifying, dealienating process which would liberate them as
individuals so they would be freer to take part in collective,
political activity. Our fight should be to bring proper, professional psychotherapy to everybody who needs it.

Person 3:
No, we should deprofessionalise. We should fight for the setting up
of self-help groups where working-class people can share and by
sharing strengthen their realisation of individual powerlessness and
collective potency.

Person 4:
Well, that might be better than nothing but even then it only goes
part of the way. Alienation isn't to do with particular forms of
society it's universal and it's to do with the fantasy of individual
self-hood. What we should be doing is working towards that
realisation.

Person 1:
This has all got a bit beyond me. Most working-class people don't
want psychotherapy, want to use drugs or be taught or told what to
do, want to be dependent on us. Why can't we just give them what
they want. Anyway, I think it's time for us to give the author the
last word.

Author enters L. He is dressed, if you will, as a normal author. He
speaks to the audience.

Author:

Epilogue

The discussion we have heard went on for many hours, many days, in
fact probably until his death. The discussion went into fields
which lecturer had only lightly touched on:
The role and difficulties of the upwardly mobile helping professional
from a working-class background;
The subjective reality represented and the feelings engendered by
the opening quotation from Meltzer;
The reality of concrete inequality between classes compared to all
this vague stuff about alienation;
The objective and subjective aspects of class identification;
And many other issues.

But the author wanted to finish to watch the world cup final on TV
and to dream about the darkroom he was making and to go on holiday so
the later parts of that discussion must wait.

NOTES

1 The empirical foundation is at least arguably shaky and hence the
   theoretical superstructure somewhat unstable. A good, brief,
   critique of Bernstein's ideas in particular and cultural deprivation
   in general is provided by Westergaard and Resler (1976), pp. 336-42
   (with footnotes). Perhaps one quotation therefrom will give the
   right flavour:
       the weight of interpretation placed upon limited data is some-
       times excessive, the refinements of interpretation tortured in
       their obscurity. There is a risk ... of promoting a caricature
       image of manual working class perspectives and life orientations
       as essentially limited to the here and now; as lacking the vision
       and the capacity to take off from the particular to the general,
       from the present to the future, from the known to the unknown.
2 This lack of specification is highlighted in Baum and Felzer (1964).
   They argue that there needs to be a more active therapist role with
   lower class patients. Their description of activity is 'a
   flexibility and spontaneous initiative applied to the particular
   needs of the particular patient at a given time' - surely a statement that most psychotherapists would attach to psychotherapy in
   general.
3 Barman: He's quite right. Genetics determines how an individual
   reacts to and is moulded by, his or her environment. There are two
   simple models, the environment has no effect or environmental
   effects are the same for different individuals. The first of these
   can be represented as:

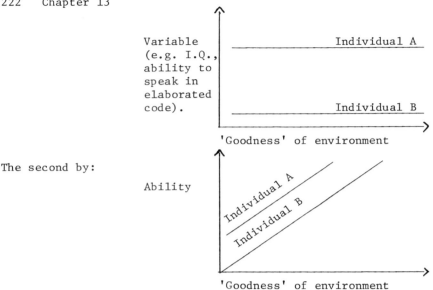

'Goodness' of environment

The second by:

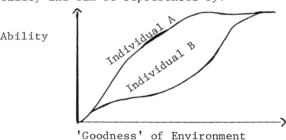

'Goodness' of environment

The first is clearly nonsense. Even the second, simplistic though it is, implies that Individual B, given a sufficiently 'good' environment will have the ability to speak elaborated code and, conversely, that Individual A, if given (over their life-span) a sufficiently poor environment, would not be able to.

But a third model, with non-linear interactions, is almost certainly closer to reality and can be represented by:

Ability

'Goodness' of Environment

In very poor environments (e.g. being reared without any verbal interaction with anybody) neither individual has the ability, given an ideally perfect environment, both would have the same ability. Two things follow:
  (i)   Any analysis of the degree of genetic involvement depends on a presupposition of what present inequalities of environment represent as a proportion of the range of possible inequalities in environment, and;
  (ii)   Differences in abilities between groups (e.g. in elaborated code ability between social classes) will similarly depend on the range of inter- and intra-group inequalities in environment.

REFERENCES

ALBEE, G.W. (1977), Does including Psychotherapy in Health Insurance represent a Subsidy to the Rich from the Poor? 'American Psychologist', vol. 32, no. 9, pp. 719-21.
ALBRONDE, H.F. et al. (1964), Social Class and Psychotherapy, 'Archives of General Psychiatry', vol. 10, pp. 276-83.
ARANA GALLEGOS, J. (1974), Psychotherapy and Poverty: 1 Psychotherapy and Social Forces, 'Revista de Neuro-Psiquiatria', vol. 37, pp. 169-76.
ARONSON, H. and OVERALL, B. (1966), 'Social Work', vol. 11, no. 1, pp. 35-41.
BAILEY, M.A. et al. (1959), A Study in Factors related to Length of Stay in Psychotherapy, 'Journal of Clinical Psychology', vol. 15, pp. 442-4.
BALCH, P. and MILLER, K. (1974), Social Class and the Community Mental Health Center, 'American Journal of Community Psychology', vol. 2, no. 3, pp. 243-53.
BAUM, O.E. and FELZER, S.B. (1964), Activity in Initial Interviews with Lower Class Patients, 'Archives of General Psychiatry', vol. 10, pp 345-53.
BERNSTEIN, B. (1964), Social Class, Speech Systems and Psychotherapy, 'British Journal of Sociology', vol. 15, no. 1, pp. 54-64.
BERNSTEIN, B. (1971 and 1973), 'Class, Codes and Control', vols 1 and 2, London, Routledge & Kegan Paul.
BOOKBINDER, L.J. and GUSSMAN, L.J. (1964), Social Attainment, Pre-morbid Adjustment and Participation in Inpatient Psychiatric Treatment, 'Journal of Clinical Psychology', vol. 20, pp. 513-5.
BRILL, N.Q. and STORROW, H.A. (1960), Social Class and Psychiatric Treatment, 'Archives of General Psychiatry', vol. 3, pp. 340-4.
BROMLEY, E. (1983), Social Class and Psychotherapy, in Pilgrim, D., 'Psychology and Psychotherapy: Current Trends and Issues', London, Routledge & Kegan Paul.
BUGLASS, D. (1976), The Relation of Social Class to the Characteristics and Treatment of Parasuicides, 'Social Psychiatry', vol. 11, no. 3, pp. 107-19.
BURSTEIN, A.G. (1976), Psychotherapy for the Poor, in 'Successful Psychotherapy', New York, Brunner-Mazel, 1976.
BUTLER, P. (1978), Continuance in Psychotherapy - Working Class Clients, 'Dissertation Abstracts International', vol. 39, no. 2-8, p. 972.
CALIGOR, L. (1969), Report on a Clinical Conference held at Solidarity House by the International Union, United Automobile, Aerospace and Agricultural Implement Workers of America, Detroit, 6 February, 1969 (unpublished).
CANTER, F.M. (1971), Authoritian Attitudes, Degree of Pathology and Preference for Structured versus Unstructured Psychotherapy in Hosptialised Mental Patients, 'Psychological Reports', vol. 28, no. 1, pp. 231-4.
CARKHUFF, R.R. and PIERCE, R. (1964), Differential Effects of Therapist Race and Social Class upon Depth of Self-exploration in the Initial Clinical Interview, 'Journal of Consulting Psychology', vol. 31, no. 6, pp. 632-4.
CARSON, R.C. (1967), A and B Therapist 'Types': A Possible Critical Variable in Psychotherapy, 'Journal of Nervous and Mental Disease', vol. 144, pp. 47-54.

COLE, N. et al. (1962), Some Relationships between Social Class and the Practice of Dynamic Psychotherapy, 'American Journal of Psychiatry', vol. 118, pp. 1004-12.

CROCETTI, G. et al. (1976), Psychiatry and Social Class, 'Social Psychiatry', vol. 11, no. 3, pp. 99-105.

DALY, R.W. and JOHNSON, F.A. (1970), The Effects of Age, Education and Occupation on Psychiatric Disposition, 'Social Science and Medicine', vol. 4, no. 6, pp. 619-28.

DAVID, K. (1938), Mental Hygiene and the Class Structure, 'Psychiatry', vol. 1, pp. 55-65.

DAY, L. and REZNIKOFF, M. (1980), Social Class, the Treatment Process, and Parents' and Children' Expectations about Child Psychotherapy, 'Journal of Clinical Child Psychology', vol. 9, no. 3, pp. 195-8.

DOWDS, B.N. et al. (1977), Cognitive Mediators between Patients' Social Class and Therapists' Evaluations, 'Archives of General Psychiatry', vol. 34, pp. 917-20.

FITZGIBBONS, D.J. et al. (1971), Patients' Self-perceived Treatment Needs and their Relationship to Background Variables, 'Journal of Consulting and Clinical Psychology', vol. 37, no. 2, pp. 253-8.

FITZGIBBONS, D.J. (1972), Social Class Differences in Patients' perceived Treatment Needs, 'Psychological Reports, vol. 31, no. 3, pp. 987-97.

FONTANA, A.F. et al. (1980), Social Class and Suitability for Psycho-dynamic Psychotherapy - A Causal Model. 'Journal of Nervous and Mental Disease', vol. 157, pp. 658-65.

FRANK, A. et al. (1978), Are there Social Class Differences in Patients' Treatment Conceptions?. 'Archives of General Psychiatry', vol. 35, no. 1, pp. 61-9.

FRANK, J.D. et al. (1957), Why Patients leave Psychotherapy, 'Archives of General Neurology and Psychiatry', vol. 77, no. 3, pp. 283-99.

FREEMAN, T. (1967), Psychoanalytic Psychotherapy in the N.H.S., 'British Journal of Psychiatry', vol. 113, pp. 321-7.

FREUD, S. (1905), 'On Psychotherapy', in 'Standard Edition of the Complete Psychological Works', vol. 7, London, Hogarth Press (1953).

GARFIELD, S.L. (1977), A Note on the Confounding of Personality and Social Class Characteristics in Research on Premature Termination, 'Journal of Consulting and Clinical Psychology', vol. 45, no. 3, pp. 483-5.

GISIN, S. et al. (1978), Social Class and Psychic Illness: An Empirical Study in Zurich Canton, 'Schweizer Archiv für Neurologie, Neurochirurgie und Psychiatrie', vol. 122, no. 2, pp. 253-69.

GOIN, M.K. et al. (1965), Therapy Congruent with Class-linked Expectations, 'Archives of General Psychiatry', vol. 13, pp. 133-7.

GOLDSTEIN, A.P. (1973a), 'Psychotherapeutic Attraction', New York, Pergamon.

GOLDSTEIN, A.P. (1973b), 'Structured Learning Therapy - Toward a Psycho-therapy for the Poor', New York, Academic Press.

GOTTSCHALK, L.A. et al. (1967), Prediction and Evaluation of Outcome in an Emergency Brief Psychotherapy Clinic, 'Journal of Nervous and Mental Disease', vol. 144, pp. 77-96.

HAASE, W. (1964), The Role of Socio-economic Class in Examiner Bias, in Riessman et al., 'Mental Health of the Poor', New York, Free Press.

HALLUM, K.C. (1978), Social Class and Psychotherapy - Sociolinguistic Approach, 'Clinical Social Work Journal', vol. 6, no. 3, pp. 188-201.

HARRISON, S. et al. (1970), Socia
Practices: The Influences of the
'American Journal of Psychiatry'
HEITLER, J.B. (1973), Preparatio
Expressive Group Psychotherapy,
Psychology', vol. 41, no. 2, pp
HEITLER, J.B. (1974), Clinical
to prepare Lower-class Patients
'International Journal of Grou
pp. 308-22.
HOEHN-SARIC, R. et al. (1964)
Psychotherapy: 1 Effects on T
Psychiatric Research', vol. 7
HOLLINGSHEAD, A.B. and REDLI
Illness', New York, John Wil
IMBER, S.D. et al. (1955), Soc
'Journal of Clinical Psychology', vol. 11,
JONES, E. (1974), Social Class and Psychotherapy,
pp. 307-20.
KANDEL, D.B. (1971), Status Homophily, Social Context and Participation
in Psychotherapy, 'American Journal of Sociology', vol. 71 (May),
pp. 640-50.
KEISER, S. (1974), Sociologic Variables and their Effect on the Language
of the Psychoanalytic Patients, 'Journal of the American Psychoanalytic
Association', vol. 22, no. 2, pp. 329-43.
LABOV, W. (1969), The Logic of Non-standard English, 'Georgetown
Monographs on Language and Linguistics', vol. 22, pp. 1-31.
LEE, S.D. et al. (1970), Social Class, Diagnosis and Prognosis for
Psychotherapy, 'Psychotherapy, Theory, Research and Practice', vol. 7,
no. 3, pp. 181-5.
LORION, R.P. (1974), Social Class, Treatment Attitudes and Expectations,
'Journal of Consulting and Clinical Psychology', vol. 42, no. 6, p. 920.
LORR, M. et al. (1958), The Prediction of Length of Stay in Psychotherapy,
'Journal of Consulting Psychology', vol. 22, pp. 321-7.
LOVE, L.R. et al. (1972), Differential Effectiveness of Three Clinical
Interventions for Different Socio-economic Groupings, 'Journal of
Consulting and Clinical Psychology', vol. 39, no. 3, pp. 347-60.
LOWE, C.D. and ZIGLIN, A.L. (1973), Social Class and the Treatment of
Alcoholic Patients, 'Quarterly Journal of Studies on Alcohol', vol. 34,
pp. 173-84.
McCUE, P.A. (1977), Uniform for Clinical Psychologists, 'Bulletin of
the British Psychological Society', vol. 30, p. 401.
McNAIR, D.M. et al. (1962), Therapist 'Type' and Patient Responses to
Psychotherapy, 'Journal of Consulting Psychology', vol. 26, pp. 425-9.
MARX, J.H. and SPRAY, S.L. (1972), Psychotherapeutic 'Birds of a Feather'
Social Class Status - Religio-cultural Value Homophily in the Mental
Health Field, 'Journal of Health and Social Behaviour', vol. 13,
pp. 413-28.
MELTZER, J.D. (1978), A Semiotic Approach to Suitability for Psycho-
therapy, 'Psychiatry', vol. 41, no. 4, pp. 360-76.
MILLER, H. (1964), 'Tropic of Capricorn', London, John Calder.
MILLER, S.M. and GRIGG, (1966), Mental Health and the Lower Social
Classes, 'Florida State University Studies', no. 49.

H. (1968), Expectations of Psychotherapy in
economic Class, 'American Journal of Ortho-
pp. 88-93.

(1974), Relationship between Values, Social Class
chotherapy, 'Journal of Consulting and Clinical
42, no. 4, pp. 482-90.

al. (1955), Social Class Differences in Attitudes
atry, 'American Journal of Orthopsychiatry' vol. 25,

D. and FRANK, J.D. (1958), The Fate of Psychiatric Clinic
ts assigned to Psychotherapy, 'Journal of Nervous and Mental
, vol. 127, pp. 330-42.

, D.W. et al. (1970), Judgments about Candidates for Psychotherapy:
Influence of Social Class and Insight-verbal Ability, 'Journal of
alth and Social Behaviour', vol. 11, no. 1, pp. 51-8.

SCHAFFER, L. and MYERS, J.L. (1954), Psychotherapy and Social
Stratification, 'Psychiatry', vol. 17, pp. 83-93.

SCHMIDT, J.P. and HANCEY, R.,Class and Psychiatric Treatment:
Applications of a Decision-making Model to Use Patterns in a Cost-free
Clinic, 'Journal of Consulting and Clinical Psychology', vol. 47,
no. 4, pp. 771-2.

SETTE, P. (1972), Psychotherapy of Lower Class Patients, 'Neurobiologia',
vol. 35, no. 4, pp. 331-48.

SHADER, R.I. (1970), The Walk-In Service: An Experience in Community
Care', in Rothman, T. (ed.), 'Changing Patterns in Psychiatric Care',
New York, Crown.

SHANAN, J. and MOSES, R. (1961), The Readiness to Offer Psychotherapy:
Its Relationship to Social Background and Formulation of the Complaint,
'Archives of General Psychiatry, vol. 4, pp. 202-12.

SHAPIRO, E.T. and PINSKER, H. (1973), Shared Ethnic Scotona, 'American
Journal of Psychiatry', vol. 130, no. 12, pp. 1338-41.

SIASSI, I, et al. (1976), Psychotherapy with Patients from Lower Socio-
economic Groups, 'American Journal of Psychotherapy, vol. 30, no. 1,
pp. 29-40.

SPRINGER, S.M. (1977), Social Class in the Mental Health Center,
'Psychiatry', vol. 49, no. 1, pp. 62-71.

STERN, S.L. et al. (1975), Confounding of Personality and Social Class
Characteristics in Research on Premature Termination, 'Journal of
Consulting and Clinical Psychology', vol. 43, no. 3, pp. 341-4.

STERN, S.L. et al. (1977), A Reply to Garfield, 'Journal of Consulting
and Clinical Psychology', vol. 45, no. 3, pp. 486-8.

STRUPP, H.H and BLOXOM, A.L. (1973), Preparing Lower-class Patients
for Group Psychotherapy Development and Evaluation of a Role-induction
Film, 'Journal of Consulting and Clinical Psychology', vol. 41, no. 3,
pp. 373-84.

TERESTMAN, N. et al. (1974), Blue-collar Patients in a Psychoanalytic
Clinic, 'American Journal of Psychiatry', vol. 131, pp. 261-6.

THAIN, H.R. (1968), Diagnosis of Maladaptive Behavior and Prognosis for
Psychotherapy in Relation to Social Class, 'Dissertation Abstracts
International', vol. 29, no. (6-B), pp. 2211-12.

WESTERGAARD, J. and RESLER, H. (1976), 'Class in a Capitalist Society',
London, Penguin Books.

WODAK-LEODOLTER, R. (1978), Working Class Language and Psychotherapy:
A Sociolinguistic Study in Group Communication, 'Univ. Vienna 1090
Austria, Series: 15A 3025'.

WOLD, P. and STEGER, J. (1976), Social Class and Group Therapy in a
Working Class Population, 'Community Mental Health' vol. 12, no. 4,
pp. 335-41.
YANAMOTO, J. and GOIN, M.K. (1966), Social Class Factors relevant for
Psychiatric Treatment, 'Journal of Nervous and Mental Disease', vol. 142,
pp. 332-39.
ZUK, G.H. (1973), Sources of Anguish that Affect Commitment in Family
Therapy, 'Neurologia, Neurocirugia, Psiquiatria', vol. 14, pp. 107-16.
BARMAN: Truly the A to Z of Social Class and Psychotherapy.

INDEX